THE WOMEN
OF
BERKSHIRE
HATHAWAY

THE WOMEN
OF
BERKSHIRE
HATHAWAY

*Lessons from Warren Buffett's
Female CEOs and Directors*

Karen Linder

WILEY

John Wiley & Sons Inc.

Published by John Wiley & Sons, Inc., Hoboken, New Jersey.
Published simultaneously in Canada.

For general information on our other products and services or for technical support, please contact our Customer Care Department within the United States at (800) 762-2974, outside the United States at (317) 572-3993 or fax (317) 572-4002.

Wiley also publishes its books in a variety of electronic formats. Some content that appears in print may not be available in electronic books. For more information about Wiley products, visit our web site at www.wiley.com.

Library of Congress Cataloging-in-Publication Data:

Linder, Karen, 1960-
  The women of Berkshire Hathaway : lessons from Warren Buffett's female CEOs and directors / Karen Linder.
      p.   cm.
  Includes bibliographical references and index.
  ISBN 978-1-118-18262-8 (cloth); ISBN 978-1-118-22741-1 (ebk);
  ISBN 978-1-118-24034-2 (ebk); ISBN 978-1-118-26503-1 (ebk)
  1. Berkshire Hathaway Inc.—Management.   2. Women chief executive officers—United States.   3. Women executives—United States.   4. Executive ability—United States.   5. Success in business—United States.   I. Title.
HD38.25.U6L56   2012
338.092′520973—dc23

                                                                          2012004091

Printed in the United States of America

10   9   8   7   6   5   4   3   2   1

I dedicate this book to my mentors, both male and female,
that guided me in building a career and running a business,
and to my former students
who I hope have learned something from me,
either in the classroom or by example.

Contents

Foreword

This book is a collection of stories about the "women of Berkshire." All are women who my father respects and admires—because they are good managers and good people. I've had the great privilege of knowing all of the women in this book. These are stories for anyone interested in business, management, entrepreneurship, or just plain human drama.

As an only female child with two brothers, I never once heard the message that many girls of my generation heard—that the only career options for me were nurse, teacher, secretary, or, of course, homemaker. I was very lucky that both of my parents were supportive of gender equity—long before it was a widespread movement. In a 2004 *Charlie Rose* interview, my dad was quoted as saying, "Wait until women realize they are the real slaves of the world." He initially said this in the 1960s, making a pretty forward-thinking statement for a man in a time when women were expected to stay home and bake cookies.

My father's support of women's and girl's issues continues to this day. He is the only man invited to the annual Fortune Most Powerful Women Summit. He is a big fan of Girls Incorporated—a nonprofit with a mission to "inspire all girls to be strong, smart and bold." In his personal life, he surrounds himself with smart people—who happen to be mostly women—including his bridge partners, many of his closest friends, and one of his doctors. In his business life, a close circle of women function as advisers and confidantes—several of whom he speaks to on a daily basis.

After reading the book, I realized that two women are missing, both enormously important to Berkshire and my father. The first is Debbie Bosanek, who 37 years ago started at Berkshire when she was 17 years old. She has been my dad's assistant for over 18 years. Debbie is the gatekeeper: She screens the mail, keeps his calendar, organizes his travel, and manages the administrative functions in the office, all while the phone is ringing off the hook. She knows everything about him: what and how he thinks about various topics, what he will eat (and, more likely, won't eat), what he will sign, what he'll say yes to, and what he'll say no to. In all the years I've known her, I've never seen her rattled, impatient, or angry. To all of the many people from around the world who call the office each day, Debbie is the voice of Berkshire Hathaway. And there could be no better person—man or woman—in that job. My dad says that the directors and managers of Berkshire—men and women—like Debbie better than they like him. He says that there isn't anything she can't do.

The second Woman of Berkshire is *the* Woman of Berkshire: My mother. My father freely admits that there would be no Berkshire Hathaway if he had married someone else. My dad was a self-described "mess" when they got married. He credits her with changing his life. It's probably not an exaggeration to say she saved his life. When I told him I was going to do the foreword for this book and talk about Mom, he said again, "I learned as much from her as anyone." My mother described her role in my father's life as the "watering can to his flower." That my mother could see my father—an aspiring but nerdy businessman with low self-esteem—as a flower is a testament to her vision and her faith in the human spirit. That my dad allowed himself to be "watered" is a testament to his ability to recognize that he was safe with her and could trust this woman with his transformation. My dad came into the world as a mathematical genius: He sees the world in odds, percentages, and numbers (and of course dollars). My mother is the one who taught him how to be a human being—to love and be loved. Her influence made him a better man in business and in life. Until the day she died, my dad relied on my mother for advice, counsel, and support in every aspect of his life—including Berkshire Hathaway.

Today this book highlights nine talented women who have helped build Berkshire into the successful company that it is. It is important to recognize their contributions. It is my hope—and that of my father—that in the future a book about the women of Berkshire Hathaway will become irrelevant, as the number of women directors and managers grows. And it surely will.

—*Susie Buffett*
Chair of the Susan Thompson Buffett Foundation
and the Sherwood Foundation

Acknowledgments

Thank you to the women—and one man—who generously agreed to be interviewed for the chapters in this book. You are an inspiration to us all.

Thank you to the circle of family and friends that volunteered their time and skill reviewing chapter drafts: my husband Jim Linder, son Trent Allen, and kind friends Cindy and Steve Clinch. Your comments, suggestions, and revisions were invaluable. Thank you, dear friend Claire Eklund, for reviewing and editing each chapter with the thoroughness of those school nuns who drilled you into an exceptionally brilliant writer and editor.

Thank you to the Wiley team whose patience with a first time writer provided a warm, secure net: Editorial Director Debra Englander, Development Editor Kimberly Bernard, Production Editor Steven Kyritz, and Editorial Assistant Tula Batanchiev.

Thank you to Gary Rosenberg of the Douglas County Historical Society who tirelessly retrieved files of newspaper clippings covering the events and people of Omaha, Nebraska, and endured the hours I invaded his space pouring over records sitting in a creaky wooden chair.

I wish to thank my professor of Honors English at Nebraska Wesleyan University, the late Harold Hall. Despite my being a biology major, he provided top-notch education and inspiration in literature and writing. Tilde Kline M.D., Jean Triol, and Roberta Goodell all encouraged me to write, edit, and publish medical articles, something that has given me enormous pleasure.

I've had many mentors to thank that have contributed to my life's experiences and lessons. While still a student of cytotechnology, I met Laura Cook, a cytotechnologist from Omaha. She guided and pushed me to actively participate in leadership positions of our professional organizations sooner than I would have chosen. Coincidently, after boarding my flight to New York to conduct the first interview for this book with Cathy Baron Tamraz, Ms. Cook, now 80 years old, and whom I hadn't seen for the past decade, was seated across the aisle from me. As I told her about my latest project she beamed proudly, just the same as she had nearly 30 years earlier. I took it as a sign.

After 19 years of working and teaching in hospitals, I opened a private pathology laboratory where I learned a great deal about business. If not for Martha Hutchinson M.D., who graciously served as my medical director, it would not have been possible.

Finally, thank you to my parents, June and Dwaine Karr, for raising me to work hard and set ambitious goals. My husband and children are the foundation of my life. Their loving support, in addition to Butterfingers' unconditional love, is a constant presence that I cherish.

Introduction

I've attended the Berkshire Hathaway annual shareholder's meeting in Omaha, Nebraska, for the past few years and always get there early (or send my husband early) to be able to secure seats in the main arena of the 19,000-seat Qwest Center, recently renamed the CenturyLink Center. We're fortunate in having Omaha as our hometown and look forward to the event each year. The 2011 attendance was 40,000, so getting there by 6:30 A.M. is important, lest you be relegated to the folding chairs and bleachers watching simulcast monitors in the exhibit hall or across the street in a ballroom of the Hilton Hotel.

Doors open promptly at 7 A.M. to long lines of people, some of whom slept on the sidewalk outside overnight. If you didn't know better, you'd think they were waiting in line for a rock concert. The meeting always begins with the Annual Meeting Movie at 8:30 A.M. Yes, people sit in their precious seats for an hour and a half with absolutely nothing to do except laugh at the people who didn't stand in line outside the convention center and are now running up and down steep auditorium steps hoping to find two open seats together.

The movie is different each year, lasts for about an hour, and is a great mix of comedy and promotion. Chairman Warren Buffett and

Vice Chairman Charlie Munger poke fun at themselves with celebrities such as soap actress Susan Lucci, NBA star LeBron James, and the cast of television's *Desperate Housewives*. This is interspersed with debuts for some of the funnier television advertisements from Berkshire Hathaway companies, such as GEICO, Dairy Queen, and Fruit of the Loom.

At the end of the movie, a scrolling horizontal row of Berkshire Hathaway managers' portraits lists their names and companies while music of modified lyrics to the tune of "My Favorite Things" plays in the background. In this video, the managers are thanked for the previous year of hard work.

As I watch this each year, I see the headshot photos of the more than 80 Berkshire company managers scroll by and wonder, "Why are they all men?" Actually, they aren't *all* men. There are currently four women who manage Berkshire Hathaway companies: Marla Gottschalk of The Pampered Chef, Susan Jacques of Borsheims Fine Jewelry, Beryl Raff of Helzberg Diamonds, and Cathy Baron Tamraz of Business Wire. During this three- to four-minute music video, the photos of these four women appear like remote islands in a vast sea of men. It made me wonder about what made these particular women so unique and if this proportion of female leadership is typical in all of corporate America.

Berkshire Hathaway Managers

As of January 2012, a record high of 18 women (3.6 percent) hold CEO positions of a Fortune 500 company. Berkshire's current ratio of female CEOs is higher than that at 5.1 percent, increasing from just one female CEO in 2001. However, the female CEOs that run Berkshire subsidiaries are not responsible for companies as large as those in the Fortune 500. When they are compared to companies of equal budget size as themselves, they have a very similar proportion of female CEOs.

Warren Buffett has a comfortable relationship with all of the CEOs of Berkshire subsidiaries. He has let it be known what he looks for when he considers buying a company and a significant piece of the decision lies in the company's leadership. Competent management is essential. Management should possess these traits:

- Be rational.
- Be candid with the shareholders.
- Resist the institutional imperative.[1]

In published criteria of company qualities that make it an attractive asset, he lists, "Management in place. We can't supply it."[2] "If they need my help to manage the enterprise, we're probably both in trouble."[3] Charlie Munger adds, "We have decentralized power to a point just short of total abdication."[4]

Berkshire Hathaway is beloved by its shareholders and employees alike. Buffett praises his CEOs regularly. Branding the CEOs as "All-Stars" may also be a clever personnel management ploy on his part to inject so much confidence in his people that they feel they must be the best.[5]

Buffett had this to say about the managers in his 2011 Letter to Shareholders:

We possess a cadre of truly skilled managers who have an unusual commitment to their own operations and to Berkshire. Many of our CEOs are independently wealthy and work only because they love what they do. They are volunteers, not mercenaries. Because no one can offer them a job they would enjoy more, they can't be lured away.

At Berkshire, managers can focus on running their businesses: They are not subjected to meetings at headquarters nor financing worries nor Wall Street harassment. They simply get a letter from me every two years and call me when they wish. And their wishes do differ: There are managers to whom I have not talked in the last year, while there is one with whom I talk almost daily. Our trust is in people rather than process. A "hire well, manage little" code suits both them and me.

Berkshire's CEOs come in many forms. Some have MBAs; others never finished college. Some use budgets and are by-the-book types; others operate by the seat of their pants. Our team resembles a baseball squad composed of all-stars having vastly different batting styles. Changes in our lineup are seldom required.[6]

Buffett includes a letter to the managers in Berkshire's annual report every other year. In the 2010 Memo to Berkshire Hathaway Managers ("The All-Stars"), he points out,

The priority is that all of us continue to zealously guard Berkshire's reputation. We can't be perfect but we can try to be. As I've said in these memos for more than 25 years: We can afford to lose money—even a lot of money. But we can't afford to lose reputation—even a shred of reputation. We must continue to measure every act against not only what is legal but also what we would be happy to have written about on the front page of a national newspaper in an article written by an unfriendly but intelligent reporter. As a corollary, let me know promptly if there's any significant bad news. I can handle bad news but I don't like to deal with it after it has festered for awhile.[7]

The CEOs of Berkshire Hathaway subsidiaries are evaluated and compensated based on their individual company's performance. The overall performance of Berkshire, up or down, is not uniformly applied to the evaluation of each of the 79 separate subsidiaries. If the stock of Berkshire Hathaway goes down in a given year, it will not negatively impact companies that have seen gains in revenue and profit. The reverse is, of course, true also.

Regarding the compensation of CEOs, Buffett says,

"Berkshire employs many different incentive arrangements, with their terms depending on such elements as the economic potential or capital intensity of a CEO's business. Whatever the compensation arrangement, though, I try to keep it both simple and fair. When we use incentives—and these can be large—they are always tied to the operating results for which a given CEO has authority. We issue no lottery tickets that carry payoffs unrelated to business performance. If a CEO bats .300, he gets paid for being a .300 hitter, even if circumstances outside of his control cause Berkshire to perform poorly. And if he bats .150, he doesn't get a payoff just because the successes of others have enabled Berkshire to prosper mightily."[8]

Of the seven CEOs profiled in this book, four (Blumkin, Christopher, Tamraz, and Graham) were already in place as CEO at the time of acquisition by Berkshire Hathaway. Berkshire has never acquired a company and let go of the existing management team. Jacques and Raff both succeeded male CEOs after Berkshire acquisition.

It can be argued that Berkshire's subsidiary company The Pampered Chef is at the forefront of the female-dominated industries of at-home parties and kitchen utensils and so having a woman CEO is not exceptional. That is a fair argument. The company was founded by Doris Christopher. She was succeeded as CEO by Marla Gottschalk. It is very unlikely that a man will soon hold the position of CEO of The Pampered Chef.

One might also suggest that the jewelry business, including Borsheims and Helzberg Diamonds, is a woman's industry, since women own and wear significantly more jewelry than men. In this case, the argument is simply wrong. Historically, jewelers and gem experts have been male. It was only in the past 30 years that women began to enter professions in the jewelry industry. The Women's Jewelry Association was formed in 1983 to help further the careers of women in the jewelry and watch industries.

The male-dominated American furniture industry began in the southern United States. Nebraska Furniture Mart, founded by Rose Blumkin in 1937, is an anomaly in the industry.

Business Wire is a service company for public relations and investor relations. There is significant female representation in the area of public relations, but not so in the realm of investor relations.

Newspapers are traditionally led by men. Berkshire Hathaway is the majority shareholder of The Washington Post Company, but does not own it outright. Katharine Graham's father purchased the *Washington Post* when she was 16 years old. Her husband took over running it from her father and she inherited the CEO position only after the death of her husband. Of some interest is that there are at least three women who claim to be the first female publisher in the United States, all in the 1700s, and each succeeded to the post after the deaths of their respective publisher spouses.

Berkshire Hathaway Directors

Berkshire Hathaway has been listed as having one of the three best boards of directors in America, along with Amazon and Johnson & Johnson.[9] Women comprise 16.1 percent of U.S. corporate board seats.[10] The board of directors for Berkshire Hathaway has 2 seats out of 12 (16.67 percent) occupied by women: Charlotte Guyman, board member since 2003, and Susan Decker, board member since 2007 (see Figure I.1). Until her death in 2004, Susan T. Buffett, wife of Warren, was a member of the board. There are two female officers (out of eight) of Berkshire Hathaway: Sharon L. Heck, vice president, and Rebecca K. Amick, director of internal auditing.

Figure I.1 Berkshire Hathaway's Board of Directors Enjoying Root Beer Floats at Piccolo Pete's in Omaha, Nebraska

Left to right: Thomas Murphy, former CEO, Capital Cities/ABC; Ronald Olson, partner, Munger, Tolles & Olson; Susan Decker, former President, Yahoo!; Walter Scott Jr., Chairman, Level 3 Communications; Howard Buffett, President, Buffett Farms; Charlie Munger, Vice Chairman, Berkshire Hathaway; Warren Buffett, CEO, Berkshire Hathaway; David Gottesman, Senior Managing Director, First Manhattan; Bill Gates, founder and former CEO, Microsoft; Charlotte Guyman, former Chairman of the Board of Directors, UW Medicine; Stephen Burke, CEO, NBCUniversal. (Not shown: Donald Keough, Chairman, Allen & Company.)
SOURCE: Gregg Segal.

Berkshire does not have a policy regarding the consideration of diversity in identifying nominees for director. The Governance, Compensation, and Nominating Committee looks for individuals who have very high integrity, business savvy, an owner-oriented attitude, and a deep genuine interest in the company.[11]

In Warren Buffett's 2011 Letter to Shareholders he said this about the Berkshire Directors,

> To start with, the directors who represent you think and act like owners. They receive token compensation: no options, no restricted stock, and, for that matter, virtually no cash. We do not provide the directors and officers liability insurance, a given at almost every other large public company. If they mess up with your money, they will lose their money as well. Leaving my holdings aside, directors and their families own Berkshire shares worth more than $3 billion. Our directors, therefore, monitor Berkshire's actions and results with keen interest and an owner's eye. You and I are lucky to have them as stewards.[12]

It's interesting and a bit humorous to learn what Berkshire directors are paid to serve on the board. It is a mere pittance compared to typical board member compensation for large corporations. In 2010, the Berkshire board members were each paid $2,700. Three members of the Audit Committee were paid an additional $4,000. The method of compensation is defined such that each director receives a fee of $900 for each meeting attended in person and $300 for participating in any meeting conducted by telephone. A director who serves as a member of the Audit Committee receives a fee of $1,000 quarterly. Directors are reimbursed for their out-of-pocket expenses incurred in attending meetings of directors or shareholders.

Berkshire does not provide directors and officers liability insurance to its directors. Directors and officers (D&O) insurance is a policy that most public corporations purchase to cover events where the board members and officers of a corporation are sued, most likely by a shareholder, in conjunction with the performance of their duties as they relate to the company.

This is far less than the hundreds of thousands of dollars some board seats pay. For example, Stephen Burke's compensation as a Berkshire

Hathaway board member in 2010 was $2,700. His total compensation in stocks and cash in 2009 as a board member of JPMorgan Chase & Company was $245,000.

Serving on multiple boards is not unusual. Each member of the Berkshire board, with the exception of Charlotte Guyman and David Gottesman, serves on between one and six additional corporate boards.

Warren Buffett requires that all directors be truly independent. He explains:

> I say truly because many directors who are now deemed independent by various authorities and observers are far from that relying heavily as they do on directors' fees to maintain their standard of living. These payments, which come in many forms, often range between $150,000 and $250,000 annually, compensation that may approach or even exceed all other income of the independent director. And—surprise, surprise—director compensation has soared in recent years, pushed up by recommendations from corporate America's favorite consultant, Ratchet, Ratchet and Bingo. The name may be phony, but the action it conveys is not.
>
> Charlie and I believe our four criteria (owner-oriented, business savvy, interest in Berkshire, independent) are essential if directors are to do their job—which, by law, is to faithfully represent owners. Yet these criteria are usually ignored. Instead, consultants and CEOs seeking board candidates will often say, "We're looking for a woman," or "a Hispanic," or "someone from abroad," or what have you. It sometimes sounds as if the mission is to stock Noah's ark. Over the years I've been queried many times about potential directors and have yet to hear anyone ask, "Does he think like an intelligent owner?"
>
> The questions I instead get would sound ridiculous to someone seeking candidates for, say, a football team, or an arbitration panel, or a military command. In those cases, the selectors would look for people who had the specific talents and attitudes that were required for a specialized job. At Berkshire, we are in the specialized activity of running a business well, and therefore we seek business judgment.[13]

Buffett was recently asked his opinion about the low number of female members on corporate boards. His reply was,

> It's changing very slowly. It's going to change at Berkshire. I get calls from CEOs who say, "We need a woman director. Do you have any suggestions?" What they're really asking me is, "Do you have a woman whose name is quite recognizable that will reflect credit on us, and who really won't cause us to do much differently?" I've suggested quite a few that don't fit into that category, but they won't find out until they put them on their board.[14]

The current Berkshire Hathaway board members have significant personal financial interest in the welfare of the company. The total value of stock holdings for the 11 board members, aside from Warren Buffett, is just over $10 billion. The average stock ownership of those eleven members is roughly $910 million ranging from $425,000 to $6.4 billion, as of September 2011. Granted, that average is influenced by extraordinarily large stock holdings by Bill Gates and David Gottesman. But every member of the board holds in excess of $7 million worth of Berkshire stock, with the exception of the two most recent additions to the board: Susan Decker, who joined in 2007, and Stephen Burke, who joined in 2009.

The directors all purchased their Berkshire Hathaway stock from personal funds. No stock options have ever been given to a director. As Buffett says, "All eleven directors purchased their holdings in the market just as you did; we've never passed out options or restricted shares. Charlie and I love such honest-to-God ownership. After all, who ever washes a rental car?"[15]

The average age of the 12 members of the board of Berkshire Hathaway is 70. Six members of the board are over the age of 80. These directors will have to face board succession issues, as well as CEO succession issues, over the next few years.

The profiles presented in this book illustrate that there is no single "recipe for success." These women come from variable social, economic, and educational backgrounds. In general, they would be characterized as coming from a hardworking middle-class upbringing.

The exceptions to this are Katharine Graham, born into a life of privilege, and Rose Blumkin, born into extreme poverty.

Many factors contribute to who these women are at the pinnacle of their careers and the valuable lessons they learned along the way. This book travels the paths that led nine women to succeed in positions traditionally held by men and tells the stories of their working relationships with professional colleagues and Warren Buffett. They share how they balance work and private lives, the lessons they learned along the way and how they are cultivating a new corporate environment.

Chapter 1

Rose Blumkin— Magic Carpet Ride

Rose Blumkin became the first-ever female Berkshire Hathaway manager when Nebraska Furniture Mart was acquired by Berkshire Hathaway in 1983. Rose was just shy of 90 years old at the time and still working 60-plus hours per week in the store. You would assume that this change in ownership would signal retirement for Rose, Chairman of the Board of "the Mart," but she still worked for more than a decade longer, 12 to 14 hours each day, seven days a week, until she reached age 103.

Buffett later joked that he would have to alter the company's mandatory retirement age of 100. "My god. Good managers are so scarce I can't afford the luxury of letting them go just because they've added a year to their age."[1]

By the time Berkshire Hathaway acquired Nebraska Furniture Mart, Rose was already a successful executive, having founded the furniture store in Omaha in 1937, at the age of 43, and growing it to a business with an annual profit of $15 million.

My first encounter with Rose Blumkin was as a customer at Nebraska Furniture Mart in the late 1980s. At this time, "Mrs. B" was well into her nineties and drove around the store on a motorized scooter (Figure 1.1).

She was a tiny woman, standing just four foot ten when she dismounted from her scooter (which I never witnessed). She stopped to speak with customers in her thick Russian-Yiddish accent, encouraging them to make a decision and assuring them that they wouldn't get a better deal anywhere else.

There are numerous tales of her berating the employees and enjoying lively negotiations with customers. Mrs. B thrived in an era of what would now be considered a "harsh" management style. She was tough, but earned respect from her employees and the community alike.

The Mart was immense even at that time. It now occupies 77 acres of central Omaha with 500,000 square feet of retail space, including a Burger King restaurant. There are also another 500,000 square feet of warehousing and distribution and over 2,800 employees.

Figure 1.1 Mrs. B on Her Scooter in the Carpet Warehouse
SOURCE: Nebraska Furniture Mart.

Most independent and national furniture stores have found it futile to attempt to compete in Omaha with Nebraska Furniture Mart. The Electronic Mega Mart, a separate electronics department, opened in 1994, has grown substantially in recent years along with consumer demand. It occupies 102,000 square feet. The furniture department still consistently brings in the most revenue of the four divisions (furniture, flooring, electronics, and appliances).

Nebraska Furniture Mart added a second location in Des Moines, Iowa, when they purchased Homemaker's Furniture in 2001. A third store was built from scratch on 80 acres in Kansas City, Kansas, and opened in 2003. Next, Nebraska Furniture Mart plans to build a new store in suburban Dallas, Texas. The project, consisting of 1.8 million square feet of retail and warehouse space on 433 acres, is slated to open by 2016.

Although Mrs. B has been gone since 1998, her presence is still felt in Nebraska Furniture Mart and her likeness appears in photos scattered around the store. "My grandmother is still the front man of Nebraska Furniture Mart," says Mrs. B's grandson and vice-president of the Mart, Robert Batt. "She's the symbol of the company."[2]

Bob started working at the store when he was age 14. On his office walls hang photos and newspaper clippings of many of the major events of the company. There are also several "Going Out of Business" advertisements from competitors' stores framed and hanging on the wall. These, he explains, are displayed so that the company will "never forget about the other stores who put themselves out of business, how it can happen to anyone, and that it must be avoided."[3] As he explains, if you forget history, you're doomed to repeat it. And what an interesting history it is. . . .

Dosveydanya!

The tale of Rose Blumkin is a quintessential immigrant's success story. Rose was born in 1893 to Solomon and Chasia (Kimmelman) Gorelick near Minsk, Russia, in the village of Shchedrin (Scadryn/Chadrin). She and her seven siblings (three brothers and four sisters) lived in a two-room log cabin, sleeping on straw mats. Her father was a rabbi, spending his days in religious study, and her mother ran a small general store. "My father was so religious. She had to support us. He only prayed."[4]

Rose later recalled her homeland: "The trees were beautiful. I remember our little house. It was right by the lake. The mosquitoes used to eat us up." Shchedrin was governed by Russia at that time, but is now part of Belarus. Belarus is remarkably similar in geography to Nebraska, with far-flung horizons stretching over fields of corn, barley, wheat, and sugar beets. Minsk, like Omaha, is an inland river town.

According to the 1897 Russian census, Minsk had 91,494 inhabitants, of which Jews accounted for approximately one-third. The village of Shchedrin was established in about 1844 by over 300 Jewish families.[5] It consisted of two parallel streets surrounded by farmland and forests. The population was close to 4,000 at the time of Rose's birth.

It was customary in this village for the men to study and the women to earn a living for the family by selling fruit and vegetables or handiwork. Only boys received an education. Rose never attended school. But she started helping her mother in the store at the age of six and she learned arithmetic. She absorbed a valuable business education from her mother.

As a child, she once woke up in the middle of the night and saw her mother washing clothes and baking bread for the next day. Young Rose said, "When I grow up you're not going to work so hard. I can't stand it, the way you work day and night."[6]

Rose left home at age 13, walking barefoot for 18 miles to preserve the soles of her shoes. She stowed away on a train, and got off at the town of Gomel, 300 miles away, near the Ukrainian border. Gomel must have caused Rose some culture shock. It had a population of approximately 47,000 in 1906, and slightly over half were Jewish.

Rose went from shop to shop looking for a job and a place to stay. "You're a kid," one store owner said. "I'm not a beggar," Rose shot back. With only four cents in her pocket, she asked to sleep in the house that night. "Tomorrow I go to work," she said. The owner relented and Rose got up before dawn the next morning and cleaned the store. She stayed, becoming manager of the store and overseeing the work of six married men by the age of 16.[7]

She then went to a larger town, got another job in a men's clothing store, and met Itzik (Isadore) Rosevich (Blumkin), a shoe salesman. They married in 1914. Mrs. B later remembered her wedding day, saying, "My mother brought me two pounds of rice and two pounds of cookies. That was the wedding feast."[8]

World War I erupted that same year and many inhabitants of Russia fled. Isadore would have been drafted to fight in the Russian army, but was able to emigrate to the United States shortly after he and Rose married. By 1915, Minsk was a battlefront city.

"We didn't have the money for two passages, and my husband had to go." Mrs. B said. According to family legend, this was when Isadore changed his surname from Rosevich to Blumkin. The story has it that he took papers off a dead soldier named Blumkin and used them to leave the country.[9]

America had been in Rose's dreams since the age of nine when she first learned that there were people in the world who did not like Jews. "I hated the Cossacks," said Mrs. B. "I didn't want to live in Russia anymore." She worked in a dry goods store, squeezed every penny, and finally, in 1917, took a train to the Chinese-Siberian border. For three years after Isadore's departure, Rose didn't know exactly where he was. She knew only that he was in the United States. It was fortunate that she didn't delay leaving any longer, however. Minsk was governed by the Russian empire for over 100 years, but Russia had to relinquish Belarus to Germany at the close of World War I in 1918.

"I had no passport. At the China-Russia frontier a soldier was standing guard with a rifle. I said to him 'I am on the way to buy leather for the Army. When I come back I'll bring you a big bottle of vodka.' I suppose he's still there waiting for his vodka," she laughed. She made her way from China to Japan and booked passage on the freighter *Ava Maru*, a Japanese peanut boat that made several stops on the way to America.[10] The ship had been in use for several years for the purpose of exporting lumber from the state of Washington to Asia.[11]

"I bought first class, but they were crooks," she said. "Took me six weeks to get here. So many peanuts. I thought I'd never get here." After six miserable weeks, the ship docked in Seattle. Mrs. B had no entry permit. "If you were healthy, you got in," she said. "And healthy, I was." She had 200 rubles ($66) in her purse.[12]

The Red Cross helped Rose to find Isadore in Iowa. "I came to Fort Dotchivie (Fort Dodge) and the people were out of this world. I never knew such a people—how they treated me. The friendship, the devotion, the goodness. I thought that anyone in this country is the luckiest one in the world. To such a people to come. They never knew me, and they treated me like I was their only child. The best people in the world."[13]

Rose and Isadore lived in Fort Dodge, Iowa, for two years, during which their first daughter, Frances, was born. Rose learned how to cook and keep a house, but she was unable to communicate with any of the locals, so they moved to Omaha where there was a large community of people who spoke both Russian and Yiddish. "I couldn't learn to talk English. Took two years. Didn't know nothing. So, I made up my mind I'm going to a bigger city. I could talk Russian or Jewish. I was dumb. Couldn't learn to talk [English]."[14]

Small Gains

They moved to Omaha and rented a house at 2809 Seward Street for $7 a month. Isadore opened a secondhand clothing store located at 1311 Douglas Street that made $10 per week. The house was soon sold by the landlord and they had to move. The house they bought in July 1919 would be their home for 22 years.

According to the U.S. Census of 1920, the Blumkins were living at 2110 Grace Street in Omaha in the midst of a true melting pot of Russian and Irish immigrants, and a majority of native Midwesterners for neighbors. The home is no longer there and the site is now occupied by Conestoga Elementary School. Family members of the 1920 household are listed as "I., Rosie, Francis, and Luie."

By 1922, the young couple had scraped together enough money to send for Rose's family. Two brothers had come to the United States before Rose, and together with the Blumkins they bought passage for their parents, one brother, four sisters, and a cousin. The rest of the family fled Russia and put down roots in Omaha, living for a while in the Blumkin household. Rose's mother lived to age 91 and her father lived to age 75.

The Blumkins had four children in all: Frances, Louie, Cynthia, and Sylvia (nicknamed Baby). The U.S. Census of 1930 lists Isadore's occupation as the proprietor of a clothing store. Frances taught her mother how to speak English after she came home from school each day.

Rose tells the story of how she began to be involved in Isadore's store, "The Depression came and my husband came home and said, 'We'll starve to death. Nobody walks in. What will we do?' I already had my four children—in 1930." Often, Isadore would sell clothing at the same price he had paid for it. He didn't understand how to make a profit. Rose would teach him about overhead costs.

"Well, there's only one thing to do," she said. "You buy a pair of shoes for $3, sell them for $3.30. Let's sell 10 [percent] over cost and I'll come to the store and show you and help you because I did build a big business in Russia for my boss and I knew business."[15]

Rose began retailing right out of the Blumkin home with home furnishings and accessories. This practice continued throughout her lifetime. Visitors to the Blumkin's house would admire the furniture with attached price tags and lampshades still covered in plastic wrap. If a guest expressed interest in a piece, it was available for sale.

At one point, she printed 10,000 circulars offering to dress a man from head to toe for $5. The offer was for a full suit of clothes, shoes, socks, shirt, tie, and underwear. The Blumkins made $800 from that promotion.[16]

"Then, in '37, I got tired of everybody crying Depression," said Rose. "People used to ask me, can you get me this? That? I used to take them to the wholesale house and sell them 10 above cost. I never lied. I showed them the bill and they all respect me. You should see what kind of customers I have. The best in the world. They build me one of the finest businesses in the country. I always believed in honesty. Anything is wrong, I like to make it right."[17]

Mrs. B opened a furniture store in 1937 with a $500 loan from one of her brothers. It was a 30- by 100-foot basement room below Isadore's pawn shop. She called it Nebraska Furniture Mart. "The same day I opened, February 7th, another furniture store was opening. They had orchestra music and Hollywood stars and I only had three-line want ads because I was poor. I did that day a big business . . . I couldn't get over it," she said.

She decided to go into the furniture business because "It's a happy business. When people buy furniture, it's a happy time. They're just married. Or they're older people who are redoing their house and they're all excited about it."[18] Rose was 43 years old at the time and her four children were between the ages of 10 and 19. Her oldest daughter was by then away at college at the University of Nebraska in Lincoln.

The Blumkins' only son, Louie, graduated from high school in 1938 and joined the U.S. Army in 1941. He took basic training and left by ship for Hawaii on December 3, 1941. When halfway there, the ship made a

U-turn and headed back to San Francisco. "At this time we were informed that the Japanese had bombed Pearl Harbor," Louie later recalled.[19]

Louie participated in the D-Day invasion at Normandy. He landed on Omaha Beach on the coast of France to fight the German military forces and then headed east. That winter, he was assigned to General Patton's Third Armored Division and participated in the Battle of the Bulge, after which he was awarded a Purple Heart. Blumkin ended the war in Linz, Austria.

"One of our great conquests," he said, "was when we freed the concentration camp in Dachau, Germany. The Germans left before we could get there because they were on the run. It was an extremely emotional experience for me, one that I will never forget because of the conditions of both the camp and the individuals. They appeared as though they had not been fed for months."[20]

A bronze statue of Louie in military uniform currently stands guard at the door to his son's office at Nebraska Furniture Mart. The statue was created by sculptor Ron Wanek, who is also the chairman of Ashley Furniture. He made three bronze statues to honor his mentors in the industry and presented them at the High Point furniture market in 2007.

Perseverance

Isadore and Rose ran their businesses separately. He had the pawn shop and used-clothing store until World War II, when he opened a jewelry store with one of Rose's brothers, a business that he ran until his death in 1950. After Isadore died, Chasia Gorelick, who still spoke only Russian and Yiddish, moved in with her daughter Rose until Chasia's death in 1958.

Mrs. B would encounter a fair number of obstacles in growing her business throughout the years. She chose to make a small profit of 10 percent over cost, bend over backwards for customers, and grow the company by selling in large volume. This earned her many repeat customers. It also made her competitors very angry. It wasn't easy standing up to the established Midwest retail giants in the late 1930s. Everyone was struggling to make a living. Success and power were often gained by intimidation and/or bribery.

The first time she wound up in court was when she and Isadore were selling used clothing. She remembered that "in 1932, we had a pawn shop, a secondhand store. One guy came in to [borrow] money on a coat. I said, 'What do you want for your coat?' He says, '$32.' I say, 'My goodness, Brandeis is getting $100. I'll buy it.' So I bought it and put it in the want ad at $37.50. And I sold it in one day. The next day, I bought and sold another six. I thought I'd become a millionaire!

"It didn't take long. They filed suit against me—Goldsteins, Brandeis. I sell too cheap. And my daughter was about 14 years old. She came to trial with me. I don't know how to talk good English like her. She says to the judge, 'My mother, when she makes $2, she's happy. She wants to make a living for the kids. My mother hates to rob people. She wants to be honest with them. She wants to give them bargains and we surviving on account of her because she sells cheap, and all the customers buy from her. What's wrong if she don't rob the people?' The judge dismissed the case and everybody offer her a job."[21]

Later, after starting Nebraska Furniture Mart, Rose attempted to buy furniture wholesale in Chicago. Those early turf wars were still active. "The merchants were very rotten to me. When I walked in Merchandise Mart to buy furniture, to buy anything, they used to kick me out and say, "Don't bother us. We're not going to sell you nothing. Brandeis and Rogers won't let us sell you anything." I used to almost start to cry. My face would get red and I'd say, 'Someday you'll come to my store to try to sell to me, and I'll kick you out the same way that you did me.' And my wish come true. Who would ever suspect? Never. I outlived them all."[22]

Mrs. B was able to convince Marshall Field's to sell her carpet wholesale at $3 per yard. She then resold it for $3.95 per yard. The competition was selling the very same carpet at $7.95 per yard. Naturally, carpet sold well at Nebraska Furniture Mart. Not everyone was happy about such a great deal. Her competition called her a "bootlegger." Her reply was, "You betcha. I'm the best bootlegger in town!"[23]

"Three lawyers from Mohawk take me into court, suing me for unfair trade. Three lawyers and me with my English. I can't afford a lawyer, so I go up to the judge and say 'Judge, I sell everything 10 percent above cost. What's wrong? Can't I give my customers a good deal? I don't rob my customers—I'm making a fortune as it is." The judge agreed, threw out the case, and bought $1,400 worth of carpeting from Mrs. B the next day.[24] The publicity from this trial was worth far more than Mrs. B could have afforded to purchase in advertising.

When the Korean War broke out in 1950, business slowed down and Mrs. B found that she was unable to pay her bills. She was worrying night and day. A local banker came into the store to buy a cabinet and asked why she was so upset. After listening, he gave her $50,000 of his personal money as a 90-day loan.

She had to think of a way to earn the money to pay back the loan, so she quickly rented the Omaha city auditorium for $200 per day and held a three-day sale. She took in $250,000 from the sale, paid off all her loans, and never borrowed money again.

That same year, Isadore and Rose went to visit her mother in California. Taking a vacation was unheard of for Mrs. B. Shortly after they came back to Omaha, Isadore had a heart attack and died. They were married for 36 years and Rose would be a widow for 48 years. Rose resisted taking any vacations after that and never left the United States when she did.

Mrs. B was once asked if she believed she had had a tougher time succeeding because she was a woman. "Me? No, sir," she answered. "When it comes to business, I could beat any man and any college graduate. I mean I use my own common sense. That's what I use for business, for anything. There is plenty dumb women, and there's plenty of people who use their common sense. It didn't stay in my way one bit."[25]

Her opinion of women in 1970 was along the lines of her contemporary male business owners and managers. "I wish I could find some women who want to work. They have all kinds of excuses. One day they come in and the next day you don't see them."[26]

Mrs. B had a rule for the female members of her own family: None of her daughters would work in the business. Only her son, Louie, and her sons-in-law were allowed to work at the store. This was based on Mrs. B's theory of how to preserve healthy marriages and the rule has been followed by the grandchildren as well. The company's current board of directors consists of Warren Buffett and a few male members of the family.

In 1984, a competitor's furniture store legally registered the business name "Mrs. B's Discount Furniture" with the Nebraska Secretary of State. Naturally, Mrs. B filed suit against them, claiming that there was only one Mrs. B and that her name was inextricably linked to Nebraska Furniture Mart.[27] The competitor's store eventually went out of business, and Mrs. B would remember that catchy business name for later use.

Mrs. B's sharp tongue and temper didn't get her into too much trouble until she was sued for slander by two carpet installers in 1993.

The carpet installers said she accused them of stealing $60,000 from her. They were awarded $10,000. She wasn't surprised by the verdict. She said it was a crooked deal. "As soon as I saw them in the courtroom, I knew the jury would feel sorry for them no matter who was right and who was wrong. They looked like they had no money and everyone knows that I have some money."[28]

Not all of Mrs. B's battles were fought against financial and legal villains. In August of 1961, half of Nebraska Furniture Mart was destroyed by a five-alarm fire that started in the shipping department. The resulting "fire sale" generated a line two blocks long to buy hugely discounted items that had been exposed to the smoke.

Mrs. B was so thankful to the firefighters who had saved what they could that she gave a television set to every fire station in the city. Television viewership exploded in the late 1950s and by the time of the fire in 1961, 75 percent of households owned a television, nearly all black and white. But Walt Disney debuted his *Wonderful World of Color* show in 1961, prompting customers to seek out the new and improved color televisions—which were sold at Nebraska Furniture Mart.

Tornado sirens in Omaha sounded at 4:29 on the afternoon of May 6, 1975. The tornado cut a swath of destruction a quarter-mile wide and 15 miles long. At 4:45, it took out the entire Nebraska Furniture Mart building and warehouse (Figure 1.2).

Figure 1.2 Nebraska Furniture Mart Destroyed by Tornado, 1975
Source: Nebraska Furniture Mart.

About 100 shoppers and employees were in the store at the time. They took cover in a fallout shelter that had been built during the Cold War years, which probably saved their lives. While property damage in the city was estimated anywhere from $300 million to $500 million, remarkably only three lives were lost to the storm that day. The tornado also destroyed a post office next to the Mart, so the Blumkins bought the ground and built on it to expand their business.

Mrs. B gave $10,000 to tornado relief efforts for those who lost their homes. It was a generous gesture and also a smart bit of publicity. Here was a woman whose business had been destroyed, first by flames and then by wind, yet she remembered those who were less fortunate. "We have turned every tragedy into a positive," says Bob Batt today.

Workaholic Widow

With her children grown and out of the house, Mrs. B devoted her entire existence to growing Nebraska Furniture Mart. She loved the game of selling. She didn't care a bit about the money; it was all about making a sale. As one of the Mart's sales associates said, "Work was her narcotic." Louie came back after the war in 1945 and joined the business, showing the same intelligence and business acumen as his mother. His calm management style balanced out Mrs. B's quick temper and he would often hire back employees who had been freshly fired by Rose.

Mrs. B had a passion for work. Success was already hers by the mid-1950s. She could have quit working at any time, letting Louis and other members of the family run the business, but the simple action of going to work and being productive kept her interested in life and energized.

"When I was poor, I wanted [things], sure. I was ambitious," she said. "I always wanted my kids should have what I didn't have, and I wanted to show poor people there is a future in life. Even if you don't have money, if you try, you could have it. I only had ambition, that's all. Money doesn't bother me. I don't get thrill out of money."[29]

In 1957, Mrs. B took time out to take classes to become a U.S. citizen. An immigrant from Britain who was a fellow member of Mrs. B's class recalls asking her: "You mean you were here for 37 years before becoming a citizen? How come you waited so long?" "Well, I was busy," said Mrs. B.[30]

She was busy strategizing, figuring expenses and revenues, and selling to her customers. "I want to do all the business I can and get every customer I can," she said. "Business is like raising a child—you want a good one. A child needs a mother and a business needs a boss.[31] . . . My hobby is figuring out how to advertise, how to undersell, how much hell to give my competitors. I'll never forget how they treated us when we were poor."[32]

A 1977 local newspaper article, of the sort you see in the human-interest section of the paper, sums up Mrs. B's temperament and work ethic.[33]

Getting Personal

Favorite thing to do on a Sunday afternoon: Visit with customers at my store.

Favorite thing to do on a nice evening: Drive around to check the competition and plan my next attack.

Favorite movie in the last year: Too busy.

Favorite book in the last year: Don't have time.

Favorite dessert: Fresh fruit.

Favorite cocktail: None. Drinkers go broke. If you want to be in business, be sober.

Favorite singer: Beverly Sills.

Favorite sport in which you take part: Not interested.

Pet peeve: Deadbeats.

Favorite TV show: *60 Minutes.*

Favorite place: My stores.

What one thing most needs to be done, either locally or in our state or nation: Clean out all the lazy ones. There are plenty of jobs for those who want to work. Unemployment payments should be only for the sick and elderly.

Mrs. B was able to stretch out time and delay aging by keeping busy doing what she loved. But eventually her legs threatened to force her to slow down. Rather than accept that, Mrs. B started driving a motorized cart in the store. She had a lot of territory to cover: three square city blocks of floor space on each of two floors. "Besides," she said, "it's fun and I'm making up for lost time. I never had a bicycle or even a kiddy car."

A friend of mine was in the Mart while Mrs. B was zipping through the aisles on her scooter. He watched as she backed into a glass curio cabinet. The entire cabinet and glass shelves all came crashing down behind her. "Why did you put that there?" she yelled at the nearest salesperson. The employee rushed over to clean up the mess, apologizing. It was his fault, clearly, that the accident had happened.

One day in 1990, Mrs. B drove her cart into a metal post and broke her ankle. "I got mad. I drove the cart too fast and I drove into a post." She didn't go to the hospital until the next day when she couldn't stand up. "It was just a crack, it didn't hurt." She was back at work the next day.[34] The next year she took a corner with too much speed and turned the cart completely over, gashing her head on a grandfather clock. The wound required several stitches, yet she was back in the store two hours later.

Bob Batt remembered a luncheon where both he and Mrs. B were being honored. The luncheon was dragging on. At about 1:15 Mrs. B stood up and hollered, "What's wrong with you people? Don't you have jobs? I'm going back to work." And she left.[35] And as Warren Buffett said during opening remarks at the 1993 Berkshire Hathaway Annual Meeting, "I'd like to introduce Berkshire's managers, except Mrs. B couldn't take time off from work for foolishness like a share-holders' meeting."

Mrs. B developed successful merchandising practices long before they were adopted by mainstream retailers. She established the idea of a discount store making small profits on large volumes, undercutting the competition and giving the consumer a bargain. Sam Walton didn't open his first discount store, leading to the Wal-Mart empire, until 1962.

The company still follows these principles. It is run very fiscally conservatively. Mrs. B always felt that the days of the Depression could return at any time. "We still run the company like the Depression is coming back," says Bob Batt. The administrative offices are no bigger than necessary. There is no debt and, therefore, the company was able to survive the economic downturn of 2008. There have never been any layoffs.

Mrs. B realized that forming a bond with employees was important to retaining them and fostering loyalty. She loved hiring immigrants. To make new employees feel more comfortable, they would be placed in work areas with others who spoke their native tongue. This had the added bonus of training the new employee better and quicker. Rose never forgot how kind people had helped her adjust to a new life in America. Nonetheless, personnel problems arise in every business, and Nebraska Furniture Mart was no exception.

Thieves and Stupes

For about a decade during the 1970s there were two Furniture Mart locations in Omaha. Mrs. B was always devoted to the downtown store where the business was originally incubated and flourished. Then, when the tornado destroyed the store out west on 72nd Street, Mrs. B's initial response was not to rebuild on the site. Those preferences changed and they did rebuild the western store bigger and better, and in 1980 decided to close the downtown store. Says Mrs. B,

> The crucial decision was one reason. I had a manager and 20 employees in a warehouse and they were stealing for 17 years. And they divided partnership. I never knew. You know, we trust people. They stole maybe a half a million a year. You know, we made money; we didn't notice as much. We knew they were stealing, but we didn't know so much. A lady comes in and buys a television for $400, and she goes to pick it up and they say, "Lady, you go take the money back. We'll give you for $150." She says, "I'm a Christian and I don't buy stolen stuff." She came and told my son and we arrested the three. The three says, "Everybody be our partner. Everything we steal, we split—with the manager, with everybody. So, why should we suffer?"
>
> Anyway, we had a trial for them. We fired them all. They signed a statement who they stole, and how they did, so the judge give them two years probation. He said, "I haven't got no more jail. The jails are full. So I'll give them parole." What can you do? They didn't give me a penny. So when we find out

they steal so much, and when the government was dealing to buy our property you know, for the new Federal Reserve Bank, we sold it too cheap. We decided to have one store, and watch the thieves and not work for them.

We have insurance, even on thieves, you see, you have to put everyone in jail. Some of them got a wife and kids. It's heartbreaking, you know. So, we let them go. Some of them died off from cancer—the thieves. I told them they going to get cancer. I don't like monkey business. And you know, that's what help the success. Only the truth.[36]

Though she never spent a single day in a classroom, Mrs. B had a savant's capacity for arithmetic. She could not read or write, or even sign her name, but she could work with numbers—in her head! This skill was extremely useful in the carpet department where she spent most of her time. It was an incredible talent that she was blessed with that made selling carpet her specialized niche. As she said, "It's not that I love carpet. I don't love carpet. I just know how to figure the prices."

Larry Batt, Mrs. B's oldest grandson, said, "At the point where a price was about to be decided, a race would commence between her and a salesman with a calculator. The salesman always lost."[37]

In fact, her skill was witnessed by the entire country on a television broadcast of ABC's *20/20* in July 1990. Bob Brown of ABC interviewed Rose, following her through the store as she drove around on her scooter. He threw out random numbers to her, "Okay, say the carpet's $12.95 a yard. I want 30 yards. How much is that?" In less than one second, Mrs. B replied, "390."

"And if my room is 12 by 14 feet. How many . . . ?" asked Bob. "Nineteen yards," replied Mrs. B before Brown had even finished his sentence. She performed these feats of mathematical skill at the age of 96! She had little tolerance for salespeople who were unable to keep up with her both physically and mentally. "Such a bunch of stupes," was her favorite expression when referring to them.

Jerry Pearson, a former carpet salesman, said, "People jump when she yells. Her favorite word in describing employees who don't meet her standard is 'stupes.' She has very little respect for anybody whose mind power is lower than hers, and that's everyone. She's the most brilliant salesperson I've ever met, but she's a lousy manager. She is terribly abusive of her employees. She charms her customers. She's a workaholic. She operates on almost zip margin. She is one tough, feisty woman."[38]

"Salesmanship is a special talent," she said. "I'm having a very hard time getting good help. They watch the clock, they don't have brains. It makes me sick."

Mrs. B's Hero

How is it that the laidback, even-tempered Warren Buffett would be interested in dealing with the hypercritical and ruthless Mrs. B? He had known of the business and was aware of its success from living in Omaha for many years. He admired the Blumkin's business savvy. In the late 1960s, he had offered $7 million for Nebraska Furniture Mart, an amount that Mrs. B turned down while calling him cheap. The Blumkins had rejected other offers to buy the store, as well. "Who could afford to buy a store this big?" said Mrs. B.

But two decades later, on his 53rd birthday in 1983, Warren came into the Mart again for the purpose of making Mrs. B another offer: $60 million for 90 percent of the company. This time, she accepted. The Louie Blumkin family subsequently bought back a 10 percent share and Berkshire's final purchase price was approximately $55 million. Mrs. B and Buffett shook hands on the deal. No lawyers were involved, there was no audit, and no inventory was taken of the merchandise.

After the handshake, Buffett and the Blumkins put in writing an agreement that was about one page in length. Buffett said, "The document mainly says that we shook hands. If she ran a popcorn stand, I'd want to be in the business with her."[39] "First of all, A, she's just plain smart, B, she's a fierce competitor, C, she's a tireless worker, and D, she has a realistic attitude."[40]

"One question I always ask myself in appraising a business is how I would like, assuming I had ample capital and skilled personnel, to compete with it. I'd rather wrestle grizzlies than compete with Mrs. B and her progeny. They buy brilliantly, they operate at expense ratios competitors don't even dream about, and they then pass on to their customers much of the savings. It's the ideal business—one built upon exceptional value to the customer that in turn translates into exceptional economics for its owners."[41]

Mrs. B viewed the sale as a way to avoid family conflict after her death. She split the proceeds of the sale five ways between her four children and herself.[42] Only the Blumkin family branch, of son Louie, retained any ownership of Nebraska Furniture Mart, at ten percent.

An announcement of the deal took place at a press conference in the carpet department (Figure 1.3).

The announcement had little impact on the price of Berkshire Hathaway stock. It increased from $1,145 a share to $1,155 a share on the day of the announcement. Perhaps Mrs. B's biggest mistake in her business career was not selling for part cash and part stock. She knew cash, but she did not know stocks, though her sister Rebecca was a whiz in the stock market. She was content with the $55 million and Buffett was happy to hang onto Berkshire shares, so for them it was a win-win deal.

Figure 1.3 Warren Buffett and Rose Blumkin Announce Their Handshake Deal, 1983
Source: Nebraska Furniture Mart.

But for the sake of entertainment, let's say that Mrs. B had taken just $1 million of the $55 million in stock rather than cash on that day in 1983. She would have received around 870 shares of Berkshire Hathaway, today valued at $87 million. If the deal had been $35 million in cash and $20 million in stock (an absurd, but fun scenario to consider), the stock would be worth $1.75 billion today or $349 million for each of the five Blumkin family units.

Until Mrs. B's death, there was little evidence of a Berkshire Hathaway presence in Nebraska Furniture Mart. Now, there are photos of Warren Buffett in the bedding department, with a Berkshire mattress collection featuring a deluxe model that bears the name "The Warren."

Of Buffett, Mrs. B said, "My hero is the middle class, the immigrants, and Warren Buffett. He's a genius. I respect him a lot. He is very honest, very plain and his word is as good as gold. I think there's not another one in the city who is so gentle, so nice, so honest, and so friendly."[43]

Mrs. B spoke regularly with Buffett after the purchase. Today, he is involved in strategic decisions. Having the connection to Berkshire Hathaway is a great asset to the Mart. As Vice President Bob Batt says, "When you have Warren Buffett for your business advisor, it's like getting physics lessons from Albert Einstein."[44]

Buffett conducted an experiment in collaboration between Berkshire subsidiary companies when, in 1990, he placed See's Candy inside Nebraska Furniture Mart. As he reported to his shareholders, it was an instant success.

> Last year at the Mart there occurred an historic event: I experienced a counter revelation. Regular readers of this report know that I have long scorned the boasts of corporate executives about synergy, deriding such claims as the last refuge of scoundrels defending foolish acquisitions. But now I know better: In Berkshire's first synergistic explosion, NFM put a See's candy cart in the store late last year and sold more candy than that moved by some of the full-fledged stores See's operates in California. This success contradicts all tenets of retailing. With the Blumkins, though, the impossible is routine.[45]

Shortly after the sale that year, Buffett sent Mrs. B two dozen roses and a box of candy for her 90th birthday. Rose said, "I got a young boyfriend. And a smart one."[46] He continued this birthday tradition for a few years, most often delivering the presents in person. "I just want her to know that I will always admire and like her. I like to see her face when she sees me coming," he said. The birthday roses for Rose continued until an unfortunate family business conflict erupted.

Multigenerational Relations

The workplace dispute in May 1989 that led Mrs. B to quit the company she founded and start a new competing store was publicized far beyond its true impact. It was, however, newsworthy, and it gave the public another glimpse into the character and persona of Mrs. B. She was applauded on ABC's *20/20* television show for her nonagenarian chutzpah. It's even possible that the story inspired other elderly persons or retirees to return to work or become entrepreneurs.

The simple fact is that she got mad one day and walked out of the store. What drove her to this point of exasperation is a lesson in multigenerational interaction. Mrs. B felt that her authority was being eroded by her two grandsons, Irv and Ron Blumkin, who had taken over running the business from their father, Louie. Mrs. B was a hands-on manager. She was aware of everything going on in the store, involving all purchases and sales. There had been a series of small annoyances in the running of the store that aggravated Mrs. B and that probably all contributed to her rash action.

She felt that improving the physical appearance of the store was a waste of money. "All the remodeling is the stupidest thing," she said. "The customers don't need remodeling. They need service and attention." But the final blow came when she wasn't consulted in a major carpeting decision.

"They had priced carpeting that cost the store $14 a square yard at $6," she said. "I say, 'How can you do it?' " Louie and Ronald Blumkin confirmed that the store had spent $14 for carpeting it sold for $6.

"That's what teed her off, I guess," Louie Blumkin said. But the decision was correct, he insisted. The carpeting was four years old and the pattern was obsolete. It's somewhat ironic that this incident would anger the woman whose philosophy had been to sell cheap.[47] And it now seems rather trivial in the gigantic world of Nebraska Furniture Mart.

"Nobody wanted her to leave," said her son, Louie. Mrs. B said she was not upset with Louie. "He's one in a million," she said. However, she said she has used the name "Hitler" to refer to grandsons Ronald and Irvin.[48]

Of this conflict, Warren Buffett said, "It's such a marvelous family. And such a generational gap." Mrs. B wanted to buy back the carpet department from Berkshire. "I would buy it in a minute," she said. "I would pay him a high price—$5 million, $8 million, whatever it takes. If Buffett doesn't sell it back, I want to run the carpet department for Buffett, independently from my grandsons. If I can't talk Buffett into either of those options, I can open a new store."

Buffett declined to respond to Mrs. B's offers, except to say that there is no noncompete clause that would prevent her from opening another store. She acknowledged, "It probably would be a first for a 96-year-old woman to start a business. But I feel capable of doing it and want to prove to Buffett and my grandsons that I can do it. I could outsmart any 25-year-old."[49] Ronald said that he would like to see his grandmother happy and fulfilled once again.

Mrs. B quickly became bored after leaving the store. She hired a chauffeur who drove her around Omaha each day from 9:00 until noon, from 1:00 to 3:30, and in the evenings from 6:00 to 8:00. The driver took her to other stores. She looked in the windows and checked to see how many cars were in their parking lots. It didn't take long for her to plan her revenge.

By September, she had decided to open a discount furniture store. "I want to be my own boss. Nobody's going to tell me what to do. I had enough. I'm going to let 'em have it. Thank God, I've still got my brains. I've got health, money, and strength and common sense. I know how to beat everybody."[50]

She placed an advertisement in the *Omaha World Herald* on February 11, 1990, announcing the grand opening of Mrs. B's Warehouse. It read, "Now I'm starting over again. The same way . . . struggling. The only difference, now I got the money and I don't need credit. I've made terrific buys on good quality merchandise. Come see me for great deals and the best prices in town." The new store was directly adjacent to Nebraska Furniture Mart in a converted grocery distribution center.

That's when the television news crews came calling. ABC's Bob Brown came to Omaha, interviewing Mrs. B for a *20/20* episode that aired in July 1990. Mrs. B was particularly feisty on the day of Bob Brown's interview. He asked if she would ever retire. She said, "No. I love to be with people. And my customers are so wonderful people. Show me one person 96 years old should go in business. I'm the only one in the country."

"And would you like to see Nebraska Furniture Mart go out of business?," he asked. "I would it should go in a smoke. I like they should go down to hell," she replied.[51] This shocking statement is an accurate representation of Mrs. B's typical response to life. Everything was black and white. Good or bad. Decisions were easily made with a yes or no. There were no grey areas with her.

Says Buffett, "Everything Mrs. B knew how to do, she would do fast. She didn't hesitate and there was no second-guessing. She'd buy five thousand tables or sign a thirty-year lease or buy real estate or hire people. There was no looking back. She just swung."[52]

She lived by her own set of rules, extremely organized, that gave her and her family's lives structure and a strong foundation. The rules of running her business were similarly simple. Sell cheap. Tell the truth. Fortunately, Mrs. B lived long enough to reconcile with her family. But the first relationship to be patched up was with Warren Buffett. Rose was angry with him after she felt he had sided with her grandsons. They hadn't spoken since the day she walked out of the Mart. But two days before her 98th birthday in 1991, Buffett once again brought roses and chocolates to her at work. "He's a real gentleman," she said, after accepting Buffett's peace offering.

She settled her differences with her grandsons in 1992 and sold Mrs. B's Warehouse to Nebraska Furniture Mart in January 1993 for $4.94 million with a provision that she could keep control of the carpet department. This time Buffett made sure to have Mrs. B, age 99, sign a noncompete agreement lasting for five years beyond her separation from the company.

"I thought she might go on forever," Buffett said. "I needed five years beyond forever with her. And then I made sure she never got mad."[53]

"Maybe I was wrong. Maybe I was too hard on them," Mrs. B said of the feud with her grandsons. "I'm very independent. If things aren't run the way I want it, I don't like it. I get mad."[54]

Nebraska Furniture Mart nurtures relationships with multiple generations of employees and customers. Currently, three of Mrs. B's grandsons and three great-grandchildren work for the company. There are also three and four generations of unrelated families who have worked at Nebraska Furniture Mart. Examples of longevity and continuity are evident in all areas of the organization. One of the current employees, Jack Diamond, started in 1954.

Giving and Receiving

Rose Blumkin was extremely generous throughout her life, although she said, "Everything I made stayed in the business. I never had a vacation, never went any place, never made parties. Accumulated penny by penny."[55] It's true that she did not spend on herself, but she donated money and merchandise to many recipients.

After struggling in the first half of her life, Mrs. B lived comfortably in the second half, but she was never frivolous with her earnings. She lived in modest houses and owned modest cars. Besides her success with Nebraska Furniture Mart, she also had real estate investments that accumulated millions for her when she sold Nebraska farmland to city developers.

Even during the Depression when they were struggling themselves, she and Isadore helped people who came into the pawn shop. In the late 1930s she was visited by a woman who talked about an impossible dream of a Jewish homeland in Palestine. The woman was raising money for that cause, and needed a place where she could call together prospective donors. Mrs. B believed the woman's goal to be doomed to failure, but she offered her own home as a meeting place.

"She was a very good speaker, very bright, very smart," Mrs. B recalled years later. It turned out, of course, that the woman's dream was not impossible. Israel was founded a decade after that meeting in Mrs. B's Omaha home, and the woman who partook of Mrs. B's hospitality later served as prime minister. She was Golda Meir.[56]

In 1956, Mrs. B established the Blumkin Foundation for worthwhile charity and educational purposes. "I like to give to good causes. I believe in giving before I die," she said. If there was a fire or flood that destroyed a home, she would give them new furniture and carpeting. One day, when a customer at Nebraska Furniture Mart remarked that he was from Fort Dodge, Iowa, Mrs. B immediately gave him a check for $500 for the Fort Dodge community fund. She was forever grateful to the residents of Fort Dodge for their kindness when she first arrived in the United States.[57]

In 1972, she helped flood victims in Rapid City, South Dakota, by buying up the contents of the Omaha Hadassah Bargain Store for $5,000. She had the clothing shipped to the flood victims and the proceeds from the sale were sent to medical organizations in Israel for cancer research.

Rose Blumkin received many honors and awards, including the Omaha Sertoma Club Service to Mankind Award; 1979 Free Enterprise Person of the Year from the Rotary Club of Omaha, Nebraska; 1985 Retailer of the Year, Nebraska Chamber Hall of Fame; Distinguished Nebraska Award from the Nebraska Society of Washington, D.C.; and the Omaha Press Club's Face on the Ballroom Floor. This latter award entails the creation of a caricature of the recipient. Mrs. B requested that her portrait be hung in the club next to Warren Buffett's.

She purchased the Astro Theater from Creighton University in 1981 for $205,000 because she didn't want the building to be torn down. It was one of the few buildings in the Midwest possessing a unique combination of Moorish and Classical architecture, constructed in 1927, and Creighton had plans to raze the structure. All that stood in the way was a designation of the building as a local historic landmark. The university filed a lawsuit against the City of Omaha over the issue.

The Blumkins subsequently donated $1 million for renovation of the building and there was much discussion about what should be done with it. Buffett also donated $1 million toward the renovation efforts on the occasion of Rose's 100th birthday in 1993.[58] Finally, in November 1995, the theater reopened as the Rose Blumkin Performing Arts Center, now commonly referred to as "The Rose."

The year 1981 was also when the Blumkin family helped break ground on the Rose Blumkin Jewish Home, built with $1 million donated by Rose and her children. On that day, Rose said, "I respect elderly people. I treated my mother like a queen and God repaid me. I want elderly people to be treated right. So I want to give my love to the elderly people, especially those who have no one to care for them.

If I'll be able to live longer, I'll try to do my best to help them all I can. When you get older, you can't take anything with you. Let people think before they die to do the best they can for others while they are still alive. A new home for the elderly will be like adding life to their years. They deserve a *haimeshe* place to live in comfort and dignity and having the Home at the Jewish Community Center will be like reuniting the Jewish family—all the generations will be coming home."[59]

She was honored by the Omaha Public Schools, The State of Israel Bonds, The Omaha Education Association, and The Omaha Fire-fighter's Association. The woman who never attended school and couldn't read or write was the recipient of some distinguished college degrees. In 1984, Mrs. B was the first woman to receive an Honorary Doctorate Degree in Commercial Science from New York University. Also, in 1984, she received an Honorary Doctorate of Law degree from Creighton University.

Rose instilled charitable giving in her children's lives, also, although she wasn't always aligned with their selection of recipients. "My kids have a heart in them to help people who needs. Sometimes, I'm not so crazy when they give to symphony and to the dance. I don't care for it. The arts. I like people who needs it worse. You can't tell 'em nothing."[60]

On Christmas Day in 1987, she went out with her granddaughter and great-grandson to deliver a Meals On Wheels lunch to a housebound woman. Posthumously, the Omaha City Council approved the renaming of 76th Drive, a three-quarter-mile-long street running along the west edge of Nebraska Furniture Mart property, as "Rose Blumkin Drive."

God Bless America

Rose Blumkin's long life allowed her to accumulate numerous experiences in the community and business. She was forever grateful that she was able to come to the United States and loved her adopted homeland. Mrs. B's favorite song was "God Bless America." She would listen to it in her CD player at home and on a cassette tape in her car. "The people who were born in this country don't appreciate all these wonderful things, like those who came from out of the darkness," she said. "I love the United States since the day I come here.[61]

"The American people—nobody's better. Like this country's people. I wouldn't talk about liars or thieves—the average middle class are the best people—the ones that work and like to pay their bills. That's the kind I like. Not the real big shots."[62] "I respect the middle class. They stick to their kids. There's nobody like the middle class in America. Many, many immigrants raised wonderful families. They struggled for something better. I love the American people—the immigrants who went through a struggle."[63]

She said she never had any problems with anti-Semitism. "I'll tell you one thing. I think most of the Omaha people, the Gentiles, built my business. They showed me nothing but goodness and friendship. I never met such a wonderful people."[64]

On her 100th birthday (celebrated at Mrs. B's Clearance Warehouse), she said, "All my wishes come true. American people were wonderful to me. They are the best in the world. And I made a success. I never expected that much. I did a pretty good job."

In the last three years of her life, Mrs. B was in and out of the hospital for pneumonia and heart problems. She was fitted with a pacemaker at age 103.

She had cataract surgery years earlier and had knee replacements. She officially retired in October 1997[65] and died at the age of 104 in August 1998. Upon hearing of her death, Warren Buffett said, "We are partners. And in most ways, she's the senior partner. She's forgotten more than I'll ever know."

Green was her favorite color. It appears throughout Nebraska Furniture Mart's signage and logos. But it had nothing to do with the color of money. She really didn't care about money. It was the thrill of making a sale that gave her happiness. Many of the 1,000 attendees at her funeral wore green ribbons on their lapels.

Although Mrs. B lived in a time and place that most of us cannot personally experience, there are some parallels to the current economic status that we can recognize. Her perseverance through adversity is a lesson that all twenty-first century entrepreneurs must learn. Having intense passion for whatever you pursue is invaluable and will bring happiness to your life. There are always ways to circumvent roadblocks. And there are times when one must admit that they are wrong—or at least acknowledge that their opinion is simply a differing opinion—and get on with doing what's best for the business.

Chapter 2

Susan Jacques—
Puttin' On the Glitz

S usan Jacques is fortunate to work each day surrounded by exquisite jewels, fine art glass, and precious metals. It's easy for one to envy her job as president and CEO of Borsheims Fine Jewelry and Gifts in Omaha, Nebraska, a subsidiary of Berkshire Hathaway, Inc. The simple act of going to work each day presents the opportunity to behold beauty. That's an employment benefit that's not easy to find, but one that over 200 Borsheims employees can claim.

Exploring the 62,500-square-foot store, which was remodeled in 2006, is itself a wondrous experience. Furnishings include hand-polished plaster walls, glass-beaded wall coverings, and light fixtures from Lalique, Waterford, Strongwater, and Baccarat. The floor is laid with marble tile. The display cases holding a feast of diamonds, gemstones, and watches are crafted from lyptus wood. Lyptus is a sustainable natural hybrid of eucalyptus that thrives in the warm climate of Brazil, permitting harvesting in just 14 to 16 years, one-third of the growing time required for mahogany. A salon in the heart of the space, wrapped in glass that is etched with subtle images of blowing prairie grass, offers clients a place where they can try on and purchase items with relative privacy.

Fine jewelry lasts far longer than our short human existence. It is often passed from generation to generation or sold to new owners. For example, Christie's auctioned the complete 269-piece jewelry collection of Elizabeth Taylor in December 2011. Taylor recognized her role as steward of her gems, once saying, "I've never thought of my jewelry as trophies. I'm here to take care of it and to love it, for we are only temporary custodians of beauty."[1]

"I work with a beautiful product and almost invariably deal with happy people as they celebrate the milestones of their lives," says Jacques (Figure 2.1). She joined Borsheims in 1982 as a $4-per-hour sales associate. At that time, the store was still a family owned and run business, and Susan decided to commit a year to the job to gain experience in the retail jewelry business. Things rarely go as planned, though, and she stayed with the company, working her way up through management and was appointed CEO by Warren Buffett in 1994.

As Buffett explains, the jewelry business is unique.

My sense of helplessness (in buying jewelry) led me to an obvious conclusion: "If you don't know jewelry, know your jeweler." For that reason, I made all of my jewelry purchases at Borsheims for many years before Berkshire Hathaway bought the company.

You don't need to understand the economics of a generating plant in order to intelligently buy electricity. If your neighbor is an expert on that subject and you are a neophyte, your electric rates will be identical. But jewelry purchases are different. What you pay for an item versus what your neighbor pays for a comparable item can be, and often is, widely different. Understanding the economics of the business will tell you why.

To begin with, all jewelers turn their inventory very slowly, and that ties up a lot of capital. A once-a-year turn is par for the course. Given that their turnover is low, a jeweler must obtain a

Figure 2.1   Susan Jacques, President and CEO of Borsheims
SOURCE: Borsheims Fine Jewelry and Gifts.

relatively wide profit margin on sales in order to achieve even a
mediocre return on their investment. In this respect, the jewelry
business is just the opposite of the grocery business, in which
rapid turnover of inventory allows good returns on investment
though profit margins are low.

In order to establish a selling price for their merchandise, a
jeweler must add to the price they pay for that merchandise,
both their operating costs and desired profit margin. Operating
costs seldom run less than 40 percent of sales and often exceed that
level. This fact requires most jewelers to price their merchandise

at double its cost to them or even more. The math is simple: Jewelers charge $1 for merchandise that has cost them 50 cents. Then, from their gross profit of 50 cents they typically pay 40 cents for operating costs, which leaves 10 cents of pretax earnings for every $1 of sales. Taking into account the massive investment in inventory, the 10-cent profit is adequate but far from exciting.

At Borsheims the equation is far different from what I have just described. Because of its single location and the huge volume generated, the operating expense ratio is usually around 20 percent of sales. As a percentage of sales, rent costs alone are fully five points below those of the typical competitor. Therefore, goods are priced far below the prices charged by other jewelers.[2]

I visited Susan and Adrienne Fay, Director of Marketing, at the Borsheims store, a quick five-minute trip from my home. They were both very helpful and informative in sharing their career experiences and knowledge of the jewelry industry.

Tiffany's on the Prairie

Borsheims is regarded as a leader in the jewelry and fine gifts industries. With over 100,000 items in inventory, Borsheims is second only to Tiffany's in terms of the range and volume of merchandise sold from a single location. There is a wide selection in all categories of merchandise and a correspondingly wide range of prices. Where a typical jewelry store may have four different lines of watches, Borsheims carries 21 different brands, representing 11 percent of the total inventory of the store. In the recent remodel, the store increased the size of its watch department from 1,500 square feet to 4,500 square feet.

Tip to Shoppers #1

The price is not the price! There is something called the Borsheims Price, which is lower than what is marked on the price tag. There must be hundreds of people who have strolled in over the years, turned over an item to look at the price and walked right out. Don't let this happen to you! Ask a sales associate for the *real* price. They won't be offended. Nothing is sold for the marked price. I don't understand the system, but I've learned to play their game.

It actually took me about 10 years to set foot in Borsheims after I moved to Omaha. I was intimidated by its quiet, elite atmosphere. I wasn't in a position to purchase fine jewelry at that time, anyway. But now, it's the first place I think of for wedding, anniversary, and retirement gifts. In Nebraska, we jump up and down when we see the familiar silver box with burgundy ribbon. It's the same physiological response that New Yorkers have when they receive a baby blue box with a white bow.

Says Jacques, "This jewelry store is like no other jewelry store in the United States. And there is an intimidation factor; we understand that. And we work very hard to counteract that as often as we possibly can. Here, they have to go through a fairly upscale mall and they've got to walk past a security officer. We cater to the customer. If it is a $20 wedding gift they want to buy . . . or a $3,000 diamond anniversary gift, they know they can buy it here."[3]

Security guards are an unfortunate necessity for the company, but to a customer, and certainly to employees, the guards can also give a sense of safety. Security is paramount when there are millions of dollars of assets in plain sight. But if you still don't feel comfortable shopping in the store, there is another option.

Tip to Shoppers #2

You can request that items be shipped to you for review before purchasing. Yes! They will send you several items in your price range that you can touch . . . hold . . . *fondle* without ever leaving your home.

Susan confirms this unusual sales practice, saying, "If you are recommended to me by a very good customer, we will send inventory to people in their homes, or in their offices." She adds that, "The Internet has assisted us, in that we no longer have to ship out as much inventory because we can e-mail pictures back and forth. [Our clients] can narrow their selection. [When] somebody calls, we used to send 12 diamond necklaces because we didn't know what they wanted to look at.

Now we say, 'Focus it. Tell me your top three candidates.' And we'll ship those out. We do a lot of that. It's not something we promote heavily for security reasons. You know, we definitely qualify the customers before we start sending packages out to people that just happen to call up and say that they're Warren's best friend."[4]

About 45 percent of Borsheims's business comes from out-of state clients, but there are several channels of sales, including Internet, catalog, phone, e-mail, and in-store purchases. One limitation is that international sales and shipping are difficult. There are duty charges and excise taxes to be paid. Most of Borsheims's international clients shop at the store in person when they happen to be in the States.

A Civil War Youth

Susan is not a native corn-fed Nebraska Husker, a fact you will quickly discover as soon as she speaks a few syllables of the Queen's English. Jacques was born and raised in Salisbury, Rhodesia, in Africa, known as the city of Harare in the country of Zimbabwe since gaining independence in 1980. Susan is the second of three daughters of a British father and Australian mother. Harare is the largest city and capital of the country. Victoria Falls, one of the world's most spectacular waterfalls, is located in the country's northwestern region. Zimbabwe experienced tumultuous and complicated changes during the twentieth century political history.

In 1888, Cecil Rhodes, namesake of Rhodesia, obtained a concession for mineral rights from local African chiefs. Later that year, the area that became Southern and Northern Rhodesia was proclaimed a British colony. It became a self-governing state in 1923, and the Federation of Rhodesia and Nyasaland came into being in 1953. The creation of the Federation had almost immediate positive effects on the Rhodesian economy. The country entered a boom period and immigration from the United Kingdom and South Africa surged.[5]

It was during this period of growth, in 1958, that Susan's parents immigrated to Rhodesia after getting married and having their first child in Southern India. The Jacques family started a timber business and Susan was born the following year. Susan's mother worked in the office of the small family company, keeping the books. "She was certainly a role model for me, working and raising a family. She waited to get married and had her children later in life," says Susan. Susan knows some basic greeting phrases in Shona, the native language, but she went to a segregated girl's school. "It was, unfortunately, a very segregated society," says Jacques.

As a child, Susan Jacques was fascinated with colorful rocks and shells. She used to spend her allowance every Friday on jewelry. "We'd go to the store, and they used to sell those inexpensive little rings—the 5-cent, 10-cent rings. Every Friday I bought a ring. Even back then, I loved jewelry."[6]

Susan had no particular career interest after graduating from high school. "My mother insisted that I take a one-year secretarial course because 'you can always be a secretary, you can always fall back on that.' And, now that I actually type on a computer I'm delighted to have my typing skills, because I can do it a little faster," says Jacques.[7]

Following the year of secretarial training, she got a job as junior secretary at Scottish Jewellers, the largest jewelry company in Rhodesia at the time. In the late 1970s, the political situation in Rhodesia deteriorated. In 1976, there was a tremendous escalation of terrorist activity. The southeastern border with Mozambique became a major battlefield. Rhodesia became Zimbabwe-Rhodesia and a black Methodist bishop, Abel Muzorewa, won a large and very credible majority in the general elections in March 1979. Britain refused to recognize this election.[8]

At Christmastime in 1978, during the height of the turmoil, Susan's father sent his three daughters to live in England for safety reasons. Susan worked for EMI Leisure Hotels in London as a secretary. She did not enjoy her time in England because her heart was back home. She was 19 years old and the young man she was dating was still in Zimbabwe fighting in the Civil War.

Zimbabwe gained internationally recognized independence in 1980 and Robert Mugabe has been President since that time. Since the mid-1990s, Zimbabwe's infrastructure has been collapsing. Political turmoil and poor management of the economy have led to considerable hardships. The country currently faces severe economic, health, and food crises. The average life expectancy of 49 years is one of the lowest in the world.[9] Susan no longer has any family in Zimbabwe, although both of her parents are buried there. Her older sister lives in Cyprus and her younger sister is in England.

Susan's mother didn't see her own parents and siblings for a period of 15 years, from departing India through establishing a family and home in Rhodesia. So she asked her own three grown daughters to make a pact that they would continue to see each other frequently, and they've indeed remained very close. Now the three sisters and their families get together for two weeks each summer, selecting different locations in which to meet. Susan has not been back to Zimbabwe since 1997, and she travels on a British passport.

"My dream had always been to go back there, but I never want to travel and take my children anywhere where they may come into harm's way. There are plenty of other great places to go visit."

A Gem of a Career

Susan lived in London for the 1979 calendar year, then returned to Rhodesia. Scottish Jewellers had another secretarial position open and also a position in marketing. Susan recalls, "I said, 'Well, I'm young and foolish and I don't know the difference,' so I joined the marketing department and soon realized this was fascinating. It had great potential, and now I knew what I actually probably wanted to study."[10]

Her childhood interest in rocks and shells had evolved into a keen interest in beautiful gems and jewelry. "After a few months of doing product design and inventory levels, some of the merchandising and marketing, I realized that I knew very little and needed to get some knowledge if I was going to stay in the field," she said.[11]

Some of her associates in the company had taken a correspondence course offered by the Gemological Institute of America (GIA). Her parents agreed to send her to the campus in Santa Monica, California, for the six-month graduate gemology program in 1980. Besides the identification of gems, the institute teaches the legends and lore about each stone. The GIA has 11 educational campuses worldwide and now also provides online long-distance education.

"Santa Monica is a pretty delightful part of the Earth to land in and there were actually five of us from Zimbabwe who came over at one time. The course is incredible," she adds. "It is like a college career done in six months."[12]

She was taught by excellent professionals and received a thorough education. "I was very much influenced by my colored gemstone instructor, William E. (Bill) Boyajian," says Susan. "He really inspired in me the deep interest I have to this day in gemstones, particularly rare and unusual stones, and the jewelry industry as a whole. He was, and is, one of the most energetic, enthusiastic, and dynamic people I have had the privilege to know."[13]

"In all my years teaching, I never saw anyone who was so intelligent and personable," says Bill Boyajian, who is also a former president of the Gemological Institute of America. "Her positive attitude helped her get where she is today."[14]

There was also a young man who sat in front of her in class who would greatly influence the path of her life. His name was Alan Friedman, and his father, Ike Friedman, owned a jewelry store in Omaha, Nebraska, called Borsheims, and they became good friends. Jacques graduated at the top of her class with one of the highest grades ever earned at the school. Susan and Alan kept in touch after their 1980 graduation and Jacques moved back home to Zimbabwe.

"I went back for three months. My heart was there and still is," she says, "but there wasn't a promising future at that time." In 1981, she left Zimbabwe once again and went back to California. She started working at United States Gemological Services, Inc. (USGSI) in Santa Ana, California, a small grading and certification laboratory. She says, "We did a lot of certification at that time of colored gem stones, which are one of my great passions. I loved that job, sitting at a microscope, grading stones."

In 1982, Susan became a Fellow of the Gemmological Association of Great Britain, where she was awarded the Raynor Diploma prize as outstanding student worldwide. She said it is somewhat rare for a person to hold both the GIA and British titles. The latter is more technical, while the American degree is designed for people in the sales end of the jewelry industry.

The height of the investment boom in gemstones and gold occurred in 1981. Says Susan, "It's not too dissimilar to what we are experiencing right now. Gold went to $800 an ounce and silver went to $60 an ounce. A one-carat grade D flawless diamond went from $9,000 per carat to $60,000 per carat in an 18-month period. Everybody chose to cash in on it and the prices just tumbled." The bottom had dropped out of the market.

She had been at USGSI for about a year and a half when the lab began to struggle and had to reduce employees' hours. "They cut us back to a four-day week," she says. "I was studying for the British exams at the time and then they cut us back even more, to a three-day week. My parents back in Africa were unable to fund my living expenses and I couldn't figure out how I was going to make my rent and car payments."

When she discussed the situation with her friend and former class-mate, Friedman, he invited her to come work at Borsheims. She had no desire to leave southern California for Nebraska. But she did need the job, so she decided to give it a year so that she could gain some retail sales experience.

"If you had asked me in 1982, when I first moved here, 'Where do you see yourself 20 years from now?' I probably would have given a variety of answers. I don't think any of them would have included still being here in Omaha."[15] She began as a sales associate at $4 per hour in the fall of 1982, was promoted to jewelry merchandise manager and buyer in 1986, and became a senior vice president in 1991.

"I got in on the ground level at a perfect time," she said.[16] "I had never done sales. So I said to Ike, 'I'm going to work at watching people for about a week or so, and see how everything goes, and then what I'll do is I'll try and do some sales.' And he was like 'No, it doesn't work like that, honey. You get out on the sales floor today. You get out there and you make some sales.' It was amazing to me." She credits Ike Friedman and his son-in-law Marvin Cohn, executive vice president at the time, for being tremendous mentors who taught her all she knows about sales.[17]

Jacques is now a leading force in the jewelry industry, playing an active role in professional organizations. She is currently the chair of the Board of Governors of the Gemological Institute of America. She has served on the boards of the Jewelers of America, the Jewelers Vigilance Committee, and the Jewelers' Circular Keystone Advisory Council.

Jacques was inducted into the National Jeweler's Hall of Fame in 1997, the third female in the industry ever to receive the honor. She was the recipient of the 1999 Annual Award for Excellence in Retail, a distinction presented by the Women's Jewelry Association.

She is a member of the 62-member Board of Jewelers for Children, an organization founded in 1999 by the U.S. jewelry industry with the mission of helping children in need. She was honored by the organization at their 2004 Facet of Hope dinner.

Susan received the Lifetime Achievement Award from the Women's Jewelry Association in July 2010. The honor is bestowed on a woman who has made an extraordinary contribution to the jewelry industry.

Aside from her professional leadership roles, Jacques has also served on several community boards, including the Greater Omaha Chamber of Commerce, the Omaha Theater Company for Young People, the University of Nebraska Medical Center Board of Counselors, and the American Lung Association. She was elected to Creighton University's Board of Directors in 2001 and was featured in the book *A Celebration of Women*, produced by the Women's Fund of Greater Omaha.

From Old West to Glitzy Glamour

Borsheims Jewelry Store was founded in 1870 in Omaha by Louis A. Borsheim. Nebraska had become a state only three years earlier, but Omaha was incorporated in 1857, and by 1870 it had a population of 16,000.

The first transcontinental railroad opened in May 1869 and many settlers traveled through Omaha on their way westward. Some put down roots and stayed in the riverbank town. What type of jewelry Louis sold can only be imagined. At the height of Victorian fashion in 1870, cameos and jewelry made from human hair were particularly popular.

Borsheim's business had a strong connection with the railroad. For many years, it served as the official railroad watch inspector for eight railroads. This activity was vital to the railroad, which commonly operated on single-track routes with strict timetables. All stations and train conductors had to have their watches synchronized to avoid trains crashing into one another.

Following Louis's retirement, the store was operated by his son, John Louis Borshiem, and grandson, Louis C. Borsheim. During the depression in the early 1930s, the family sold majority ownership of 51 percent of the Borsheims store to a Pittsburgh firm. In 1948, Louis Friedman and his brother-in-law Simon Gorelick bought the store.

Borsheims and the Nebraska Furniture Mart are inextricably connected by their Gorelick family origins. Rose Gorelick Blumkin (Mrs. B) was the founder of Nebraska Furniture Mart. Simon Gorelick was her brother, and her sister Rebecca was the wife of Louis Friedman. The two companies also share similar retailing philosophies of "sell cheap and tell the truth."

Rebecca Gorelick married Louis Friedman while still living in Russia. In December 1922, with Rebecca six months pregnant, the Friedmans left. They traveled part of the way by train and a portion by horse and buggy. Additionally, at least 10 miles were made on foot to complete the journey from Minsk to the Russian border with Latvia. Rebecca later lost the baby.[18]

With the help of Mrs. B and other relatives, the Friedmans came to the United States, arriving in Omaha on July 10, 1923. Louis started working at 25 cents per hour at the Swift meat-packing plant, and Rebecca sold furniture scarves door to door. Their son, Isadore (Ike), was born July 10, 1924, exactly one year later. After the first year, they had saved up enough money to open a pawnshop.

Louis helped Rose Blumkin open the Nebraska Furniture Mart in 1937 and worked there. When Ike returned from the war in 1946, he started working at the furniture store as well. Ike later remembered, "I was selling, delivering, cleaning up, everything. I got quite a lot of business philosophy from my aunt and my mother. My aunt is very successful. She's a phenomenon."

After the Blumkin and Friedman sons returned from World War II, it became clear that the furniture store might be a little crowded for both families, so Friedman sold his share back to Mrs. B and purchased Borsheims with Gorelick. Ike joined Borsheims in 1950.

Simon Gorelick died in 1952, and the Friedmans became the sole owner of Borsheims. Ike bought out his father in 1973, but the elder Friedman continued to work at the store each and every day until his death at age 89. Ike said he got his work habits from his father.

"Dad would always say, 'Just keep working.'"[19] Louis went to work at Borsheims on a Saturday in August 1989 and died the following Monday.

Ike started working at 11 years old, selling the *Omaha World Herald* newspaper on the street outside the Paxton Hotel, and later devoted most of his waking hours to Borsheims. "I don't even go out for lunch," he said. "I usually have a sandwich brought in. If you're not here, attending to business, you miss phone calls."[20]

Ike's mother, Rebecca, also worked at Borsheims, but had a passion for playing the stock market. She, like her sister Rose, had a knack for numbers. During the 1970s, she could be found each day at Dain, Kalman & Quail, watching the electronic board flash the latest stock quotes. Known to the brokers as "Becky," she brought them cookies on holidays.

"I come every day," she said. "I love it. I understand everything. I have to watch how they go up and down,"[21] Bob Batt, Rebecca's great-nephew, and vice-president at the Nebraska Furniture Mart, said. "We always called her Auntie Ticker Tape. She could give you the current stock quote on any stock."[22]

In 1976, she was interviewed and said, "Look at IBM. It once was 150¾. Now it's 242. It used to be 400." She shrugs. "You take your chances in this game." She said she'd been interested in the market since 1929. She didn't recall exactly how much she made or lost. "American Motors was pretty good. I made a little," she said.[23] Rebecca lived to age 91.

Ike Friedman grew Borsheims from a small downtown store with 30 employees to the suburban mall phenomenon that it is today. "Ike Friedman was a remarkable character," says Susan Jacques. "A computer mind who knew people by their jewelry, knew people by their previous purchases, knew exactly what everybody had, incredible negotiator, incredible buyer, and incredible salesman."[24]

Being a jeweler is a potentially risky profession. The store in downtown Omaha was robbed at least six times between 1956 and 1980, sometimes with a gun prodding the chest of Louis or Ike. One time, Ike hopped into his car to follow two boys who had taken a display tray of rings. The boys were on foot and Ike followed them in the car for about a mile, turning up and down the streets and driving through an alley until a policeman intercepted the boys.[25]

In 1980, a security guard, working for $3.27 per hour, was injured when he was repeatedly hit on the head with a revolver during a scuffle. The thief ran out the front door with 18 bridal ring sets. The security guard, 70 years old, was planning to retire the following week, but said, "I think I'll go back (to work). They might think I was chicken if I didn't and nobody is going to call me chicken."[26]

By 1986, Borsheims had outgrown its downtown facility, thus prompting a move of six miles to the west to its current location in Regency Court, an upscale shopping mall that now hosts Williams Sonoma, Christian Nobel Furs, and Fleming's Steakhouse.

Sell Him the Store!

A couple of years later, Warren Buffett heard through the Blumkin family that the Friedmans might be interested in selling their jewelry store. He came into the store in December 1988 to shop for Christmas presents. While he was looking at the merchandise with a salesperson, Donald Yale, who was Ike Friedman's son-in-law, spotted him. He shouted to the salesperson, "Don't sell him the ring, sell him the store!"[27]

In January 1989, after very little discussion and apparently no negotiation, Borsheims became part of the Berkshire Hathaway family. Through a simple handshake, Warren E. Buffett purchased 80 percent of Borsheims's stock from Ike Friedman, at a price estimated to be something over $60 million.[28] Friedman told Buffett what the business was worth, and that was that. No audit or inventory. "What Ike said is so, is so," Buffett said.[29]

Buffett was excited to add Borsheims to the Berkshire family. As he said in his 1989 Letter to Shareholders, "It was in 1983 that Berkshire purchased an 80 percent interest in The Nebraska Furniture Mart. Your Chairman blundered then by neglecting to ask Mrs. B a question any schoolboy would have thought of: 'Are there any more at home like you?' Last month I corrected the error: We are now 80 percent partners with another branch of the family."

Buffett went on to praise the Friedmans for their forthrightness, business sense, and retailing abilities. "It is great fun to be in business with people you have long admired," he said. "The Friedmans, like the

Blumkins, have achieved success because they have deserved success. Both families focus on what's right for the customer and that inevitably, works out well for them, also."[30]

Buffett shared a story about Ike. "A story will illustrate why I enjoy Ike so much: Every two years I'm part of an informal group that gathers to have fun and explore a few subjects. Last September, meeting at Bishop's Lodge in Santa Fe, we asked Ike, his wife Roz, and his son Alan to come by and educate us on jewels and the jewelry business.

"Ike decided to dazzle the group, so he brought from Omaha about $20 million of particularly fancy merchandise. I was somewhat apprehensive—Bishop's Lodge is no Fort Knox—and I mentioned my concern to Ike at our opening party the evening before his presentation. Ike took me aside. 'See that safe?' he said. 'This afternoon we changed the combination and now even the hotel management doesn't know what it is.' I breathed easier. Ike went on: 'See those two big fellows with guns on their hips? They'll be guarding the safe all night.' I now was ready to rejoin the party. But Ike leaned closer: 'And besides, Warren,' he confided, 'the jewels aren't in the safe.'"[31]

"Becoming a subsidiary of Berkshire Hathaway opened our market to a whole new group of people who previously may not have been aware of us," says Susan.[32]

As usual in Berkshire acquisitions, Buffett chose to leave the current management team in place. "We'd have to be damn fools to alter anything" said Buffett. Buffett said he and Charlie will "stay in the stands and cheer."[33] Buffett gave the management team straightforward directions, "Don't change a thing." Unfortunately, things would change very soon as Louis died eight months later and Ike, himself, lived for just two years more.

Ike, a longtime smoker, was diagnosed with lung cancer in March 1991 and died the following September. Says Jacques, "Ike was a remarkable, remarkable genius in our industry. He was a great mentor to me for nine years until he passed away. I was very blessed to work really close beside him. I learned so much about how to treat your customer."[34]

Upon Ike's death, Warren Buffett said, "Ike was a business genius and a showman of style and imagination. I loved Ike as a personal pal."[35] After Ike's death, Donald Yale took over as president of Borsheims. Alan Friedman sold his share of the company to Berkshire and left to open his own jewelry store in Beverly Hills. Susan was promoted to senior vice president.

Summoned to Headquarters

Two years later, in 1993, Yale's wife Janis was diagnosed with cancer and he resigned to take care of her and their five young children. The Yale family later sold their share of the company to Berkshire.

A few weeks after Yale gave notice, Buffett made a phone call to Jacques. She remembers, "Warren called me at about 10 o'clock one morning, and said something like, 'Is there any chance you can come down to the office this afternoon to meet with me?' and I assumed he was meeting with all of the executives on the team for an update on how things were going, so I told him that I'd be happy to go down and see him. But then I realized that I wasn't wearing one of my favorite suits. And, you know, I wanted to look very professional if I was going to have a meeting with Warren."

At that time, Jacques lived on a farm near Fort Calhoun—about a 30-minute drive from Borsheims—and she and her husband also had a small apartment close to the store. "So, I called up my husband," she recalls, "and I said, 'Warren's asked me to go down to his office and I have to go home and change, but my shoes are at the farm and my suit is at the apartment.' So Gene said, 'You go get the suit and I'll run to the farm and get the shoes for you.' So Gene is speeding along the Interstate to get my shoes and he gets pulled over by a cop. And he says to the cop, 'You are never going to believe this, but my wife has an appointment with Warren Buffett this afternoon and I've got to go get her shoes.' And the cop said, 'That's a good one, I haven't heard that one today,' and he let Gene off with a warning."[36]

After changing into her suit and shoes, Jacques went to her meeting with Buffett. Soon after they began talking, she discovered that he hadn't just called her in for an update, he was offering her the position of president. She was 34 years old at the time.

"Never in a million years would I have anticipated that I would someday hold the position of Borsheims' president," says Susan.

"When Warren Buffett asked me to meet him at his office. I thought nothing of the call except that perhaps he wanted to discuss store operations. When he offered me the position, I was completely stunned." It was an offer not without some concerns. She was enjoying her current job with its duties and was concerned about taking on too much. She negotiated for Buffett to find a Chief of Operations to take over some of her former duties. "In fact, I accepted the presidency with the caveat that if I didn't like it, I could go back to what I had been doing!"[37]

Susan became the second woman to hold the CEO position for a Berkshire Hathaway subsidiary, following in the footsteps of Rose Blumkin. Mrs. B retired in 1997 and Jacques would be the only Berkshire Hathaway female CEO after that for the next five years until Berkshire acquired The Pampered Chef, founded and led by Doris Christopher.

"He told me when he offered me the position that he had no problem with either my gender or my age," she says. "I joke with Warren every now and then that he needs a greater representation of women at the helm."[38]

In announcing Jacques's appointment, Buffett said, "Susan's rise from a $4-per-hour salesperson to president in 11 years reflects her exceptional customer focus and business skills. It's a particular pleasure to promote from within, a policy consistently favored by Berkshire Hathaway."[39] He later noted that in appointing Jacques, "This move ranks as one of my best managerial decisions."[40] When it was announced that she had become president, she received a congratulatory phone call from the cop who had stopped her speeding husband.

Susan acknowledges that Buffett is the individual who has had the greatest impact on her professional life. "He's influenced me in a positive manner with respect to really caring about what I do, and in regard to believing in myself, having self-confidence, and always doing what I think is right."[41] She describes him as a hands-off but accessible owner.

"Mr. Buffett used to come by a lot more than he does now," she says. "There were many Saturday mornings when the doors would open at 10 and he'd drop in, but he has never interfered. Things are different now due to his celebrity. I miss seeing him, actually."[42]

"It is an extraordinary blessing and privilege to be able to say that you report to Warren Buffett, that you've got Warren Buffett as a boss," she says. "The integrity, the honesty, the trustworthiness of the man matches the ethics of this business so well. I have the ability to visit with him as little or as much as I like. I get a one-page letter in January, giving me my goals for the year, and anytime I have a question he is always readily available, as much as I need to speak with him."[43]

Having the backing and resources of Berkshire Hathaway also allows Borsheims unique purchasing power. "When we go to market, when we work with our vendors, we do everything in our power to own our inventory at the very best price we can own it at. And so, consequently, we will prepay orders if we have to. I mean, they can work with our money for eight weeks if they need to. There are very few people in the jewelry industry that do that. Most people try to draw out their payments as long as they can. And again, coupled with our operating expense ratio, we are able to sell at even better prices."[44]

Operating as one of 79 subsidiaries enhances the opportunity for collaboration with sister companies. While each CEO is evaluated on his or her individual performance, partnering can boost the efficacy of marketing efforts, resulting in simultaneous gains for multiple business units.

Berkshire Siblings

Borsheims was Berkshire Hathaway's first foray into the jewelry business. Subsequently, Berkshire purchased Helzberg Diamonds in 1995, a company with over 230 stores nationwide, and Ben Bridge Jeweler in 2000, with over 70 store locations in 10 states.

In 2007, Berkshire Hathaway bought jewelry companies Bel-Oro International and Aurafin LLC, combining the two into the newly formed Richline Group, based in Arezzo, Italy, a geographic area known for gold jewelry manufacturing and design. Richline, with $500 million in sales, continues to acquire a diversity of jewelry brands, manufacturers, and designers.[45] Says Dennis Ulrich, chief executive officer of Richline Group. "A bigger acquisition is not excluded."[46] Richline is a supplier, although a small one, to Borsheims.

Helzberg Diamonds is the only Berkshire jewelry sibling to have a presence in Omaha. Helzberg currently operates two shopping mall stores, down from four stores in town just a few years ago. Of the relationship, Susan says, "There is great friendship. There is competition between Helzberg and us because we are in the same market. Ben Bridges is not in our market. . . . Ours is a competitive industry, but we are also very, very friendly and like to help one another. There aren't too many people that I truly deem as my competitor."[47]

"Our biggest competition is travel and electronics," says Adrienne Fay, 31, Director of Marketing (Figure 2.2). "It's not necessarily other jewelers." Adrienne was born and raised in Omaha and began working at Borsheims in 2004. She received an Honors Bachelor of Arts in Public Relations and English from Marquette University in Milwaukee, Wisconsin. Following graduation, she marketed 401(k) plans for a financial services firm in Milwaukee before moving back to Nebraska.

Susan adds, "I'll tell customers that if they don't want to buy from me, then they should buy from Helzberg. I'm not about to give them sales and they're not about to give me sales, but I will certainly recommend a

Figure 2.2   Adrienne Fay, Borsheims' Director of Marketing
Source: Borsheims Fine Jewelry and Gifts.

sister company before I'd recommend anybody else. At least they'll be buying from another Berkshire company."[48]

Borsheims has teamed up with See's Candies and NetJets to promote their products to clients, by hosting a dinner during the Berkshire shareholder's weekend. In this way, NetJets customers are introduced to Borsheims and vice versa, while everyone can enjoy some See's candy.

"The Berkshire affiliation has helped us to grow our customer base tremendously," says Jacques. Hosting visiting shareholders each spring during the Berkshire Hathaway annual meeting is a successful marketing tactic for the store. When attendees return home, the Borsheims experience is shared with friends and family.

Spring Bling Fling

Borsheims is a very small asset in the Berkshire Hathaway portfolio, but it enjoys a high profile with shareholders. Each year, during the Berkshire Hathaway annual shareholder's meeting in May, there are shareholder discount shopping days at Borsheims and Nebraska Furniture Mart. Warren Buffett and Charlie Munger stop by to chat with shareholders in the stores.

Getting to Borsheims from the annual meeting at the convention center isn't difficult, since complimentary shuttle buses depart every 20 minutes and drive between the CenturyLink Center and the Borsheims store. Three buses continually circle the route, which is about 15 to 20 minutes one way.

Borsheims hosts a cocktail reception on the Friday evening prior to the Saturday meeting, with live music and dancing until 9 P.M. "We love the opportunity to show people our store," says Susan. Adrienne's first day of employment at Borsheims was the day of the shareholder's reception in 2004. It was, she says, "baptism by fire!"

We brought our visiting Boston friend, Dan Bracco, to the 2011 reception. He had not yet seen the crowd that would show up the next day at the convention center and did not know at all what to expect. When we arrived, the store and adjacent tent in the parking lot were packed with people, young and old. The drink glasses were full of beer and wine, and the jewelry counters were full of shopping customers.

Dan's impression of the Borsheims party was that it was "like a college frat party, although much more controlled. Great marketing concept— drinks and jewelry!"

Susan says, "Every year, we bring in thousands of extra pieces of amazing jewelry just for our Berkshire Hathaway shareholders' weekend." The weekend's revenues vary year to year, but contribute from 8 to 15 percent of annual revenue each year. In addition to the jewelry, there is popular Berkshire Hathaway memorabilia for sale, including items such as a Monopoly game, puzzle, bank, pen, travel mug, and a Warren and Charlie's Magic Answer Ball that reveals answers like "HOLD!," "I have nothing to add," and "Buy a Diamond."

"Sometimes, we might highlight a jewelry item," says Adrienne. "For example, two years ago we had the Tudor Rose Brooch. This item was commissioned by Napoleon Bonaparte's granddaughter. Around 1920, it became part of the collection of the Vanderbilts. That piece was a phenomenal museum-quality piece."

In 2001, they featured a 134-carat diamond necklace worn by Nicole Kidman in the film *Moulin Rouge*, released in theaters that year. The 545.67 carat Golden Jubilee diamond made an appearance in 1996.

Borsheims opens at 9 A.M. on Sunday of the shareholder's weekend for a brunch. It's the only Sunday of the year when the store is open, and then only to shareholders. Warren Buffett took a turn at selling during the 2011 Sunday brunch. He made dozens of sales, including necklaces, watches, and anniversary rings for couples celebrating their 30th and 50th anniversaries.

"Buffett definitely closed some sales that wouldn't have happened without him," said Jacques, including a $30,000 ring for one woman and a diamond bracelet for a man who held up his credit card and said he just wanted to buy something from Buffett. It was Borsheims' best weekend of sales ever. "We knew Warren would be a successful salesman and he did not disappoint," Jacques said. "We'll welcome him back to our expert sales team anytime."[49]

In all, sales at Borsheims for the Berkshire Hathaway shareholder discount period were up 45 percent over last year, in part because of Buffett's one-hour stint as a salesman on Sunday afternoon and in part because of a decision to sell jewelry for the first time during the annual meeting at the Qwest Center.

Borsheims has always had an exhibit booth at the convention center during the annual meeting, but until this year, they sold only Berkshire Hathaway memorabilia. This year, they integrated some basic jewelry box staples, such as pearl necklaces and diamond stud earrings. Shareholders eagerly bought up the one-carat earrings priced at $2,000. The offering was very successful and the company plans to expand their selection at the convention center in future years. In this way, they can show some representative items to the shareholders who never make it out to the store.

The main store attracted 14,000 people Friday evening and a record 8,000 on Sunday, Jacques said. "And they were more eager to buy than in recent years. Sales in 2010 were up only slightly from 2009," she said, "but this year, I was pleasantly surprised. It was an extraordinary crowd."[50]

Planning for the next shareholder's weekend begins the day after the last one has ended. Says Adrienne, "The shareholders' event for us is Christmas in May. We always want to make sure that we create the best atmosphere and the best experience for shareholders. We're always tweaking. We have a great partner within Regency Court. We are feeding over 7,000 people, so it requires really wonderful partners. From a marketing perspective, it is probably the best return on investment that we have out of our entire year."

The O! Factor

Borsheims will always be based in Omaha and only in one location. Even though they have a very large proportion of sales to individuals outside of the state, there is no need to move or open additional stores.

The Greater Omaha Chamber created the symbol O! to represent the city's passion for progress and Borsheims is very happy with their Omaha location. "It has been a terrific location for our business," says Jacques. "It has afforded us the ability to become one of the largest independent jewelry stores in the country. We are able to maintain an incredible cost structure based in Omaha that we could not manage if we were on Madison Avenue in New York or Rodeo Drive in Beverly Hills. We could never afford the 62,500-square-foot store we're allowed to have here."[51]

The availability of shipping makes Borsheims's physical location irrelevant. Transporting jewelry around the country to buyers is far easier than other products, such as furniture, cars, or artwork. Adrienne Fay says, "We love being a local Omaha business, but we're also very proud at how wide-ranging our customers are from all over the world."

Susan adds, "The work ethic plays a lot into our success. Our mission statement is to provide exemplary customer service and the Midwest attitude, the Midwest mindset enables us to do that. People that come from the coasts, we particularly notice this for the Berkshire Hathaway meetings, are always flabbergasted at how friendly, how wonderful, how personable the people are at the store."

"I've had a truly blessed life in Omaha. I enjoy the fact I have a five-minute commute to work. There are so many benefits to having a balanced life in Omaha, and I think in the business world today, most people are trying to find that balance, between family and work. In Omaha, we're afforded that balance really, really well by the lifestyle we're allowed."[52]

Figure 2.3 Borsheims's Fundraiser Event for Henry Doorly Zoo, 2011
Left to right: Brandon Greaves, Lead Keeper of Reptiles and Amphibians; Warren Buffett; and Susan Jacques.
SOURCE: Borsheims Fine Jewelry and Gifts.

Borsheims supports many events and organizations in the Omaha community. In July 2011, there was a fundraiser party in the store for Omaha's Henry Doorly Zoo. A portion of the sale of selected pieces of animal-themed jewelry went to raise funds for renovation and expansion of the zoo. The shoppers mingled with a tarantula, an alligator, a penguin, a snake, and Warren Buffett (Figure 2.3). "We love to cobrand with other strong brands, particularly other local brands," says Susan. "It's a win–win for both."

Family Life

Jacques met her future husband, Gene Dunn, while he was working at Borsheims as extra Christmas help in 1987. Dunn is one of 10 children of a prominent Irish-Catholic family in Omaha. He had given up his early career as a commercial diver, played the stock market for a while, and was buying a cabinetry and casework company, Mica Mecca, when they met.

"His joke is that he had to give up a budding career in gemology to ask me out because I wouldn't date him if he worked here."[53] They dated a couple of years and then he proposed, giving her a "three-carrot ring," with three little orange carrots, that the store used to give out to children. Her initial engagement ring was actually a white diamond ring that had belonged to her mother. She later upgraded to her current wedding ring, a fancy vivid yellow diamond flanked by white diamonds.

They married in 1990 and now have three boys. Gene is now part-owner of Goldberg's Restaurant in the Dundee neighborhood of Omaha. Referring to her husband, Susan says, "He is the backbone of my success. He's very, very supportive of women in business and is very gracious with his support, I must say."[54]

Susan's hobbies include the study of jewelry, world travel, and collecting antiques and gemstone specimens. She says, "When time permits, I love to go walking. It is great mental and physical therapy. I also love to eat, preferably candy, dessert, and most things in which I should not indulge.[55] We have a great circle of friends—a number of circles of friends that we love to get together with."

"My life is fairly busy," she says. "I have three children. They keep me busy. I have a young son who just got a bicycle for his fifth birthday, so we go to the park every night. He rides his bike and I walk. I used to play tennis and haven't played it in a long time, but that's one of my passions I would like to get back to."

Her philosophy on maintaining physical and mental wellness is to "Be happy! You should live life with a positive attitude and always look on the bright side. I have been extremely blessed in the life, for which I am extremely grateful, I have good health, a love of life, and a warm and loving family."[56]

Pearls Gone Wild

When I visited with her recently at the store, Susan was wearing a black-and-white abstract patterned skirt with a black jacket. She was draped in ropes of pearls. "My fashion style is conservative and classic. I wear tailored suits to work each day, and naturally accessorize with tasteful jewelry. I love to dress up and I'm not very good at dressing down. For years, I never even owned a pair of jeans."[57]

Almost every piece of jewelry that she is wearing on this day has a memory or significant meaning to her. On her left wrist is a pearl bracelet. "I bought this with my gift certificate from Borsheims for celebrating 20 years of service at the company," she says. On her right finger is a gorgeous diamond ring. "This was my 40th birthday present from my husband. It's a 4.04-carat diamond ring, which sym-bolized at the time my fortieth birthday and the four members of our family. We had two children then. Now with three, I told him we have to add some weight to it," she says with a chuckle. "Gene gave it to me on the millennium. I was a big fan of the millennium and the celebration. We were at a friend's party and he gave it to me on the dance floor at midnight December 31, 1999."

On Susan's right wrist is another pearl and diamond bracelet. "This was a very special gift a number of years ago for a wedding anniversary," she says, and then describes her gray pearl drop earrings. "Oh, these are fairly new. These are a *Susan* purchase. And my ropes of pearls . . . ," three strands, 97 inches long, white, oval shape, "We love ropes of pearls!" Adrienne Fay, wearing three strands of large white pearls the size of small marbles, agrees, "We do!"

Susan adds, "We think pearls are just one of those most classic gorgeous fashions. As you notice, I play with them all the time." Adrienne, who has a new baby says, "My daughter has discovered them and puts them in her mouth." Susan joins in, saying, "My sons all teethed on my pearls. They're great teething beads."

"I'm a big believer that everything has meaning," she says. "I have a gorgeous pin that I don't have on today, that was my 25th Borsheims anniversary pin. My jewelry is not just an accessory. It's the commemoration of those timelines."

Family Friendly

After Susan had her first child, her decision to return to full-time work wasn't easy. "I know a lot of people that struggle with the balance of family and career," she said. "When Luke was born, I had a grave decision to make as to whether I should return on a full-time basis and pursue the career that I had chosen."[58] "At times, it is difficult when my commitments necessitate traveling such as when on a jewelry buying trip or when attending board meetings that take time away from home and family."[59]

It helps that Borsheims was voted one of the 10 most family-friendly companies in Omaha. They provide partial payment for membership at the Henry Doorly Zoo and Joslyn Art Museum. They sponsor fitness activities, provide low cost lunches on site, and give prenatal kits to pregnant employees. The jewelry store awards prizes to employees who contribute to the United Way and March of Dimes, and offers complimentary tickets to sporting and charity events.

Borsheims has always supported its female employees, who outnumber the male employees. Several of the female members of the Friedman and Blumkin families have worked at Borsheims. My own Aunt Phyllis has worked part-time as a bookkeeper at Borsheims for the past 16 years. At 77 years old, she loves the flexibility the company gives her to take time off when she wants to travel.

"We have a lot of young women in our management team, and family is a very important focus," she says. "We feel that if you have a very, very good home life and a good family life and devote the necessary time to it, that you'll be more productive at work, as long as you've made the decision to work," says Jacques.

Borsheims's executive management team includes seven women out of eight total, four of whom are officers. Jacques is President and CEO. Erin Limas is Chief Financial Officer. Jennifer Johnson is Vice President of Human Resources and Administration. Sean Moore is Director of Jewelry Sales. Ginny Mathey is Director of the gifts division. Janet Saar is Treasurer and Controller. Adrienne Fay is Director of Marketing and Karen Goracke is Director of Merchandising.

Susan praises them, saying, "I surround myself with people that have talent in areas [where] I am not as talented. We have a great team here."[60] "I enjoy working with an incredible management team who assist in setting and striving to exceed our company goals, plus the truly professional, enthusiastic, and hard-working staff who have helped Borsheims grow to what it is today."[61]

Warren Buffett serves as Chairman of the Board of Borsheims. The only remaining minority owner is the Marvin and Susie Cohn family. Susie is Ike and Roz Friedman's youngest daughter. Marv was the diamond buyer for the company for 25 years, and is now semi-retired, but still comes in to help out during the holidays and the Berkshire shareholder's weekend, and continues to assist his personal clients.

Employees do not work for commission. Serving the customer is the focus, not making a sale. Employees receive Borsheims gift certificates as they reach service milestones with the company. Susan says, "I tell people, 'Don't just apply it to your account. Pick out something that's going to have meaning. And every time you look at it, and every time you see it, you're going to be reminded that it's a reward for all of your hard work and the contributions you've made to the company."

Borsheims has stuck fast to their policy of being closed on Sundays, despite pressure from the mall's management company to open their doors seven days a week. "I don't shop on Sundays. If everyone would just stop shopping on Sundays, there would be no reason for stores to stay open," Jacques explains. "I see stores open on holidays and someone has to work on those days so that someone else can shop. It's just not necessary. We all need one day a week that is *family* day."

Susan enjoys the opportunity to mentor the professional growth of the Borsheims staff. The company has a continuing education program to help more of its employees become graduate gemologists, certified by the Gemological Institute of America. "It can be a long process. They start with diamonds and learn diamond grading. Then they move on to gemstone identification. It basically gives you the skills to identify gems and grade them. Once you have a graduate gemologist degree you have the rudimentary skills to become an appraiser."[62]

Jacques also mentors Creighton University students. She has served on the Creighton board of directors for a decade and participates in their Executive Partnership Program. "I avail myself to anyone to whom I can be of assistance to, quite frankly. If I can help them negotiate and navigate their way through a new career path, I'm happy to do so. I think that giving back and mentoring is important and helping others to find their way is something that we do. We do some of it internally in the company and some of it externally."

Susan places her family as first priority above her job. She and her husband just celebrated "21 fabulous years of marriage." She says she will "continue working on a great marriage and raising a beautiful healthy family. That's my number one goal."

Our Lips Are Sealed

In jewelry retailing, confidentiality is of utmost importance and Jacques advises young jewelry professionals, "Don't ever tell anyone about an engagement after making the ring sale, and don't assume that someone is buying [it] for whom you think they are buying for. Many a retailer has lost a client after asking his wife how she liked a piece of jewelry."[63]

"Confidentiality is an extraordinarily big part of our business and so we do not discuss who buys what," says Jacques.[64] But it's already been leaked that a few "Berkies" and other celebrities have made purchases at Borsheims. Stanford Lipsey, Berkshire manager and publisher of the *Buffalo News*, bought his wife's engagement ring there, as did Chuck Huggins, CEO of See's Candies.

A *New York Times* editorial by Maureen Dowd, published on December 24, 2000, reported satirically, bordering on spiteful, that

Hillary Clinton had a Borsheims gift registry when she moved out of the White House, but Jacques denies it.[65] Clinton's spokeswoman states that Hilary's silver and china patterns can be found at Borsheims.[66] That fact may be true, but in itself does not a gift registry make.

Warren Buffett's friend and Berkshire Hathaway board member Bill Gates was able to shop in private on Easter Sunday in 1993. Gates brought his fiancée, Melinda French, on a surprise trip to Omaha. Buffett greeted their private jet and drove them to Borsheims. Susan was there while the couple selected a wedding ring.[67]

Buffett, himself, bought the engagement ring and wedding band for his second wife, Astrid Menks, at Borsheims before their marriage in 2006.[68] The store has a huge database of customers, but isn't about to name-drop or brag about their celebrity clients.

An Evolving Business Model

Borsheims launched its e-commerce website in June 1999, and sales and traffic on the site grow each year. The decision to provide Internet sales at that time must have been a difficult one. Buying jewelry, as with any artistic creation, often requires an emotional connection to the product. Would photos on a monitor provide such a connection? Apparently, that hasn't been a problem.

"The Internet is a challenge," admits Susan. "It is huge for our Bridal Registry division—our table-top division, we do sell jewelry on it. We utilize the site also for our diamonds. We have some of our loose diamond inventory registered on there."[69] There's a full-time photographer on staff who not only documents the inventory, but also communicates with clients by e-mail to send photos of possible purchases.

The website includes educational information for clients to teach them about diamonds, pearls, precious metals, and other gemstones. There's also an area to custom-design your own diamond ring, which allows you to separately choose the setting and stone. There is also an Internet *Deal of the Day*.

Borsheims has a Facebook page with a small following of fans and also a Facebook application called "Borsheims—What's New."

These are simple inexpensive methods of reaching potential clients. Borsheims does not expend a lot of resources on advertising.

"Our marketing budget is 2 percent annual revenues," says Susan. "The industry norm is in the 8 to 10 percent range. We're not going to take out a $10,000 advertisement in *Town and Country* magazine. You are fishing in a very big pond. It is much, much easier to have an extraordinarily happy customer, a satisfied customer, refer friends and family, and continually build the business."

Susan regularly evaluates comparative sales for each jewelry line. In 2009, 12 lines were discontinued and six lines were picked up.[70] The store just added two *shops within a shop* to the store: a Cartier boutique and a Pandora shop. Corporate gifts are a new trend. Items in that category are typically used as incentives or awards, such as clocks, desk accessories, and gift cards. The corporate gift division grew 27 percent in sales in 2010.[71]

Another new revenue source for the store is acquiring scrap gold, silver, and platinum, offering cash as well as trade-ins for new jewelry. "We always allow trade-ins on diamonds . . . a lot of customers upgrade their jewelry. But they can also trade back for something less expensive."[72]

Tip to Shoppers #3

Stop in person at the customer service counter and appraisers will weigh your old, unwanted jewelry and give you a value. You can choose to take the value in cash or in store credit. Cash is given on the spot and credit must be used the same day as the trade-in.

A Role Model

In a business dominated largely by middle-aged Jewish men, Jacques says, "One of the jokes I made when I first got my position was that I had three strikes against me: I was young. I was a woman. And I was a *goy*, a non-Jew." She does not feel that being a woman has hindered her. "I think people are taken for their abilities," she says.[73]

Jacques reflects on how she became a female leader in a male-dominated industry. "I'm in retail and that's very different from corporate America, but I've been very blessed because it opened a tremendous number of doors for me. When I became a woman leader in the industry, at the time there were very few. I was asked to serve on a number of boards. I was invited in because they needed and wanted diversification," she says.

"I think it's very encouraging for young women to see that the jewelry business is no longer the very male-dominated business it used to be," she says. "Having gone through the ranks and been named CEO gives hope to a lot of people. When I've given a speech at a jeweler's conference and a young woman comes up to me and says, 'You are such an inspiration,' that really makes me feel good."[74]

Susan was one of the 2011 honorees at the YWCA Omaha Tribute to Women. Selection is based on the following criteria: living, working, and volunteering in the Omaha metropolitan area; achievement and impact on and involvement within the community; and a demonstrated commitment to helping women and their families build lives of strength, growth, and self-sufficiency.

Susan describes her management style as "passionate" and she is truly devoted to the Borsheims store and its employees. She is just as passionate and knowledgeable about the career of a jewelry professional as she is about gemstones and jewelry.

Susan's typical day is hectic. Each and every day brings new challenges and opportunities. Says Jacques, "My office is located directly on Borsheims's sales floor so that I can maintain a presence for customers and so that I am accessible to all employees throughout the day. At any given moment, I may be greeting customers as they arrive at our store, waiting on a catalog customer, assisting an associate with closing a sale, calculating a customer's 'Borsheims price,' procuring special items for customers, inspecting the work of our bench jewelry shop, reviewing a jewelry appraisal, or responding to a website customer."[75]

In fact, our interview was briefly interrupted because Susan was needed to give a Borsheims price. It was fascinating to witness her while she evaluated the multiple items to determine the purchase prices. Her many years of experience and high level of confidence were reflected in her swift, methodical decisiveness.

"On an average day, from a corporate operations perspective, I may meet with members of my executive staff regarding security, human resources, customer service, financial, inventory, or marketing matters.

Plus, at certain times of the year, I may be traveling on a product-buying trip or to attend various board or customer meetings."[76]

Challenges of a Recession

Borsheims's sales peaked in 2007, the best year ever in its 141-year history. Then in 2008, the bottom fell out of many retail industries, including jewelry. It's been a struggle in subsequent years to regain the revenue ground that was lost. "I was optimistic. I thought it would take three years," said Jacques. "2010 was moderately better than 2009, and 2011 is much stronger, but truthfully it has taken longer than we wanted or anticipated."[77]

It can be tough to sell luxury items in volatile economic times. Most jewelry items are purchased as gifts and there is a sentimental value attached. "We are the first to realize that there is nothing in the store that anybody needs," Susan says, "with the possible exception of a timepiece."[78]

Says Susan, "The opulence of the 1990s and early 2000s has shifted from being how big can something be to how rare and unique it is. There's a different mindset in the affluent market." And Adrienne Fay adds, "The luxury customers have shifted away from conspicuous consumption. I think that's a direct result of what happened to the economy."

Berkshire's retailing revenues were $3.1 billion in 2008, a decrease of 9 percent from 2007. Retailing revenues continued to decline for 2009 at 2.9 billion. The Borsheims store is one retailer within a group of eight companies, as shown in Table 2.1. In 2008, seven out of eight

Table 2.1   Berkshire Hathaway's Retail Companies

Furniture	Jewelry	Candy
Jordan's	Ben Bridge	See's
Nebraska Furniture Mart	Borsheims	
R.C. Willey	Helzberg Diamonds	
Star Furniture		

retailing companies had revenue declines and all eight had earnings declines compared to 2007. In 2009, revenues of the three companies in the jewelry sector dropped 12 percent.[79]

Susan had the unfortunate experience in 2009 of issuing the first layoffs in the company's history of 100-plus years. Sales began to decline in November 2008 necessitating cost-cutting measures. "The loss of our staff members is devastating," says Jacques. "This is the absolute last thing we wanted to do. While we are hopeful that we might see signs of an economic recovery in the fourth quarter of 2009, we had to make extremely difficult decisions out of a fiduciary responsibility to Berkshire Hathaway and its shareholders to continue to remain profitable despite the challenging times."[80]

"The message for us was that we would have to work harder with fewer people and less sales, but . . . we had a strong foundation to build on," Jacques said. "We know that discretionary income will come back, but it will likely take three to five years to get it back to the level of 2007."[81]

The store employed 267 people at that time. The cost-cutting measures included a hiring freeze, elimination of merit raises, reduced hours for full-time hourly employees, removal of all bonus and incentive programs, and significant cuts in the marketing and advertising budgets as well as in charitable donations. As openings have reappeared, some of these employees have been rehired.

In Buffett's 2009 Annual Report, he wrote, "We had a number of companies at which profits improved even as sales contracted, always an exceptional managerial achievement. Here are the CEOs who made it happen . . . Borsheims' (jewelry retailing) Susan Jacques."[82] Eight other companies and their managers were similarly recognized.

Retail sales began to look up in 2010. As Buffett reported, "In 2010, revenues were $2.9 billion, an increase of 2 percent compared to 2009, and pretax earnings were $197 million, an increase of 22 percent compared to 2009. The increase in earnings in 2010 was due to the modest increase in sales and ongoing cost containment efforts. Throughout 2008, as the impact of the economic recession in the United States worsened, consumer spending declined and these conditions continued in 2009.[83]

Today's Must-Haves

According to Susan and Adrienne, jewelry trends closely follow the fashion industry. The clothes we see on the runway today dictate how women accessorize. But with money tight, shopping habits have changed. "The recession has made purchasing a very significant occasion. If someone is going to part with their dollars, they want to make sure it's for something rare and special," says Adrienne.

"Those rare and exotic gems remain popular," says Adrienne. "There is sustained interest in something that is nature's rarest treasure. We have a wonderful relationship with the Argyle diamond mine in Western Australia where the world's pink and purple diamonds are. The entire amount of pink and purple diamonds that are mined in one year could fit into the palm of your hand. So, they're exceptionally rare with amazing color. The fact nature made this perfectly pink diamond and there are very few of them, that is what customers gravitate toward."

The Argyle Mine came online in 1980. After discovery, it takes about ten years to get a mine up and running and then they usually have about a 25-year life. Susan explains, "The Argyle mine has about a decade left and after that the mine will cease. It will likely become a big hole with water in it like the Kimberley in South Africa. Then those rare gems that are currently in the marketplace will become that much rarer because there's no new production replacing the inventories. There's far greater demand than there is supply. And as the Asian markets, India and China, become very strong, they're driving a tremendous demand for extremely rare gemstones. They have a cultural affinity to gems and jewelry."

Celebrities have always influenced jewelry trends. "Now, with Kate Middleton being married with Princess Diana's ring, there's a huge resurgence of sapphires surrounded by diamonds. We've seen that here in the store, whether it's an actual sapphire or something similar looking like iolite or tanzanite or some other gem that has that same feel to it," says Susan.

"Another gem that we've seen a trend towards recently is the conch pearl," she says. Only 1 in 10,000 queen conch mollusks will produce a conch pearl and of those only 1 in 10 is of gem quality. These extremely rare pearls range from pastel pinks to peach in color and are typically oval or pear shaped. The rarest and most expensive conch pearls have a *flame structure* patterned on the surface.

Borsheims's large inventory covers all the bases. "The more traditional categories are there, but they get updated," explains Susan. "Pearls are no longer the graduated strand, they are long ropes. There's a great resurgence in pins. Stacked bangles, cuff bracelets are popular. Big rings are back, not necessarily cocktail. It's big colored stones, micropave. There's a lot of nature themes happening right now."

Jacques has a particular fondness for antique and estate jewelry and her knowledge of jewelry's history through the ages and its form and function in different cultures is impressive. Borsheims' Estate Collection even contains items that might have been sold by Louis Borsheim when he founded the store in 1870, although I'm uncertain if human hair jewelry is currently in stock.

"We have a lot of pieces of Victorian jewelry," says Susan. "1870 to 1880 is what became known as the *grand period*. It's a popular period for estate and antique jewelry. This was when Queen Victoria came out of mourning and it became fashionable again to wear jewelry. Prior to this, everyone associated with the court could wear only black, dark gray, or dark purple clothing and consequently, the jewelry was very dark, not ostentatious."

This does not explain why all three of us sitting at the Borsheims's conference table are wearing black, though two of us are draped with ropes of pearls. "She lightened up after mourning for 27 years," continues Susan. "British families were going on the grand tour to Italy and visiting archaeological sites. You get beautiful micro-mosaics and beautiful cameos from that period. It was a fascinating and evolving period of time. Queen Victoria loved cameos and whatever the monarch loves, becomes very popular."

Doorways

"The greatest lesson I learned came from Warren: 'Don't say or do anything that you wouldn't want to read the next day in the newspapers.' That is my mantra, both in my personal life and in my professional life.

It keeps you focused on doing what's ethical. Have a high set of standards and live up to them," Jacques advises.

"Find something that you're passionate about and follow it. To achieve your dream, you must give your absolute best effort each and every day and seize the opportunities presented to you. Never be afraid of a problem, as there is always a solution to be found. When you strive to persistently work though problems, you'll find that your achievements will be that much more rewarding."[84]

Obstacles guide us through life. They aren't insurmountable, they simply give us new direction, and at the time it might be difficult to envision where that path will lead. "You never dream the life you will lead," Jacques says. "I tell my staff that all the time, that you have no idea how the decisions you make will alter your path in life."[85]

"The opportunity when I drove out here was not to work for Warren Buffett. It was to get a $4-per-hour sales job at a jewelry store that would get me some great retail experience, of which I had none," Susan says.

"I'm a big believer that opportunities come your way, but they are not the end result. The door will open and it's a question of whether or not you choose to enter it and step out of your comfort zone and maybe go down a different road for awhile or whether you just stay in a zone where it's comfortable."

"My parents were, somewhat, risk-takers . . . for example, moving the way we did. When my mother became very ill, I was in Omaha and I desperately wanted to move back to Zimbabwe. My father said, 'We left our families and we started this new life for ourselves and you've begun that. So, why would you step out of that now? Come back to visit whenever you need to and whenever you want to, but you're setting your own path and your own destiny now.' So, I think you can always step back to that comfort zone because it's always there. If you're not going to step out of that comfort zone, you're perhaps not going to reach the same levels."

She advises young professionals to treat all coworkers with respect and know the names of colleagues all along the corporate ladder. It's good to be a team player since it takes many people for a business to be a success. "Take the initiative to do the best job that you could do," Jacques said.

She suggests above all, "Bring enthusiasm to the job," and quotes Buffett, who said that you ought to "tap dance into work every single day." Jacques advises employees to "Make the choice to be optimistic and passionate in whatever you do." She emphasizes the importance of company loyalty. "If you're dissatisfied with your job, don't take a paycheck and complain," she says. "Make a change and move out of there."[86]

She believes that her most admirable trait is her optimism. "I think a positive attitude is contagious," she says, "and I act that way at home as well as at work, because a smile costs nothing and a cheery hello means the world. I think that your attitude, and the attitude of the people around you, makes a big difference in your life. I think having a positive attitude is important, and I work really hard at it."[87]

Susan Jacques faces a challenging but interesting future as CEO of Borsheims. "My business goals are to continue to grow the sales and profitability of the company," she states. "We are judged by Warren basically on our profitability increases."

"I want to develop a really strong, terrific team. I get the accolades, which is unfair because there are 200 terrific people at Borsheims who work really hard every single day to make it the success that it is. It's not me. I'm the face of Borsheims in many respects, but it's truly not about me. It's about the commitment that every single one of those individuals has to their job and to ensuring that they are following our vision and our mission."

As Warren Buffett often says, "If you don't know jewelry, know your jeweler." That's a statement reflecting the trust you must have as a buyer. But aside from that, if Susan Jacques is your jeweler, you literally don't have to know anything about jewelry. She has an enormous body of knowledge and the inventory to go with it.

Tip to Shoppers #4

Go to Borsheims, say "Hello" to Susan, and ask her to tell you about a particular colored stone or estate piece. It will be a fascinating and educational experience.

Chapter 3

Doris Christopher—
Kitchen
Counter Culture

Doris Christopher is an entrepreneur who founded The
Pampered Chef® in 1980 and currently serves as chairman
emeritus of the board. The Pampered Chef utilizes independent consultants to sell its kitchen accessories at home-cooking shows.
The company has approximately 800 employees and is headquartered in
the Chicago suburb of Addison. The number of employees is dwarfed
by the 60,000 consultants selling approximately 300 kitchen items in the
United States, Canada, the United Kingdom, Germany, and Mexico.

The company's mission has been the same for over 25 years:

> The Pampered Chef is committed to providing opportunities
> for individuals to develop their God-given talents and skills to
> their fullest potential for the benefit of themselves, their families,

our customers, and the company. We are dedicated to enhancing the quality of family life by providing quality kitchen products, supported by service and information for our consultants and customers.

Berkshire Hathaway acquired The Pampered Chef from the Christopher family in 2002 for an estimated $900 million.[1] In a press release at the time, Warren Buffett, chairman of Berkshire Hathaway, said, "We are extremely excited by The Pampered Chef. Doris Christopher has created from scratch an absolutely wonderful business and Sheila O'Connell Cooper [president and COO at that time] is exactly the type of manager Berkshire admires. They both clearly love the business and the people they work with. We are delighted to add The Pampered Chef to the family of Berkshire businesses."[2]

In Buffett's annual Letter to Shareholders, he summarized Berkshire Hathaway's purchases of 2002:

> Berkshire acquired some important new businesses—with economic characteristics ranging from good to great, run by managers ranging from great to great. Those attributes are two legs of our "entrance" strategy, the third being a sensible purchase price. Unlike LBO operators and private equity firms, we have no "exit" strategy—we buy to keep. That's one reason why Berkshire is usually the first—and sometimes the only—choice for sellers and their managers.[3]

Doris (Figure 3.1), 66 years old, has the appearance of a silver-haired cookie-baking grandmother, attired in a business suit. Educated as a home economist, she did not create The Pampered Chef with the intent of it becoming a multimillion-dollar direct-selling enterprise. She was simply looking for a way to make some money for her family while spending her days at home with her two children when they were not in school. She was unable to find a job that allowed her the flexibility she desired, so she started her own business, where she could be the sole proprietor and schedule her time to meet personal needs. Doris discovered the perfect niche for her talents and temperament. When inspiration, passion, and action find a common goal, significant achievements often follow.

Figure 3.1 Doris Christopher, Founder and Chairman Emeritus of The Pampered Chef
SOURCE: The Pampered Chef.

Failure Led to Success

Doris was born June 2, 1945, the youngest of Ted and Jane Kelley's three daughters. The family lived in Oak Lawn, Illinois, an unincorporated rural area 12 miles southwest of downtown Chicago. Ted and Jane had both grown up in farm families, but now they lived and worked in the city. Her father owned a one-man gas and service station in Logan Square, on the North Side of Chicago. The station was open 12 hours a day, 7 A.M. to 7 P.M., six days a week, and Ted was the only employee.

Doris's mother worked part-time around her daughters' schedules, and went back to work full-time when Doris went to first grade. During her career, Jane Kelley worked as a typist for several insurance companies in downtown Chicago. Having a mother who worked full-time was unusual in the 1950s. Most households had only a single wage-earner and women worked only until they started having children.

"The fact that I never felt the least bit shortchanged is a testament to how well my mother managed to juggle her various roles," says Doris. "Most of what I know about keeping my balance I learned from my own working mother. With three daughters, a husband, and a full-time job, she still managed to cook us all dinner, a nightly triumph of efficiency and organization. She was the original make-ahead cook, forming meatballs today for tomorrow's spaghetti, browning Monday's beef for Tuesday's Swiss steak. More hearty than elaborate, her recipes were nonetheless delicious. And these meals accomplished one important thing—they brought us to the table for dinner as a family."[4]

Jane Kelley showed her daughters how to organize a household by example. "It was my mother who ran the house. I don't mean to imply that my father was oblivious to us, but his work was so demanding, he just wasn't home enough to get involved in our activities," says Doris.[5]

Christopher took her first home economics class at Walther Lutheran High School because she needed to make up credit after withdrawing from a typing class that she was failing. This was particularly distressing to Doris and her family given her mother's job as a typist. But her weakness in this one area of academics led to discovery of talent in another. She excelled in her home economics class and took two full years of high school home economics courses. Had she been a better typist, she likely would not have found her career passion and wouldn't have created The Pampered Chef.

Doris entered the University of Illinois as a home economics major. One of her favorite classes was Home Management. In this course, eight seniors lived in the same residence for eight weeks, managing the house, taking turns cooking, cleaning, and managing the budget. She graduated in 1967 and in that same year married her high school sweetheart, Jay Christopher.

Itchy Domesticity

After college graduation, Doris taught home economics to junior high and high school students at Liberty Township High School in Valparaiso, Indiana, for a year. She and Jay then moved back to the Chicago area. She found a job working as a home economist for the DuPage County (IL)

Cooperative Extension Service, where she taught adult education classes. She had found her niche. She knew a great deal about quality kitchen tools, which were hard to find in retail stores, and she could instruct people on the proper and most efficient methods of food preparation. She enjoyed teaching these classes and did it for six years, up until her first daughter, Julie, was born in 1972.

The Christopher's second daughter, Kelley, was born three years later and Doris stayed home with both of them until Kelley started school. In 1980, after eight years as a stay-at-home mom, she was ready to find a part-time job. Julie and Kelley were eight and five, so they would be in school most of the day, but Doris wanted to be with them when they were at home.

Drawing upon her past experience and education, Doris searched for an idea of what to do. She considered many options related to food service, sewing, and hospitality. Her priority of putting her family first eliminated a lot of jobs, such as opening a restaurant, catering, or retail sales, which required long hours and weekends away from home. Any of these would also require more start-up funds and continuous overhead expenses.

For a time, she provided alteration services and demonstrated appliances at sales events. She also taught a one-hour sewing class at Montgomery Ward on Saturday mornings. "None of these jobs gave me the flexibility," she says. "I wasn't in control of my schedule."[6]

"I wanted the best of all worlds. I wanted the flexibility to be there and nurture my children, but I was ready to get back into my own career. My husband and I talked about it and realized the way to do that was to start a business."[7]

She had always prepared wonderful family meals and also knew how to throw a good dinner party. When the female guests came into her kitchen, they were impressed by her high-quality kitchen tools.

"My friend's kitchens were very attractive," Christopher says. "Mine wasn't fancy or pretty, but it was very efficient. When people came over, they always made a fuss about things I thought were ordinary."[8]

They gushed over her professional-grade knives, heavy baking sheets, and other utensils. "They'd say, 'Where did you get this pan? Why don't you pick up one for me next time you're there?' " Doris remembers.[9] That request would lead to a brilliant business idea.

"People I knew didn't like to cook, because it wasn't easy for them," she says. "Part of me said, 'Maybe I can never convert them.' But another part said, 'They're using knives that aren't sharp and forks with missing tines. If they had the right tools, it would be fun.'"[10]

It was then that she realized there was a market for high-grade kitchen supplies and that she could turn her knowledge and skills into a business. She knew that in order to sell her favorite products, she would need to demonstrate them. Not everyone can intuitively use unique kitchen gadgets correctly. "I thought if I could show cooks, in their kitchens, quality tools that would make their lives easier, I could earn an income and still care for my family."[11]

However, she wasn't too keen at first about selling at home parties. "I always avoided home parties," admits Doris. "There's always an obligation and they were always a little pushy and aggressive."[12]

She devised a plan that included a considerable dose of education and demonstration, offering recipes, similar to the courses she previously taught as a home economist. She created her role in the venture as more of a teacher than a salesperson. It was a business concept that took an element from the direct selling industry and enhanced it with education, entertainment, and social interaction.

She decided that she would not attempt to enter the haute cuisine market, but would keep things simple and fast and show people that it was easy to use the tools that she offered. She also made a conscious decision to offer several items priced under $10. She wanted the people who attended the parties to have options that didn't force them to spend a lot if they really just wanted to support the hostess by being there. That's why The Pampered Chef still offers a citrus peeler for $1 and Quikut paring knives for $2.

"Although I didn't like some things that went on at direct-selling parties, I owe a great debt of gratitude to early companies in the industry because I didn't come up with the idea on my own. Clearly they created the model. I just altered it to fit my own personal style," says Doris.[13]

"I can say from the moment I realized that I could redefine the direct-selling technique, I plowed straight ahead. At the first kitchen show I found people were hungry for this kind of information. Then I knew. This is easy," recalls Christopher.[14]

Bootstrapping a Start-Up

To get started, Doris borrowed $3,000 against a life insurance policy on her husband, Jay. Says Jay, "I teased Doris that diverting those funds for her new business meant she'd only be able to bury half of me."[15]

She used this money to buy a desk, install a separate phone jack in the house, have business cards printed, and buy some inventory. She visited the showroom of every kitchen-product wholesaler at Chicago's Merchandise Mart. She picked up a dozen each of this and that, paid cash up front, and then went home to set up operations in her 400-square-foot basement. She never borrowed money again after the initial $3,000 startup costs.

"I made several more trips back to the Mart during the next few weeks. Had I lived farther away, it would have been too expensive to travel to Chicago that many times. So this is one of those blessings I received, a piece of my life's puzzle that fell into place," she says.[16]

"I picked things I knew and loved," she says. "It was exciting to me to introduce people to something new in their kitchen that did make a difference. Stoneware became a big component of our line."[17] Her basic pricing formula was to take the amount she paid for an item and multiply it by two.

"Everyone lives a very hectic busy life. It's hard to be motivated to do something creative in the kitchen," says Doris. "It's a business from the heart.[18] . . . What's important is that by saving time and frustration in the kitchen, people have more time and energy to enjoy a meal with their families."[19]

While driving to her first kitchen show at the home of a friend, Doris almost talked herself into returning home, convinced she was doomed to fail. But the women she faced that evening loved her and her products, and purchased $178 worth of kitchen tools. Best of all, four more women who were interested in hosting parties came forward.

Doris did not start slowly. She conducted a whopping 18 home shows in the first two months of her business, averaging $372 in sales per show. She made $67,000 in sales in 1981, her first full year in business.

"That first year, I was overwhelmed, not to mention excited, by the newness of it all. I'm afraid there were times when I grew quite obsessed with my new role as a fledgling entrepreneur, letting it consume too much family time. Over the years, I became busier and busier with my business. At first, my goals were modest, but my company took on a life of its own. I'd set out to help families share more mealtimes by making cooking faster and easier—and it was working. However, it was limiting the time I could spend with my own family."[20]

The Pampered Chef took on its first consultant nine months after inception. The company served a regional clientele for most of the 1980s. It was doing well and Doris could certainly have been content with making $1 million annually, but she made a decision to take the company a step further. She started traveling and advertising for new consultants in other cities, first within driving distance of Chicago, and then beyond.

"I had to step outside my comfort zone, leave my family, drive to those places, stay in a hotel room, and figure out how to interview people in a safe setting," she remembers. "It took persistence. I think I went to St. Louis 12 times."[21]

"When you have a business in your home, you tend to work all hours. I'd work during the day and then do a kitchen show at night. I'd come home when everybody was asleep, so I'd go down to the basement and get back to my desk. When you hit 80 hours [per week], an alarm goes off, and you say, 'This is too much, there's no balance in life.' "[22]

Doris didn't take a salary for the first five years. She and Jay reinvested everything they made back into the business, building sweat equity. They put some of the early money into more inventory, a distribution center, and consultant incentives.

After four years in the basement, she bought a nearby building and revised the inventory system. Items were lined up on shelves in the same order as on the order form. Pickers used shopping carts to pack orders. The company's first office furnishings were secondhand.

The Christophers would eventually move their family out of the River Forest home where it all began. The company later bought back their original home and named it Heritage House, and now uses it for special functions.

The story of The Pampered Chef serves as a classic model of entrepreneurship in the United States. It doesn't matter what you start with. If you have talent or knowledge in an area, belief in your business service and/or product, and the courage to take the necessary actions to build it, a business is born. When Doris was unable to find a job that matched her specifications, she created one for herself. Dissatisfaction with the status quo led to the realization of a new opportunity for Doris and tens of thousands of others who have joined The Pampered Chef as consultants.

In hindsight, Doris would start out exactly the same. "I wouldn't have done it any other way. I would never have been a risk taker by taking out a huge loan, starting in a facility. For me, this was the only way it would work. To really start small and make do with what we have and to grow the business little by little, always putting back into the business any profit that we had, especially for the first five years or so."[23]

Doris continues to think with an entrepreneurial mindset. "When things are going well, we all have a tendency to go with the flow," she says. "In other words, if it's not broken, don't fix it. We must be sure that we are encouraging and recognizing creative and innovative ideas from our people—within our home-office team and in the sales field. Be supersensitive to looking at your business creatively to see what innovation will be the right response to this market. There are great ideas that are worthy of taking a risk for. Our job, as leaders, is to open the door to creativity and to allow the ideas to flow—to keep rocking the boat!"[24]

Ladies' Night Out

The clearest memory I have about the first Pampered Chef party that I attended is cellulose. Yes, *cellulose*. It was the mid-1990s and I lived in a small rural town of less than 1,000 people in Iowa with my husband and three young boys.

My friend, Deb, from the local women's society club invited me to her home for a Pampered Chef party. It seemed as though every month someone in our town had a party of some sort, for Tupperware, PartyLite, silk flowers, or home décor. I went to about half of these events, mostly for the social aspect. Personal contact with adult women was lacking in my home.

I wasn't too keen on being sold cooking utensils because I had a limited kitchen repertoire, but Deb was a good friend and I wanted to see what she was getting herself into by hosting this party. I still remember the demonstrator asking if any of us knew what cellulose was. I have a science background and that quickly caught my attention.

"It's wood shavings—like sawdust," said the demonstrator, pointing to the list of ingredients on a package of shredded cheese. "It's listed as the ninth ingredient. They put it in the cheese to keep it from sticking together and you eat the sawdust right along with the cheese." She was correct. The party guests made *icky* faces.

Then, she brought out a shiny new chopper and chopped up a fresh block of cheddar cheese in no time at all. Save your fingers from a grater! Save money by buying cheese in blocks! Preserve the health of your family! I was sold.

I've used the grater on a few occasions, some successful and some not so much. But that comment about eating sawdust has stuck with me all this time. I think of it whenever I sprinkle my conveniently preshredded cheese into an omelet while the grater sits in its dark, quiet drawer.

The First PC Spouse

Doris' husband, Jay, was instrumental in the creation of The Pampered Chef. He first asked her out on a date during Doris's sophomore year of high school, when he was a junior. "Jay surprised me by asking me to be his date for the school's homecoming dance. Poor Jay didn't know it, but nobody at Walther lived farther away than I did. As we continued to date, I'm sure his parents wondered why Jay couldn't have found a girl who lived closer."[25]

She and Jay went to different colleges and dated others while they were apart. Doris explains, "If our love was true love, we reasoned, dating would make us appreciate each other all the more."[26] They both graduated from college in 1967 and got married the same year.

Right from the start, Jay was very supportive of Doris' plan to start a business. He helped her list the pros and cons of various business options to arrive at a final decision on what to pursue.

"My husband is my mentor," says Doris. "He coached me. He was always right there."[27] Jay recalls, "When Doris started The Pampered

Chef in 1980, both of us had a lot to learn about the business. In my role as the first Pampered Chef Spouse, I learned one lesson over and over: A supportive spouse can be a critical asset in the success of any Pampered Chef business. Every day, I had an opportunity to do something that would help build the business: for example, something as simple as handing someone a catalog or suggesting they host a Kitchen Show."[28]

Jay wrote a book entitled *Come to the Basement*. Judging the book by its cover gives one an ominous feeling that this is a scary horror novel. But it makes sense if you're familiar with Doris' book, published two years earlier, entitled *Come to the Table*. Doris' book was written to encourage families to share mealtimes. Jay's book describes how to be supportive as a Pampered Chef spouse, and the book's title is a reference to the location in their home where The Pampered Chef inventory and office was first located. "Come to the basement" was frequently shouted up the stairs when one Christopher needed the assistance of the other.

Jay was willing to be the primary caregiver to their children while Doris gave kitchen shows or was busy with other aspects of the company. "I started thinking of my evenings with the girls as a blessing," says Jay, "not an inconvenience. In our evenings by ourselves, we created a fund of shared memories that will last all our lives. We still laugh about the quest for the perfect pizza, they still roll their eyes at my stumbling efforts to help them with their spelling, and Julie is still unsure what to think of my unique style of power basketball."[29]

As the company grew, it hired employees to take over some of Jay's previous tasks. He says, "Most of my support functions have been turned over to professionals by now. It's comforting to know that it's taken hundreds of people to replace me in maintenance, logistics, marketing, accounting, and all the other behind the scenes functions."[30]

Hockey Stick Growth

The Pampered Chef experienced steady growth for its first seven years. By the end of 1981, its first full year in business, The Pampered Chef had 12 Kitchen Consultants and revenues of $67,000. In 1985, with

32 Kitchen Consultants, sales reached $592,700. The Pampered Chef was gaining momentum. Then sales hit the $1 million mark in 1988 and from that point on revenues shot upward meteorically. Adjusting for a rapid change in sales, either up or down, is a challenge. Because Pampered Chef customers pay for products before delivery, cash flow is not a problem.

"One of the greatest blessings for me was the slow growth in the beginning," says Doris, "because it gave me the opportunity to experience some of the decisions I made, whether they were right or wrong. I could get comfortable with my decision-making ability, make mistakes and learn from those, and have small successes and hope to repeat those. It let me slowly step up the business while my children were small, which was so important to me."[31]

The Pampered Chef made *Inc.* magazine's list of fastest-growing companies in 1994, ranked at number 131. Over a four-year period, its revenues grew 1,760 percent, from $3.5 million in 1989, to $10 million in 1991, and to $65.3 million in 1993.

By 1994, the company was a multimillion-dollar business and had over 200 employees. Revenues were $200 million in 1995. In 1999, sales hit $580 million and in 2001 they were $740 million. As a Berkshire Hathaway subsidiary, the company's annual revenues are now pooled with other companies in Berkshire Hathaway's annual reports and tax filings. So it is no longer possible to monitor the company's level of sales. Revenues from 1981 to 2001 are shown in Figure 3.2.

In 1996, Doris was amazed at the company's growth and said that back in 1980, when she first stated the company, "If I had looked at what my job is today, I couldn't handle it."[32] Several employees who started out with the company in the early days did not foresee how large it would become. Many felt they wouldn't have been qualified to work for such a large company when they started, but along with Doris, they grew professionally as the company grew.

"I have a nice problem at this time," Christopher explained, in 1996. "While we have grown so fast, I strive to keep our focus where it always has been: on our product and on our people."[33]

What decisions were made in the company that caused its rapid growth in the mid-1990s? Were there new strategic initiatives or was it simply an unforeseen, unplanned growth spurt?

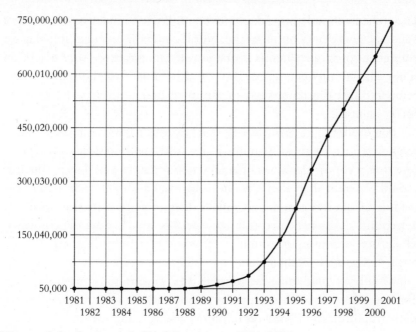

Figure 3.2   Pampered Chef Revenues, 1981–2001

There may not be a single cause for the company's rapid growth. Rather, it may have been related to several factors, including but not limited to:

- A good economy
- Increased recruitment of consultants
- Expanded geographic market penetration

Personal spending on discretionary items often correlates with a period of economic expansion and rising Gross Domestic Product (GDP). The GDP of 1991 to 2000 rose 40.1 percent.[34] This coincides with the rapid growth period of The Pampered Chef. By contrast, the GDP rose only 15.3 percent from 2001 to 2010. As previously explained, company revenues for years 2002 and later are not publically available.

The number of consultants in 1996 was 25,000 and in 2001 there were 71,000. Increasing the number of independent consultants does not contribute significantly to company expenses, but does enhance profits.

The consultants are not paid employees. It is the cumulative sales total of all consultants that determines the overall company revenue. It makes no difference to overhead costs if one consultant generates only $1,000 in sales while another generates $100,000. Revenues from both flow to the company and the company's expenses related to each consultant are nearly identical.

For example, in 1996, when there were 25,000 consultants, company revenues were $330 million. In 2001, with 70,000 consultants, revenues were $740 million. The 2001 consultants were less productive at $10,571 each than the 1996 consultants at $13,200 each. While the volume of sales per person may reflect changes in the economic health of our country, it's only the combined total sales that impact the company. Therefore, increasing the number of consultants, even if their sales are small, benefits the company.

Multilevel marketing is the structure of earning commissions on the sales of recruited individuals by the consultant who recruited them. This structure incentivizes consultants to recruit and mentor their team members to, in turn, recruit others. Multilevel marketing benefits independent consultants more than it does the company directly, because it increases the consultant's commission rate. However, by nurturing the team concept, more consultants are recruited and overall revenues are increased for the company.

An expanding geographic area may have been a factor in The Pampered Chef's pace of growth in the 1990s. With the increase in numbers of consultants, their geographic territories expanded. Households exposed to The Pampered Chef for the first time are more likely to purchase products and spend larger amounts than those in markets where individuals have had prior exposure and are previous customers. The challenge of maintaining repeat customers is discussed later.

Headquarters

A growing business requires adequate physical facilities. Even a direct seller without a brick and mortar retail store needs space for operations and inventory. Pampered Chef moved to a succession of progressively larger offices and warehouses in its first 20 years. The company physically grew from a 400-square-foot basement to a 780,000-square-foot three-story facility.

Amazingly, the Pampered Chef business was located in Doris' home for four years. But at that point, handling the inventory and deliveries became unmanageable from the basement. The company took a major step when it bought a 2,500-square-foot building for $121,000, located only two miles from the house.

Moving out of Doris' house gave the company validation. Vendors treated it more like a business. For the first time, it had real business hours. The growing number of employees and consultants were more comfortable too, having felt like they might be intruding in the family's personal space when they came to the house.

In 1991, the company moved to a 40,000-square-foot building in Hillside, Illinois. Ten years later, they again needed more space. Proposals to build the new Pampered Chef headquarters in 2001 met with some resistance from residential neighbors, but the village of Addison benefits greatly from the standpoint of jobs and tax revenues from the company. The headquarters, employing 1,100 in 2002, became Addison's largest employer.

The company moved into its new headquarters in October 2002. For the grand opening, there were floats, bands, dinner, and dancing. "We like to celebrate in a way that is very visible," said Doris.[35]

The new headquarters consolidated four buildings the company occupied in Addison and nearby Carol Stream. The building is a 14-acre facility on a 43-acre campus, including a pond. The main building has 1,222 parking spaces and 50 loading docks that handled 18 semitrailer truck deliveries in and 18 shipments out of the facility each day when it was first opened. By 2006, they had outgrown it and signed a 10-year lease to occupy an additional 265,000-square-foot building, to be used for distribution, directly across the street. Construction was completed on it in September 2006.

Selling the Chef

Succession planning is essential for a family owned business. Typically, the family must identify and develop internal people who can fill key company positions as needed. A succession plan gives security to employees, clients, and vendors, by ensuring that the company will continue to exist beyond the years that its founders are running it. Family businesses look first to the next generation to assess whether they have the interest and/or capabilities to lead the company.

With the new millennium approaching, Doris and Jay began thinking about a succession plan for The Pampered Chef. "Over the years, Jay and I have seen a lot of good people hurt because they worked for, or did business with, a company that did not have a succession plan in place."[36]

"We decided to take action before we had to," she says. "I am in good health, there was no financial reason to do it—we didn't need the money. We did it because we wanted the people in our sales organization and home office to be assured that our business was secure beyond the time I would be here to run it."[37]

The Pampered Chef was unlikely to stay in the Christopher family. Initially, the Christophers met with bankers at Goldman Sachs to discuss the possibility of issuing a public offering. On their advice, Doris approached Warren Buffett about buying the company. He agreed to meet with her, and asked that in addition to providing him the typical financial reports that she send samples of Pampered Chef products.

Doris sent several big boxes of product to Berkshire Hathaway's home office, where there was a staff of about 15, all but two of whom were women. Says Doris, "Buffett told me that he had never heard such clamoring coming from the office where these boxes were being unpacked. The women told him story after story about what they had, what they liked, and what they wanted if he wasn't going to use all these things. That got his attention."[38]

On September 1, 2002, Christopher and her then-CEO, Sheila O'Connell Cooper, met with Buffett at his headquarters in Omaha for four hours. Buffett made an offer. Doris did not negotiate, but she discussed it with her family before answering. The company was attractive to Buffett because it had no debt, was well managed, was simple to understand, and was a good return on investment.

Shortly afterward, Doris reflected on her meeting with Buffett, "He's very smart, charming, warm, and his interest in people shines through," Christopher said. "I may sound like a Warren Buffett groupie, but prior to meeting him three weeks ago, I wasn't all that familiar with his working style or the way he works with companies. It was an amazing experience."[39]

Buffett remembers when Doris came to Omaha to talk to him about selling her company. "Right on the spot," he says, "I knew I wanted The Pampered Chef in the Berkshire Hathaway family. So we immediately made a deal. I saw this business for myself when I attended my first Kitchen Show. I put on my Pampered Chef apron and chopped, tasted, and tested right along with the other guests. I wasn't a star, however, coming in last in the apple-peeling contest."[40]

Buffett described to Berkshire Hathaway shareholders his reasons why The Pampered Chef was an attractive company to acquire:

> The largest acquisition we initiated in 2002 was The Pampered Chef, a company with a fascinating history dating back to 1980. I've been to a TPC party, and it's easy to see why the business is a success. The company's products, in large part proprietary, are well-styled and highly useful, and the consultants are knowledgeable and enthusiastic. Everyone has a good time.
>
> Two years ago, Doris brought in Sheila O'Connell Cooper, now CEO, to share the management load, and in August they met with me in Omaha. It took me about ten seconds to decide that these were two managers with whom I wished to partner, and we promptly made a deal. Berkshire shareholders couldn't be luckier than to be associated with Doris and Sheila.[41]

Buffett's management style allowed The Pampered Chef to operate as it always had. When the acquisition was complete, every employee received a $1,000 bonus for each year they had worked for the company as a thank-you for their service.

"The purchase is just the best possible resolution for providing for the long-term legacy of the business," said Christopher. "It allows us to continue with what we do best, and that is running Pampered Chef."[42]

"I greatly admire and respect Warren Buffett for his integrity, honesty and solid business ethics," says Doris.[43] She added, "Berkshire represents a great partner for The Pampered Chef as Sheila, our management team and I look forward to growing and building our business. We are proud to stand among the top-tier brands of Berkshire Hathaway."[44]

Sue Rusch, a business consultant at Sue Rusch & Associates said, "When Warren Buffett purchased The Pampered Chef, it validated this business (direct selling) in a way it had never been validated. That caused many corporations to take notice that this is a viable business model and decide that they wanted in."[45]

That Berkshire was interested in a direct-selling company should not have surprised business analysts. The purchase of The Pampered Chef was not Berkshire Hathaway's first foray into the direct selling industry. Berkshire Hathaway acquired the Scott Fetzer Company for about $320 million in 1986. Scott Fetzer had 17 businesses at that time (more than 20 now) including several that sold products directly to the consumer, such as World Book Encyclopedia, Kirby Vacuums, and Ginsu knives. It was by no means a stretch for Buffett to understand and appreciate the Pampered Chef business model.

Industry Icon

Doris Christopher is a superstar of the direct-selling industry. The Pampered Chef became a member of the Direct Selling Association (DSA), the national trade association for nonretail product sales, early on in 1986. Christopher was named to the Board of Directors in 1992, and later served as chairperson. The board is composed of 35 individuals from organizations such as Amway, Avon, Scentsy, Kirby, academic universities, and the county of Los Angeles.

Neil Effen, president of DSA, said, "Doris's election to the executive committee of our association's board of directors is an indication that she is, indeed, a superstar who has earned the respect of the corporate community. Her level of professional integrity is the highest. Not only does she believe in 100 percent customer satisfaction, she treats the 20,000-plus entrepreneurs who sell the company products with respect and dignity. Quite frankly, she treats them with love."[46]

The Pampered Chef has been honored with the DSA's Vision for Tomorrow Award for its efforts to help feed the nation's hungry. It has also received two DSA Industry Innovation Awards—the first for its support of entrepreneurial women, and the second for excellence for using web technology that formed an online community of Internet visitors.

Doris is also past chair of the Direct Selling Education Foundation (DSEF), a branch organization of the DSA. Among other things, the DSEF supports a Women's Entrepreneurship Initiative, promoting personal leadership skills and entrepreneurial thinking with the goal of having women maximize their contributions to the success of organizations, endeavors, and communities. They develop programs to teach self-esteem and business literacy, while highlighting direct selling as a low-risk, low-cost entry into the entrepreneurial system.

DSEF is now initiating a pilot educational program for students to earn a direct selling entrepreneur certificate. Three community colleges will offer the program of study in 2012.

Christopher is certified in Family and Consumer Services and is an active member of the business section of the American Association of Family and Consumer Sciences. She is also a member of The Committee of 200. This organization, whose membership is by invitation only, has a mission to foster, celebrate, and advance women's leadership in business. Christopher was repeatedly recognized by *Working Woman* magazine as one of the top 500 women business owners.

Buffetted

When Berkshire Hathaway acquired The Pampered Chef in 2002, it caused a bit of a ripple with Pampered Chef customers and independent consultants. There was concern about the charitable donations that Berkshire Hathaway directed on behalf of its shareholders. Some of the donations supported family planning and prolife organizations that caused boycotts of Berkshire Hathaway companies. Pampered Chef's annual revenue of $740 million was a small fraction of Berkshire's $42.4 billion in 2002 revenues, and while the boycotts and protests caused a minor annoyance for the other Berkshire holdings, it hit The Pampered Chef hard.

Buffett had long criticized chief executives for donating corporate funds to their pet charities. After all, the money belongs to the stockholders, not to the CEOs. So, in 1981, Berkshire inaugurated a shareholder-designated program. Berkshire decided to give $2 per outstanding share to charity—but to let each shareholder allocate his or her portion of the corporate gift. Thus, a stockholder owning 100 shares could designate the beneficiary of a $200 gift; one with 150 shares could allocate a gift of $300. Each shareholder was allowed to spread his or her gift over a maximum of three charities.[47]

When consultants began to quit and protesters urged boycotting of The Pampered Chef, Christopher talked about the situation with Buffett. Said Buffett, "She didn't ask me, but I could tell she was hoping I would cancel the program. And you know, I'll do it. I thought we could tough it through, but we can't. It's hurting too many people that I don't want to hurt. It hurts Doris, and these are her flock. They're getting injured, and they're innocent. They're in her office, crying."[48]

Buffett announced termination of the shareholder-designated contributions program in July 2003. Shareholders had designated about 3,500 charities annually, including about 800 different educational institutions and 400 churches and synagogues.[49] Some applauded his decision as magnanimous and others criticized him for giving in. Both before and after, it was impossible to please everyone.

Warren Buffett explained the chain of events in his 2004 Letter to Shareholders.

From 1981 through 2002, Berkshire administered a program whereby shareholders could direct Berkshire to make gifts to their favorite charitable organizations. Over the years we disbursed $197 million pursuant to this program. Churches were the most frequently named designees, and many thousands of other organizations benefited as well. We were the only major public company that offered such a program to shareholders, and Charlie and I were proud of it.

We reluctantly terminated the program in 2003 because of controversy over the abortion issue. Over the years numerous organizations on both sides of this issue had been designated by our shareholders to receive contributions. As a result, we regularly received some objections to the gifts designated for prochoice operations. A few of these came from people and organizations that proceeded to boycott products of our subsidiaries. That did not concern us. We refused all requests to limit the right of our owners to make whatever gifts they chose (as long as the recipients had 501(c)(3) status).

In 2003, however, many independent associates of The Pampered Chef began to feel the boycotts. This development meant that people who trusted us—but who were neither employees of ours nor had a voice in Berkshire decision-making—suffered serious losses of income.

For our shareholders, there was some modest tax efficiency in Berkshire doing the giving rather than their making their gifts directly. Additionally, the program was consistent with our "partnership" approach, the first principle set forth in our Owner's Manual. But these advantages paled when they were measured against damage done to loyal associates who had with great personal effort built businesses of their own. Indeed, Charlie and I see nothing charitable in harming decent, hard-working people just so we and other shareholders can gain some minor tax efficiencies.

Berkshire now makes no contributions at the parent company level. Our various subsidiaries follow philanthropic policies consistent with their practices prior to their acquisition by Berkshire, except that any personal contributions that former owners had earlier made from their corporate pocketbook are now funded by them personally.[50]

Charlie Munger, Vice Chairman of Berkshire Hathaway, also commented on the situation, stating that The Pampered Chef was "having real rebellion troubles. We just hated the idea of having a new subsidiary that was being hurt because they had joined Berkshire."[51]

Leading with Values

Like Berkshire Hathaway, The Pampered Chef holds high business ethics and has an excellent reputation among consumers. The Pampered Chef was recognized in 1998 for its highly ethical treatment of customers, suppliers, and employees when it received the Better Business Bureau's Torch Award.

"The challenge," says Christopher, "is one confronting most companies: how to provide an inspirational vision to staff and consultants and to communicate it in a way that offers clear direction but still leaves room for creative flexibility and empowerment. A true leader takes initiatives and risks, formulates ideas, and continuously offers guidance and solutions. He or she regularly interacts with the people around him or her, aligning them to their ideas, goals, and vision."[52]

It's necessary that a leader communicate effectively. "The secret is to send simple, clear, and consistent messages of what the expected business practices are to everyone in the company," Christopher said. "Eventually you establish a reputation (for being honest) and people are attracted to that. People want to do the right thing. If there is any confusion in the message, you start to lose people. The challenge is holding on to those values as the business changes and grows."[53]

Conducting business in private homes requires a heightened level of trust between the consultant and hostess. "I believe direct selling requires the highest level of integrity," says Doris. "We conduct our business in the homes of others; we are a guest along with the other guests our hosts invite. We get to know their family and friends, and share personal and professional insights and strategies for successful mealtimes. Trust is absolutely essential. The highest level of ethics is also essential."[54]

In 2006, Christopher was inducted into the Horatio Alger Association of Distinguished Americans as a lifetime member (Figure 3.3). Horatio Alger Association members are recognized as individuals who have come from humble beginnings to achieve extraordinary success.

"For me," says Christopher, "the most important aspect of this award is its focus on education. The Horatio Alger Association's tireless efforts on furthering education help to show us that here in America, hard work, perseverance, and education are truly the building blocks of future success. In America, it doesn't matter where we came from, what matters is where we are going."

The success of The Pampered Chef has allowed Doris and Jay Christopher to become philanthropic leaders. Most of their efforts are directed toward education. In 1999, they gave $15 million to Concordia University in River Forest, a Lutheran-sponsored school where Jay Christopher's father had worked as legal counsel.

Figure 3.3   Doris Christopher Receiving the Horatio Alger Award from Berkshire Hathaway Board Member and Fellow Member and Former Board Chairman of the Horatio Alger Association Walter Scott, Jr., 2006
SOURCE: The Pampered Chef.

A few years later, they gave $16 million to help fund the Valparaiso University library at Jay's alma mater. The building, opened in 2004 and recipient of several architectural design awards, is named the Christopher Center for Library and Information Resources. Jay lent his collection of railway china to Valparaiso University for its first public exhibition in 2008.

As early as 2000, The Pampered Chef made a financial commitment to the University of Illinois, Doris' alma mater, to establish The Pampered Chef Family Resiliency Program. In 2003, Doris and Jay established an endowed Chair in Family Resiliency with a $1.5 million donation and announced plans to donate $11.5 million to construct a building for the program. In 2006, Doris Kelley Christopher Hall opened on the campus to house the Family Resiliency Center, where research, education, and outreach initiatives improve the well-being of children, individuals, and families.

"Illinois has a wonderful reputation as a research university," says Doris. "But the work they are doing in Human and Community Development is equally intriguing, vitally important, and closely aligns with our company's mission to enhance the quality of family life. My vision for The Pampered Chef Family Resiliency Program is to examine ways to enrich children and families to better handle life stressors. What are the traditions to preserve? How can we pass those on to our children? Sharing information and best practices will make families stronger. Faculty can prepare students interested in this field and their research will advise families to better meet challenges. If we don't have strong families, we don't have a strong work force—we're all in this together."[55]

Other recipients of funds from the Christopher Family Foundation include Dominican University in River Forest, Illinois, with a $2 million donation to establish a Nutrition Sciences Center; the Brookfield Zoo in Chicago, with $1.5 million to support renovation of a building into a conservation learning center; and the Lutheran School of Theology at Chicago, which received $1 million in unrestricted funding, among others.

Management Challenges

Doris Christopher started Pampered Chef over 30 years ago. The company went through many stages of business growth from its humble beginning as a start-up sole proprietorship. Along the way, Doris met challenges with courage and a determination to make her company succeed. As an entrepreneur, you cannot entirely predict the direction your business will take, or know what obstacles will lie in your path. Doris learned many lessons and gained many new skills during her career.

Business Knowledge

Doris had no previous business experience when she started The Pampered Chef. There was much to learn, starting as she did from scratch as the only employee. Says Doris' husband Jay, "When she started The Pampered Chef, I was astonished. I had underestimated her. She thrived on the challenges and developed talents that certainly surprised me, and may even have surprised her."[56]

Trial and error gave Doris her business education. In retrospect, she offers the lessons she learned as *Eleven Tips for Start-Up Entrepreneurs:*[57]

1. Follow Your Passion
2. Have a Clear Idea about What You Want to Do
3. Find a Niche
4. Be the Best You Can Be
5. Make A Difference
6. Keep It Simple
7. Watch Your Overhead
8. Go with Your Instincts
9. Value Your Time and Be a Good Time Manager
10. Brush Up on Your Computer Skills
11. It's Only a Business

Recruiting Consultants

Doris was the sole party demonstrator of Pampered Chef products for the first nine months of the company's existence. When she made an agreement with another woman, Kim Bass, to operate as an independent consultant, the company was forever changed.

Working by herself, Doris was aware of the status of absolutely every aspect of the company. Bringing on additional employees presented challenges. There were concerns about stocking the inventory, because Doris always knew what she had on hand in her basement, but others wouldn't necessarily have access to that information. The consultant compensation agreement had to be defined and then later readjusted to determine the appropriate commission schedule.

Consultant education and background experience requirements were evaluated as more consultants were recruited. The original concept of consultants being home economists or teachers was abandoned as it became evident that this was not necessary. Consultants simply needed to have transportation and a circle of friends.

At one point, in 1990, the business grew at a pace that was unmanageable for the home office staff and employees. Recruitment of consultants was up 400 percent over 1989. These new consultants generated sales beyond the company's inventories and the threat of back orders became a real possibility. To avoid this undesirable situation, Doris made the tough decision to institute a four-month temporary recruitment freeze on new consultant agreements. A consultant waiting list was generated and the delay in further sales increases gave the company time to get back up to speed with its internal organization.

Selling to Noncooks

Frequently, kitchen show attendees will claim that they don't cook, or don't like to cook. I cook, but don't claim to be a *good* cook. It can be a bit intimidating to the consultant at a kitchen show to hear this from the people watching a cooking demonstration. How do you sell kitchen products to people who don't cook? The selling opportunity lies in the fact that most of these people do not own quality-grade kitchen gadgets that can make food preparation easier and save time. Pampered Chef products have the potential to inspire a noncook to try cooking something new just to experience using a fun tool or beautiful baking dish. If not that, then there's always an opportunity to sell an item to be used as a gift.

Repeat Customers

A challenge with selling kitchen tools is the creation of repeat customers. Unlike a lipstick, candles, or clothing, whisks and spatulas do not get used up or worn out—particularly not when they are the high-quality products sold by The Pampered Chef. So, once I've outfitted my kitchen and brought it from the Stone Age up to the Information Age, my need to purchase additional gadgets diminishes. And at some point, new customers will only be found when new households are established. This is possibly why The Pampered Chef is now offering edible items, such as olive oils and spices, which can be purchased again and again.

There are natural fluctuations in the number of new households related to the housing and jobs market. Population demographics also play a part. The baby boomer's children, for the most part, are now living independently in homes of their own and producing boomer grandchildren. This leaves a gap of several years for an echo peak of a population spike to occur as the grandchildren reach adulthood.

The greatest increase in new households is currently in the immigrant sector. Over one million persons obtained legal permanent resident status each year since 2007. Nearly eight million immigrants entered the United States between 2000 and 2005, nearly half illegally. U.S. Census projections show that the population will grow by 135 million in 42 years, most as a direct result of immigration.[58]

Future immigration policy could alter the reality to be quite different from the hypothetical projections. With the current U.S. fertility rate of 2.1 children per woman, the population remains stable. If the economy improves, perhaps young adults who have been sharing housing with either roommates or their parents will create new households. For whatever reason, should the number of U.S. households increase significantly in the future, there will be an expansion in The Pampered Chef's market base.

Customer Education

Customer satisfaction requires proper customer education. Kitchen tools can be a complete mystery; their purpose is not always evident by mere physical examination. It is essential that consultants selling Pampered Chef products effectively demonstrate them and communicate to potential buyers the utility and benefit of a particular product.

"Selling a product is only the first step in building a relationship with customers," says Christopher. "Many times when customers take home a product they are unsure how to use it. At The Pampered Chef we make sure this does not happen. At our kitchen shows, the customer has the opportunity to try the product before he or she buys it. We also ensure that once the customers get the product home, they know how it will meet their needs in the kitchen. With each product we provide easy-to-read instructions detailing how to properly care for and use it, along with recipes that utilize the product. Our Kitchen Consultants also offer ongoing customer service and support after the sale."[59]

Proprietary Products

Using interesting gadgets makes cooking fun and entertaining. Pampered Chef's items are designed to be easier to use, helping to eliminate the frustration that often accompanies food preparation. Owning the rights to a custom-designed product adds prestige to a company. By offering something that is not available elsewhere, the buyer has additional justification to purchase it from Pampered Chef. Exclusivity has direct value.

When Doris couldn't find exactly the right gadget, she sought out someone to manufacturer her design for her. "We've become good at examining a product," she says. "We go to a manufacturer and say, 'We'll take your product, but we want it to have a longer handle, or we want it cheaper, or we want it to do three things."[60] The Pampered Chef began designing its own products in the early 1990s. Doris is left-handed, so she made certain that the Pampered Chef peelers, scissors, and cheese graters were designed to be easy to use for everyone.

Approximately 80 percent of the products in the Pampered Chef catalog are exclusive to the company. Popularity of items is continually assessed and revisions to the catalog are frequent. "I wouldn't be without a kitchen scale," says Doris, "but it's something people don't get that excited about; it's a little scientific for some."[61] Pampered Chef formerly offered kitchen scales, but it wasn't a popular item and was discontinued.

Litigation

Successful corporations must deal with the inevitable legal issues that arise. It's not evident to the general public just how frequently litigation occurs in corporate America. The Pampered Chef is both targeted as a defendant in litigation and acts as a plaintiff in other suits.

Justified or not, many suits and countersuits arise over design infringement and wrongful copying of catalogs between a former product supplier and The Pampered Chef. The Pampered Chef has also been sued by its customers for defective design and failure to warn customers of "inherent dangers" associated with a product.

Most troubling was a lawsuit brought against the company by a customer who cut her finger when a ceramic baking pan broke. The liability settlement awarded to the plaintiff was $2.6 million.[62] That's outrageous, in my opinion. I once had an Accidental Death and Dismemberment insurance policy through my employer that would pay $500,000 if I accidently *lost my entire hand*.

The company has sued individuals over sharing trade secrets and the act of "proselyting;" that is, the recruiting of sales force members from one direct-selling company by another. The Direct Selling Association has guidelines that prohibit such action.

Dealing with litigation is time-consuming and expensive. Christopher admits that lawsuits are just a part of doing business. "Corporations have a responsibility to protect what is theirs," she says.[63]

Management Transition

For an entrepreneur, the company that they create is a treasured personal entity. It is their "baby." It can be difficult to hand off the leadership, let alone ownership, of the company to another individual. Doris's first attempt to transition out of her role as president came when she hired Sheila O'Connell Cooper as president and COO in October 2000. Cooper was a former executive with Mary Kay and BeautiControl, both of which are direct-sales cosmetics firms. She was very experienced in the direct sales industry. In 1999, as CEO of BeautiControl, Cooper engineered its sale to Tupperware.

Cooper was likewise instrumental in assisting with the sale of the Pampered Chef to Berkshire Hathaway in 2002 and was promoted to chief executive in January 2003. Of transitioning the CEO position from a company's founder Cooper said, "One of the things that Mary Kay did masterfully was transition that role so that people understood that the company was the result of a number of people's efforts," Cooper said. "We are doing that, too."[64]

Cooper made it part of her mission to reach new users, including men. The sales force, which then numbered 71,000 consultants, had been composed almost entirely of women. The company also was aiming to sell more to minorities. The product line already had begun to expand beyond chefs' tools. Sheila O'Connell Cooper left The Pampered Chef abruptly in May 2003, after only five months as CEO. Doris had to fill in again as president until Marla Gottschalk was hired and started working at the company in December 2003.

Christopher sums up her management approach simply: "If you want people to be successful, you have to give them some wings."[65]

Food for Thought

Traditionally, the great professional chefs of the world were men. Female chefs continue to fight for the position of head chef in kitchens of the finest restaurants and for professional recognition. Out of 14 James Beard Foundation Chef Awards of 2011, 4 went to women.

Why are gender roles switched in the home kitchen? Cooking is not suited more toward either gender. However, genders in both professional and home kitchens are becoming more mixed.

From its inception, The Pampered Chef independent consultants were 99 percent female, and Doris is committed to encouraging entrepreneurship in women. Gender composition of the consultant workforce is a natural process, not an intentional plan. Christopher says, "It's grown through one person sharing it with another, and women tend to share it more with other women."[66] National Executive Director Teresa Brown has a few men on her team. "If you can find a guy who takes it seriously, they do amazing," she says. "One of our top salespersons in the country for the past 10 years has been a guy."

Doris also encourages youngsters to help out and have fun in the kitchen, while learning how to cook. "Be sure to invite sons as well as daughters into your kitchen. When I was a girl, kitchens were viewed as women's places, and it was a rare man who took his turn at the stove. But these days, basic food preparation is considered a life skill that everyone needs. More couples are cooking together or taking turns fixing meals for each other. People are marrying later—therefore living on their own a lot longer. It's never too early to start."[67]

Doris and Jay Christopher created a company that has had an impact on 12 million lives—even if it's something as small as owning and using a citrus peeler. Few of us have the opportunity to make such a difference in the world. "I believe it has been God's hand at work. He has been instrumental in guiding me and the result has been an enterprise that serves tens of thousands of Pampered Chef people, whose work, in turn, enriches millions of families by bringing them together at mealtimes."[68]

The Christophers have both spent much of their lives mentoring others. As Jay says, "I'm personally committed to teaching business skills and promoting entrepreneurial thinking in young people."[69] Doris adds, "One of the tips I give to people is to find something with a purpose that goes beyond earning a living, beyond just supporting yourself. Personal fulfillment and helping others will motivate you to do your very best," she says.[70]

She adds more advice, "If you have an idea that keeps resurging in your mind, you probably have an idea that's worth at least investigating and taking some steps to figure it out. Follow your instinct. You have to be reasonable in that. You have to know that there's a niche where people want and need what you're thinking about. If it's something that you're really excited about and love, that's important too, because you're going to spend endless amount of hours pursuing this product or this idea. If you really believe in it, you have to figure out a way to go for it."[71]

Doris is the personification of an entrepreneur. She started her company from scratch, nurtured it as it grew by huge percentages, and successfully executed an exit strategy beneficial to everyone. She begins a new stage of life now, stepping down from being the full-time leader and spending more time with her family and grandchildren. She does this comfortably, knowing that the company has solid ownership and leadership.

Chapter 4

Cathy Baron Tamraz—
Distribution Evolution

I first met Cathy Baron Tamraz, President and CEO of Business Wire, at the 2011 Berkshire Hathaway annual shareholders' meeting in Omaha. Business Wire, a company that disseminates business press releases and regulatory disclosures, has been a subsidiary of Berkshire Hathaway since 2006. Tamraz, Figure 4.1, oversees the company's day-to-day operations, long-term strategic planning, international expansion, and global branding. Thirty-nine Berkshire Hathaway companies had displays set up in the 194,300-square-foot Qwest Center exhibit hall (now named the CenturyLink Center), and I was making the rounds.

On this particular day, she was working in the Business Wire exhibit booth setting up an easel for display of a portrait of Warren Buffett. It was painted by Stephane Zovko, a client service representative in

Figure 4.1 Cathy Baron Tamraz, President and CEO of Business Wire
SOURCE: Business Wire.

Business Wire's Paris bureau. The painting would be auctioned during the meeting to raise funds for CASA (Court Appointed Special Advocates) of Omaha, a charitable organization that provides a voice for abused and neglected children within the court system through the use of trained citizen volunteers. My first impression of this handy CEO was "petite and spunky." The 57-year-old Tamraz appeared fresh and energetic on a day when she was directly interacting with many of the 40,000 persons in attendance.

Showcasing a business news organization amidst exhibit booths selling diamond earrings from Borsheims Fine Jewelry, $1 Dairy Queen Dilly Bars, and $5 packs of Fruit of the Loom underwear is a daunting task. The excitement in the exhibit hall is palpable, as long lines form to buy books and Cokes, and get car insurance quotes from a gecko. During the nine hours that the exhibit hall was open at the annual meeting in 2010, attendees bought 1,053 pairs of Justin boots, 12,416 pounds of See's candy, 8,000 Dairy Queen Blizzards, and 8,800 Quikut knives.[1] But since the Berkshire meeting attendees probably have a higher level of interest in financial news compared to the general public, the Business Wire booth also hosted a lot of visitors.

We chatted about Business Wire's charity fundraising project, something they do each year at the meeting, and Cathy proudly told me how they were able to bring a dozen Business Wire employees to Omaha for the event and that this year was the 50th anniversary of the company.

From just this brief encounter, I was impressed by Cathy's warmth and approachability, her pride in her company, and her youthful enthusiasm. It was evident that she is a leader who inspires her team members.

As we spoke, I could see a hovering figure out of the corner of my eye and realized somebody was obviously very anxious to speak to Cathy. I slipped aside and heard the young man's excited greeting: "Hi Cathy. Do you remember me from last year?" There's obviously a certain level that a CEO has attained when they can claim to have a fan club. Cathy has reached that level.

Information before the Information Age

Business Wire turned 50 years old in 2011 and celebrated by ringing the bell at the New York Stock Exchange on September 30. Warren Buffett joined Tamraz for this event, as did the winner of Business Wire's College Student Video Contest who was selected for best answering the contest question, "What is the future of public relations and communications?"

As a wholly owned subsidiary of Berkshire Hathaway, with annual revenues of approximately $150 million, Business Wire each year transmits and discloses hundreds of thousands of news releases, regulatory filings, and multimedia content of its member companies and organizations to financial professionals, journalists, regulatory authorities, and the public through NX, its own electronic network.

Cathy has seen major changes in the process of press release dissemination in her 32 years with Business Wire. The company was founded by Mr. Lorry Lokey on October 3, 1961, in San Francisco. It started in a tiny 9- by 12-foot leased office with seven client members and Lokey as its only employee. The business grew rapidly, though, and within four months there were 22 members of the service. Today, there are 500 employees and tens of thousands of member companies and organizations.

In August 1979, Lokey interviewed the 25-year-old Cathy after she answered a classified advertisement in the local San Francisco newspaper. With her undergraduate degree in English and master's degree in literature, she felt she could utilize her education by working at a communications company. Lokey agreed and hired her as an editor. In this job, she took dictation over the phone, reviewed news submissions from member companies, made revisions to text to make it more comprehensible, and put it in an acceptable and standardized format ready for distribution. It's a job that requires skills in customer service and communication, as well as a heightened attention to detail.

By this time, Business Wire had grown and opened additional bureau offices in Seattle and Boston. In 1980, Lokey decided to make a further expansion on the East Coast to establish a national presence. He opened a one-room office on 42nd Street in New York City. At the same time, Cathy was getting ready to quit her job in San Francisco so that she could move back to New York to be closer to her family. The timing couldn't have been better and Cathy agreed to become the New York newsroom manager.

Cathy recognized the opportunity to get in on the ground floor of a new office and the significant role that a Manhattan bureau would play. Moving back closer to her family in Long Island, where she was born in 1953, was also a motivation. It was a moment of foresight, as the New York office is now coheadquarters with the San Francisco office. The two offices have identical operations and are similarly staffed so that if one happens to go offline for any reason, the other can take over.

Being a new employee in a company that is in an expansion phase is an opportunity that can present itself to anyone lucky enough to be in the right place at the right time. But you need to be alert enough to recognize the chance when it happens and commit to taking the risk of embracing a life-changing event if you want to reap the eventual reward. Change is almost always required if one is to progress.

Cathy did not experience any barriers to entry due to gender when she began working for Business Wire. "This is a women-friendly company," says Cathy. "Always was. And I credit that back to the founder, Lorry Lokey. It's kind of interesting, because years and years ago in the 1960s when the company was new, there was a lot of typing on the news editor job. It was great for women. Lokey did a lot of great things for women way back then. We had one of the first nurseries in our office in San Francisco. It's an innovative and entrepreneurial company. We like to break the mold and do things differently. We still hire the best person for the job, but it's women-friendly."

Lokey recently gave Mills College, a California liberal arts women's college in the San Francisco Bay area, the largest gift ever from a living donor at over $30 million. His support was recognized in 2008 in the naming of the Lorry I. Lokey Graduate School of Business.

"I have this crazy idea that women are as good as men," he says with an ironic chuckle. "When you have both women and men in your company, you get a complementary situation. I saw this very early in the game. When I got to the point where I could start hiring people, women were there to take the jobs. Bear in mind, it was teletype work all day long. Our job was to type, including me. In those days, in the 1960s, that role fit women. Some men did it, too, but only a few. As years went on, I noticed that men were not so interested in the job because they saw it as 'women's work.' So I said to myself, the heck with them."[2]

"She is doing just fine," Lokey says of Tamraz with pride, "which proves I was right. In fact, Cathy broke another barrier by succeeding me. This still doesn't happen much in business. You see lots of women vice presidents, but not enough breaking through to the top. There are still glass ceilings, but we are breaking through them."[3]

Rising Cream

Cathy has always worked hard, but she couldn't have imagined running a $150 million company back when she was driving a taxicab in Long Island during a summer college break. That experience supplemented her natural talent for getting along with people and was a successful example of a woman working in a traditionally male occupation. It wasn't simply a "male-dominated" job in the 1970s; it was *completely* occupied by males, with the exception of Cathy.[4]

"Sometimes being a woman is an advantage. You can look at it both ways. As we were growing up at Business Wire, there were a fair number of women around and we supported each other and encouraged each other. That was always good. I never thought of there being a glass ceiling. But looking back at it now, we did break some barriers, so I'm pretty happy about that. If I'm a role model to any woman, that's great."

Cathy was named manager of the company's eastern division region in 1987 where she was responsible for the operations, sales, and support staff in all the bureaus along the eastern seaboard. This job required frequent communication with multiple offices and an increased necessity for travel.

At the age of 37, in 1990, she was named a vice president and appointed to the company's executive committee. She quickly ascended through the executive ranks, being named senior vice president in 1994, executive vice president in 1998, chief operating officer in 2000, president in 2003, and CEO in December 2005.

The ability to handle increasing levels of responsibility is a skill, or may be a personality trait, that some people lack. Those who lack this capacity hold a self-perception that is rooted in fear. They avoid any significant change. They are resistant to the unknown, fearing that it will inevitably be worse than the current, known situation.

There are only two possible outcomes of accepting more responsibility:

1. You successfully handle additional responsibility.
2. You are unable to handle additional responsibility.

Since the latter is a real possibility, many choose not to accept the challenge for fear of failure. But if you don't make that attempt to accept new challenges and responsibility at all, then you have *already* failed to handle it and your fears are immediately realized.

As illustrated in Cathy's climb through the Business Wire structure, there are necessary steps where learning occurs that allow one to proceed to the next level of responsibility. Mastery of skills is achieved and experiences are gained that contribute to success in the subsequent ladder rungs.

After announcing Cathy as the new CEO at the 2005 annual meeting, Lokey said, "Cathy has been a primary mover behind Business Wire's enormous success, first in the United States, and now internationally. Her commitment to a team approach is appreciated by the entire staff, which was underscored by the standing ovation she received when her promotion was announced. It's extremely gratifying to be able to pass the CEO baton to Cathy, who successfully balances management skills with people sensitivities."

Inspiring Women

I visited Cathy in her New York office on the 14th floor above East 52nd Street. She was dressed in a charcoal gray pantsuit and greeted me warmly. The office was located in the proverbial "corner," with wonderful Manhattan views in two directions. It was furnished comfortably with a large L-shaped desk, two guest chairs, and a couch (Figure 4.2)

Cathy gave me a tour of the offices that occupy two floors and we discussed the company she leads and how she came to be one of the four current female CEOs of a Berkshire Hathaway subsidiary company. "My mother is a huge female influence in my life. Forget the fact that I got very lucky in having her for my mother. As a person, she is one of the kindest, most caring people I know and she taught me by example how

Figure 4.2   Cathy Baron Tamraz in Her New York Office
SOURCE: Karen Linder.

to treat others. Her quiet strength is something I try to emulate every day. She's 86 now, and I'm grateful that I still have her with me in this world."

Cathy's mother was a homemaker and her father an engineer. She grew up with an older brother and a younger sister, and graduated from Mineola public high school on Long Island as an honor student and an athlete. She went to SUNY Oneonta for her bachelor's degree with a double major in English and Education. She later obtained a master's degree in Literature at Stony Brook University.

Cathy entered college straight out of high school, but during breaks she traveled extensively throughout the United States and Europe. She studied in Europe during one semester of her junior year, staying there for five months. She experienced many diverse cultures in her travels and learned to interact with a variety of people from different strata of life. She benefited greatly from traveling and obtaining a liberal arts education that gave her a very broad background of knowledge and experience. These are qualities that are rewarded in her industry. Rather than requiring a specific degree for employment, Cathy recruits smart, well-rounded, hardworking individuals.[5]

Upon graduation with her bachelor's degree, she took a position teaching high school English. It had only been four years earlier that she, herself, was sitting in a high school classroom as a student. There, as a newly minted teacher, she gained her first experience in management. She was forced to quickly learn how to take command of the classroom. Losing control of a high school class quickly leads to disaster, and she knew she better not let that happen. It was a delicate balance at age 22 to be tough and yet relatable, and to foster an environment of learning. It was a duality of role, having a position of authority, yet also feeling like one of the group. "It was a bit of a yin and yang thing. I think I have carried that with me to this day," says Cathy.

Other women in the public relations industry have inspired Cathy as she pursued her career. "I actually looked around at women who had big positions when I was coming up," said Cathy. "Dorothy Brooks had a very big position at UPI (United Press International). I always respected her. She spoke her mind. She was tough. She was tough on me and eventually we broke through that and I think she saw me continuing to push forward and I think I earned her respect. She didn't mentor me specifically, but I always looked around and watched what women were doing. I got to know her better over the years. That's somebody that I look up to."

"Public relations has a good share of women in the industry, but investor relations does not. When I first came to New York with the company in 1980, this town and Wall Street was male dominated. But I never looked at it that way and I still don't look at it that way. You just work hard. I think my parents gave me that."

Cathy serves as chair of Business Wire's executive committee. There is no board of directors since the company is a subsidiary of Berkshire Hathaway. The executive committee is comprised of six individuals from within the organization. Three of those six (50 percent) are female, well above the average 16.1 percent reported to be on Fortune 500 corporate boards.[6] Cathy also serves on the board of directors of Business Wire's joint-venture company, PYMNTS.com, a website containing news releases and commentary for the payments industry launched in October 2009.

Business Wire's chief operating officer, Executive Vice President and member of the Executive Committee, Phyllis Dantuono, was a former client who joined the company in 1986 (Figure 4.3). Her responsibilities are very broad, with a focus on sales and client relations. She makes sure that the company retains clients and meets their expectations. "I communicate what can be done, making agreements with clients," she says. "The operations team runs the company. I make the policies and practice guidelines. It's important that the process is in place. Everyone needs to follow the process. Everyone needs to move in the exact same direction. New hires need to get into that flow."

Phyllis also runs interference with the media who look to Business Wire to verify the content or have questions about the company that put out the release. Cathy adds, "It's about reputation. We vet our clients. We make sure that they are who they say they are. We spend a lot of time on it. If someone's reading information on the web and it has our name on it, it's very important that it's accurate." Phyllis ensures that Business Wire's editorial standards and integrity are maintained. Unfortunately, there are instances when attempts are made to release false information. "I wouldn't say it's a daily occurrence," said Phyllis, "but just about. We have to be extremely careful in our process and practices."

Figure 4.3   Phyllis Dantuono, Business Wire Chief Operating Officer
SOURCE: Business Wire.

There are 90 employees in the New York bureau working around
the clock, but Phyllis remembers when the New York office had just
nine people working there. "Everyone had to do everything," she says.
"And when the boss has done the job, it's a big advantage for everybody.
As the leader, if you know what the staff is doing and you know what
their challenges are, then you can say 'That's not such a big deal. You
can do that. I know that, because I did that job.' It's an advantage for
both the leader and the team. None of us on the executive team are
involved in the operations now as the people on the front line are, but
most of us know what's going on there and how that job needs to be
done. I think that's what's so significant here because so many of us
started here doing all of the entry jobs and know how to do it."

About being a female and rising to the level of corporate executive, Cathy says, "It's all about moxie and confidence and not being
afraid to break through barriers, and trying new things. Sometimes
you fail. I never really thought about being a woman versus a man.
My parents taught me to work hard and keep going and look for the
opportunities."[7]

Figure 4.4   Cathy Baron Tamraz with Warren Buffett in India, 2011
SOURCE: Cathy Baron Tamraz.

Speed, Accuracy, and Technology

Business Wire now has 26 U.S. bureaus, four in Europe, one in Australia, and one in Japan. "Where we don't have direct offices, we have partners," says Cathy. "We have a partner in the Middle East and Latin America, so there isn't anywhere that someone can't have access to using our services." Cathy keeps the possibility of future expansion open. "Obviously Brazil has really been going strong. We have an office in India—the middle class is exploding there—we just visited India with Warren Buffett (Figures 4.4 and 4.5). We work with a partner in China. That's a really high interest for us. They've opened it up for establishing a business there," she explained.

Not all companies in the industry follow the local bureau model of operation. "We take a different approach from every other wire. We take the *local service, global reach* approach. We could just have salespeople in different regions and not have the full operations, such as the newsroom. But we want to process the copy locally. We take a local approach. We want to take care of our clients in these areas where they are located. We are handling market-moving news. It's all about accuracy and speed

Figure 4.5   Cathy Baron Tamraz (on right) at Reception in India, 2011
SOURCE: Cathy Baron Tamraz.

and knowing our clients well. We want to *superservice* our clients and take really good care of them. It pays off for us to do it that way, in terms of the clients we keep."

Over 1,000 news releases are disseminated by Business Wire each day in 150 countries in 45 languages. In 2006, Business Wire was awarded a U.S. patent for Business Wire NX, a simultaneous network news distribution process. The company obtained a Canadian patent for NX in 2009. A patent for a social media application has just been awarded that greatly impacts the way users interact with Business Wire's content.

Business Wire pricing is determined by the length of the press release and the chosen geographic distribution. With a base of 400 words, and overage charges for each additional 100 words, U.S. news distribution can be as low as $325 for a 400-word press release. Says Cathy, "We used to have a system of 'first in, first out.' Now there are no delays waiting your turn for dissemination. We have the best technology and the fastest. We have the capacity to process 1,000 releases per minute, but for now, today, it's running at just 150 per minute because the recipients can only read them that fast."

Financial disclosures are the largest part of Business Wire's service, including product announcements and stock splits. Cathy explains, "We are in the disclosure business. Anything that's going to affect the stock price, that's kind of our sweet spot. Public relations and investor relations go hand in hand. That's what people look for when they come to our site to do research.

"The core communications conduit, the news release, which remains at the nexus of the disclosure process, was born out of the need to reach a wide audience quickly and effectively, and to 'shine a light' on events that required context and perspective," says Cathy. "Ivy Lee issued the first press release in 1906 following a train wreck in Atlantic City, New Jersey."

Following the accident, Lee not only convinced the railroad to distribute a public statement, he also convinced them to provide a special train to get reporters to the scene of the accident. In the weeks that followed, both newspapers and public officials effusively praised Pennsylvania Railroad for its openness and honesty.[8]

"A well-written news release, spotlighting the material data points, is a concise narrative that appeals to all audiences," said Cathy. "It is clearly the information currency of choice, freely accessed by a broad range of constituents, ranging from Wall Street professionals to Main Street investors. The news release kicks off the transparency process and allows journalists, investors, analysts, regulators, et cetera to analyze, interpret, and publicize information. It, in effect, starts the conversation in an open, transparent manner."[9]

How does Cathy plan to keep Business Wire viable in an age where social media spreads the news in nanoseconds and where regulations for company financial disclosures are threatened?

"Social media is huge," she says. "Every press release we send out has social media tags in it. We also send it out to our own social media site called eon.businesswire.com for 'enhanced online news.' We're on Facebook and have Twitter feeds. We have an entire department that keeps up on that because the algorithms change all the time."

Business Wire's Facebook page currently has 26,971 "likes" and their Twitter feed (@businesswire) has over 16,000 followers. "It's really another communications vehicle," says Tamraz. "And as many vehicles as we can have, and tools, the better. It's all about the eyeballs."

Business Wire was the first in their industry to put up a website, launching it in May 1995 by simply posting the company brochure. Now, all clients come in through the website, which also includes tutorials and tools for supporting and educating writers and journalists to build press releases for search engine optimization.

A growing area of the industry is the distribution of video releases. "In 1997, we launched the 'smart news release,' where we could embed photos, video, and audio right into the press release." Back then, clients provided hard copies of photos that were scanned by Business Wire to upload to the Internet. "That's something the Internet gave us. Today, if you don't have video on the Internet, you're not going to get *the look*. It's a big push of ours to make every release 'smart.'

"There's a direct correlation between having multimedia in your release and the number of views. We had a very big tech client that recently posted a relatively long 15-minute video that was watched by an incredible number of people. We have a measurement report that counts the number of views with demographics. We push the news out and they get back a report on who looked at it with some demographics to help a company track where their markets are. So that's a big piece of the service."

"We recently added a team of accountants for XBRL reporting, tagging the releases," said Cathy. The Securities and Exchange Commission mandated a three-year phase in of the XBRL requirement beginning in 2009.[10] EXtensible Business Reporting Language (XBRL) is a technology that relies upon the input of data tags to identify and describe information in a company's financial statements. The information can then be searched, downloaded into spreadsheets, or reorganized for analytical purposes.

XBRL also allows financial statements in foreign languages to be translated into English. It's expected that the use of XBRL will facilitate the comparison of financial and business performance across companies, reporting periods, and industries; assist in automating regulatory filings and business information processing; and increase the speed, accuracy, and usability of financial disclosure.

In August 2011, Business Wire launched a mobile alert service for users to receive text messages regarding the specific companies that they are monitoring. Subscribers are immediately alerted via text message whenever a press release is issued. "Our clients tell us they want to reach audiences wherever they are—which increasingly is on the go," said Laura Sturaitis, executive vice president of New Media and Product Strategy for Business Wire.

In 2000, Cathy was invited to meet with the Securities and Exchange Commission (SEC) as they developed their landmark Regulation Fair Disclosure (FD) provisions. In 2008 she presented to the SEC's Advisory Committee, a group given the task of reviewing policies on the use of Internet technologies in the disclosure of market-moving material information. As the CEO of a major newswire service, Cathy serves as a representative of her industry to the public, the media, and the government, all of which may require her attention simultaneously.

She has been vocal in calling for the SEC to enforce its regulations requiring corporate financial disclosures to utilize recognized disclosure channels. But the U.S. stock exchanges altered their rules following SEC guidance in 2008, recognizing that disclosures on company websites can meet the broad, nonexclusionary distribution requirements of Regulation FD if they meet certain standards of prior notice, prominence, usability, timeliness, and accuracy.

Cathy wrote a scathing article in response to Microsoft's decision to simply post their reports on their own website beginning in November 2010. Google has similarly posted its earnings on its own website since July 2010. "Records are meant to be broken," said Cathy in the article. "Rules, on the other hand, aren't. And when those rules have a direct impact on both the fairness and workings of our financial markets, then an even higher standard of accountability is in order. The latest disclosure debacle involves Microsoft, which abruptly notified the market of its shift to a web-disclosure model. The company posted its earnings online, without benefit of a corresponding broadly disseminated release. Microsoft's ill-fated foray into web-based disclosure provides a textbook example of *worst practices* investor relations. There's a large investor in Omaha who doesn't want to be checking hundreds of websites minute-by-minute throughout the day. But then again, who would?"[11]

This reference to Warren Buffett is completely appropriate when discussing the impact of actions, such as those taken by Microsoft and Google, since Berkshire Hathaway closely monitors numerous company financials and disclosures. And it's also a bit ironic since Microsoft

Founder and Chairman Bill Gates is a member of the Board of Directors of Berkshire Hathaway. While, admittedly, this trend toward web disclosure poses a serious threat to the revenues of newswire services, it also handicaps investors and the media. Large investors don't have time to check multiple individual websites and small investors don't necessarily have the knowledge to obtain accurate information. Business Wire, and other investor relations services, spend a considerable amount of time verifying the accuracy of press releases. Can investors trust the information posted directly on a company's website? Can they even find it there?

"Speed, Accuracy, and Technology are the key strengths of our company," said Cathy. "And the success we have with clients is in large part because of the level of trust they have in us."

The Berkshire Bump

That Business Wire is part of the 78-member Berkshire Hathaway family is due in large part to Cathy's initiative. On Saturday, November 12, 2005, Cathy was at home with her husband, who was reading a *Wall Street Journal* article with the headline "Warren Buffett, Unplugged."[12]

"He said, 'Wow, this sounds like Business Wire—like Lorry,'" Cathy recalled. The article described Buffett as tremendously wealthy but fairly hands-off in running his business, operating on instinct and in a folksy, unpretentious manner. Cathy quickly wrote a letter and faxed it off to Buffett, offering him the business.

Warren Buffett remembers that letter. "There was something about the letter that rang true to me. Both about the business and the writer of the letter," said Buffett.[13] "By the time I finished Cathy's two-page letter, I felt Business Wire and Berkshire were a fit. I particularly liked her penultimate paragraph: 'We run a tight ship and keep unnecessary spending under wraps. No secretaries or management layers here. Yet we'll invest big dollars to gain a technological advantage and move the business forward.'"[14]

Business Wire had been quietly on the block for the past four years, and while many prominent media firms had taken a look, none had offered a high enough price.[15] Cathy admits that it was difficult to find a buyer for Business Wire. "We were private for 45 years. We did our own thing and we really liked it. We were a very entrepreneurial company. If we wanted to do something, we did it. The stakes got higher and we went global. When you have a family-run business, there are estate issues and succession issues, so we were looking at that as Lorry was getting closer to age 80 and no one else in the family was going to run it."

Within a week after Cathy faxed her letter, she received a phone call. It was Warren Buffett on the line. Remembers Cathy, "I said, 'Hello, Mr. Buffett,' and he said, 'Please call me Warren.'" He was, indeed, interested in buying Business Wire. Cathy sent him more detailed financial information, and within the month Buffett, Lokey, and Tamraz were lunching together in San Francisco and the deal for an undisclosed purchase price of the company, appraised at $600 million, was done. The acquisition closed on February 26, 2006.

"We were debt-free and didn't have to sell it, but to those of us who built our careers here and wanted to continue, we thought it made sense to look around," said Cathy. "We'd only sell to a strategic company, not a financial partner, because we didn't need the money. It was very hard to find the right fit, and it was very frustrating. We didn't fit into the typical formulas. And then I found Berkshire Hathaway. Warren said 'Keep doing what you're doing.' Berkshire doesn't want to change the companies they buy. They are buying something because they love the model. Why would they want to mess with it?"

Buffett had confidence in Cathy as a manager from the very start, stating "In making this acquisition of Business Wire, we have followed our blueprint of buying profitable companies that are industry leaders, yet have significant growth potential. A major criterion in all our investment decisions is evaluating corporate management. Business Wire's experienced management team was key to our decision."[16]

Buffett also liked Cathy's attention to detail. "When I asked her on the phone how many employees she had, she replied '504.' I love this," said Buffett. "Not 'about 500.' I think she has 505 now and is doing considerably more business. She won't be happy until she has 100 percent market share."[17]

Employees learned of the pending deal on January 16, 2006, when founder Lorry Lokey sent a companywide e-mail coauthored by Cathy with the subject line "A Renaissance: A re-birth for Business Wire." Within the memo, annoyingly far down, it read:

> Many of you might have heard rumors these last few years that Business Wire might be for sale. It's true that in order to ensure our future and continue what we've built, we have considered options such as a sale, merger, acquisition, etc. I am pleased to announce that Business Wire has been sold to Berkshire Hathaway and its leader, Warren Buffett.

At 8:55 A.M. EST on March 1, 2006, the news broke on Business Wire (of course) that Warren Buffett's Berkshire Hathaway had bought Business Wire, making it a wholly owned subsidiary.

Typically with most acquisitions, there is a fair amount of disruption and change in the acquired company's culture. And acquisitions can cause a lot of stress and uncertainty for the entire organization. But there was very little disruption when Berkshire acquired Business Wire. The day-to-day operations continued as they had before. Still, being a part of Berkshire Hathaway has had an impact—a positive one. When Berkshire buys a company, people notice.

"We already knew we had a great company," said Cathy. "So did our clients and the media. To get that accreditation from Warren and Charlie Munger, it's big. We sell on our own merits, but backing us is this corporate giant. We share the same corporate ethics. And he saw that in us as well. Did our confidence level go up a notch? Probably."

Business Wire's Chief of Operations Phyllis Dantuono adds, "As an executive team, we're aware of our identity and what we are a part of. We know our goals. There's a pressure to do well, but that's a positive impact. We're very fortunate that we've always had a great reputation, but being part of Berkshire Hathaway added to that—it was really a validation of our reputation."

Cathy appreciates the backing that a company the size of Berkshire Hathaway can provide. "If I am looking around to buy something and make an acquisition that is very sizable, I have the guy in Omaha who can help, if he agrees with it. So that's a benefit, from a financial standpoint as well. It's subtle, but it's really helpful.

Having relationships with the other Berkshire companies added a new dimension to the business after the acquisition. "I obviously want the other Berkshire Hathaway companies to use Business Wire," said Cathy. "Some of them were clients before we became part of Berkshire. Not all of them issue press releases, but NetJets, GEICO, Benjamin Moore, and Johns Manville all were clients before. You want them to believe in you. They know I will be looking out for my sister companies when they issue a press release." There is, however, no financial benefit for sister companies. "We sometimes give discounts based on the size of the company and volume of business," says Tamraz, "but that applies to any company."

Cathy talks to Warren Buffett fairly frequently. "I think he loves Business Wire. He loves the model. We're so connected to Wall Street. And we get along. We just got along from the beginning. He's such a supportive person. I speak to him a couple of times a month."

An Entrepreneurial Family Workplace

Business Wire's New York office has an open design. Individual workstations are spaced a few feet apart from each other in a large single room with no interior walls. Windows let in natural light. Everyone can interact with each other, as needed, but the atmosphere is remarkably quiet and relaxed, at least to an outside observer. The large area of computer servers and other information technology equipment is located on the floor below in a glass-enclosed room. This area, and the employees responsible for it, is isolated from the rest of the office, as is optimal for servicing and maintaining the company's computer infrastructure.

Deb Subia, Editorial Process development manager in Seattle, was one of the lucky Business Wire employees selected to attend the 2011 Berkshire Hathaway annual meeting. She said of the experience, sometimes referred to as Woodstock for Capitalists, "Business Wire has long been known as a company with a family atmosphere. I had the sense at the annual meeting, being around other Berkshire Hathaway companies, that I was part of an even bigger family."[18]

"We're a real homegrown kind of company. We're close with each other," agrees Cathy. "We run it very entrepreneurial, but we're serious about what we do. I like to know everybody's names and their families and what's going on in their lives, and I really think that builds loyalty and good morale. We have great benefits."[19] Business Wire offers the standard employee benefits, such as health insurance, 401(k) matching, and paid time-off, but they also have unique benefits including reimbursement plans for fitness, dental work, and education classes.

Any employee with 10 years or more service can receive a $1,000 vacation stipend to any Hawaiian island. "My roots to Hawaii go back 35 years, when my husband and I managed a small hotel there," said Cathy. "This is a wonderful perk that honors our Hawaiian connection." With perks like that, Tamraz has exceptional success at retaining employees.

"A lot of what we do is about longevity, so it's an encouragement to stay with the company," she says. "Coming to our organization, we want you to find a home here, and we try to match skill sets and promote and reward. Obviously money is important. Beyond that, it's feeling appreciated and noticed. We don't have a lot of layers here— we've got about 500 employees, so your work is recognized and acknowledged. It's pretty simple, you work hard, you get rewarded, and if there's other opportunities, we'll look from within first to promote."[20]

"I'm all about the people that work here and that I deal with outside, as well," says Cathy. "It's a relationship business. Knowing what motivates people and how to get them to work for you and feel good about the company, themselves—it all flows together."[21]

Business Wire survived the burst of the dot-com bubble when many of their clients went belly up. "We really ramped up in 1999 to 2000 with dot-com explosion, adding 50 editors to our staff to process copy. But then we had the correction and had to shrink back," she said. At one time Business Wire had 525 employees. It's currently back to 503.

"We had a lot of technology companies that formerly used Business Wire," says Cathy, "and we felt a trickle-down effect, but we didn't have any layoffs—not one—during that time. We said, 'We hired these people to be with us and grow with us, and we're going to find something else for them to do until we recover,' and we did. It speaks to the fact that we weren't overextended. We're a no-debt company. If we don't have the money to do something, we don't do it."[22]

In honor of its 50th anniversary, Business Wire is giving back by providing each of its employees paid time off in 2011 to volunteer with the nonprofit of their choice. The company also has a charitable match program that matches employee contributions of $100 or more at 50 percent, up to $10,000 per person. Employees get to choose their own 501(c)(3) charities, making it more personal.

As one of her personal goals, Cathy would also like to give back more in the future. She says, "I have certain charities that I like, but haven't spent the time that I'd like to spend on that. I may also write a book someday. Writing is a big deal to me due to my background in literature, and I would also like to do more traveling."

Being *Pono*

Cathy has an office at the San Francisco Business Wire bureau, but spends most of her time in New York. This New York address is the fourth that Business Wire has had in the city. Cathy discussed her daily activities that are far from routine. She commutes to work by train each day, during which time she does most of her daily reading. "I'm up pretty early. I watch the Squawk Box (CNBC). I usually read my management reports on the train. I read the *Wall Street Journal*, and I have Google alerts set for news topics I'm interested in."

Cathy is a hands-on deeply involved manager. "My day is varied," she says. "I think that's why I like it so much. I will talk to Europe early. We also have Monday morning meetings a couple days a month to just catch up. I may have some outside calls with our partners. I speak to my CFO frequently in California. I work closely with the CIO. It's a close-knit team. I'm extremely hands-on. I've got my hands in everything. I don't know any other way. Obviously I delegate, but I like to know all the details. I'm big on knowing what's going on in sales and I deal with personnel issues."

Being involved in every aspect of a business can cause stress and lead to burnout. "Balance is important and one has to find the way to be the most productive in work and life. In Hawaiian, we call it *pono*," she says. In the Hawaiian thought, being *pono* means being in perfect alignment and balance with all things in life. "We've owned a home on Maui since 1999 and I try to get there whenever I can because it is so rejuvenating for me. I have a full office set up over there, so I'm not out of touch. Health is everything . . . body, mind, and spirit!"

"I have a little newspaper clipping headline on my PC, and it says, 'Nerves of steel.' It's stressful. Lots of things happen, and you have to be prepared, but you can't anticipate everything that's going to happen on a given day." She advises, "You've got to be flexible, and you need to be able to take that deep breath and think about it rationally before reacting. Then you address the issue head-on, you deal with it straight up, and you move on. The one thing I do is, when we have a problem, I immediately communicate. That takes a lot of the sting out of the problem. You take your lumps and you fix your problems and you just move on. That kind of attitude serves everybody well."[23]

Cathy was in New York City during the 9/11 attack. Two of the Business Wire staff were in the vicinity of the World Trade Center that morning. They were okay, but there were stressful hours of uncertainty while communications were impossible. "That day and the ensuing weeks were much more dramatic for me than the recent financial crisis," said Cathy.[24]

Security of a company and safety of the company's employees is yet another concern for a CEO. Cathy says, "Life changed after 9/11. This is one of the most secure buildings. We've been here for 17 years. It's a nice part of town, we have a great landlord, and we plan to stay here."

Cathy's immediate family includes her husband Stephen Tamraz, whom she married in 1982. She has no children, but enjoys her pets and extended family. There's a balance that we all attempt to maintain between work and personal lives. To keep that balance, Cathy practices yoga and is an avid tennis player. "I'm a big tennis player," she says. "It's the greatest stress reliever in the world, hitting that little yellow ball."

"A lot of people have aging parents. I have that as well," says Cathy. "There are some years where the balance isn't there. There are sacrifices and compromises that are made. I actually have gotten better at balance. If you have support in your life, it's possible. Yeah, it's hard at times. But I can't think of a situation where it's not hard. Anybody building a career has to figure it out. It's tough at times."

Appreciation of others is a quality that Cathy would like to see continue with Warren Buffett's eventual successor. "Those are big shoes to fill. I have never worked for anyone like him. It's such an enormous gift, both personally and professionally. He's got this style that makes you think that you know everything and can do no wrong. He motivates me. I've studied that style and it works. I've taken that into my own management style. His belief in us is so big that it's tough to sleep at night. I say that tongue-in-cheek, but that's how it is. I don't need outside motivation, but everybody likes to be complimented."

"He has appreciation for his managers. Those qualities are important and it works well for Berkshire. It's obviously a serious-minded company, and it wants to be the best, but it's family in a certain way. And I love that. I think that has to exist going forward."

The Business Wire executive team meets quarterly to discuss strategy. There is no advisory board. "We have no outside advisors," says Cathy, "other than Mr. Buffett, that I might bounce some ideas off of. We do have a steering committee to connect with each other and come up with ideas. We're a crisis de jour business. We don't look even five years down the road. There are certain things that we want to have happen and we put a plan in place to get that done."

"We don't make projections. That's one of things that made it difficult when we wanted to sell the company. They all wanted to see projections, but it doesn't work like that. The interesting thing about Warren Buffett was that he looked at how we had performed. And he made a decision about how we would perform in the future based on how we performed in the past. It makes a lot of sense because that is *reality*."

Buffett's buy-and-hold mantra is mirrored by Cathy's 32-year career with Business Wire. She strongly advises young people to begin thinking about the long term and to persist in the same job, especially if you love the work and the company. She doesn't believe that a magic formula exists for achieving success, other than hard work.

She recommends that one should be open to challenging or even distasteful jobs. She advises, "Sometimes there's a certain job that you don't want to take on, or within a company there are certain tasks you don't like. But you don't know where that road is going to take you. Keep going! Don't judge things or say 'No' to them. There's no road around hard work. Look for the opportunities. I am living proof that it does work out. The cream does rise to the top." Good advice from one who, herself, worked hard, rose through the ranks, and is now at the top.

It has been said that Cathy Baron Tamraz is one of the most prominent women in the public relations and investor relations industries. However, it's not necessary to qualify that statement with gender. In fact, it is more appropriate and completely accurate to say that Tamraz is one of the most prominent and influential *persons* in the public relations and investor relations industries.

Chapter 5

Marla Gottschalk—Consuming Passion

Marla Gottschalk, Chief Executive Officer (CEO) of The Pampered Chef®, a direct seller of high-quality kitchen tools and a Berkshire Hathaway subsidiary, was named CEO on May 1, 2006, after having been COO of the company for the previous three years. The Pampered Chef was bought by Berkshire Hathaway in 2002.

When Gottschalk's appointment was announced, founder of the company Doris K. Christopher said, "I value Marla's judgment and decision making without hesitation. From the beginning she demonstrated respect for our corporate history and values as she introduced changes to keep the brand vital for years to come. With Marla at the helm, I see great things for our future. Our sales leaders have warmly welcomed her leadership, and I feel it's a privilege to work with her."[1]

After Marla became CEO, Doris retained a relationship with the company as chairman. Marla continued to work in close partnership with Doris and both Gottschalk and Christopher reported directly to Warren Buffett, chairman and CEO of Berkshire Hathaway. In 2011, Doris's title was revised to Chairman Emeritus, a change that signals further transition toward Doris's retirement.

Since joining Pampered Chef, Gottschalk (Figure 5.1) has implemented numerous strategic initiatives to take the already successful company to the next level. She simplified the business for the sales field and focused on the fundamentals.

Gottschalk leads The Pampered Chef's executive team, and is responsible for the overall direction of the business. In addition to day-to-day decision-making, she oversees long-range planning and defines corporate strategy for the company. The executive team includes Jim Bresingham, CFO, and Rob Sarkis, CIO. Jean Jonas is a visible presence as senior vice president of sales.

My personal encounter with Marla Gottschalk was very brief. At the Berkshire Hathaway 2011 annual meeting, The Pampered Chef had a large booth in the exhibit hall of the convention center. Gottschalk and Christopher were working in the booth selling kitchen utensils from their current line. And when I say they were *working*, I mean they were

Figure 5.1   CEO of The Pampered Chef, Marla Gottschalk
SOURCE: The Pampered Chef.

working their tushies off! The booth was packed with people loading up on gadgets to make their lives in the kitchen easier and more fun.

I had hoped to speak with both Marla and Doris, but they were obviously far too busy. Instead, I introduced myself to Doris and asked for her autograph inside the cover of my newly purchased copy of her book *The Pampered Chef*.

I waited in line at Marla's counter and when it was my turn, showing my ignorance and stammering, asked her what she was selling. I selected the Breast Cancer Awareness Pink Zebra High Heel Cake Server. The encounter was a mere minute or two. I discovered nothing about Gottschalk's leadership, except that she is comfortable and confident ringing up sales. Cakes and pies are rarely served at my table, but I love my new stainless steel pink zebra server. The "heel" magnetically attaches and detaches for easy storage in my kitchen drawer and it's just so darned cute.

Finding the Right Fit

We know Doris was a home economist. But what was Marla before joining The Pampered Chef? Marla's background and training is in accounting, finance, and management. She followed a nontraditional education and employment path in the early years of her career.

Marla was born and raised in Bloomington, Indiana, a town whose metropolitan area has a population of roughly 175,000, located 50 miles south of Indianapolis. Her father was the third generation owner of a car dealership, and her mother was a homemaker. She had three older brothers.

She had no particular career interest in mind while in high school, and by the time she was a senior, she had enough credit to attend class for just half of the day. The rest of the day, she worked at her father's dealership, Curry Buick Cadillac, started by W.S. Curry in 1915. The dealership is now operated by the fourth generation.

"My dad had a tremendous work ethic," says Marla. "He worked more hours than any of my friends' parents did. I made the mental connection that working hard would help me be more successful. He was a fabulous role model. He looked at the dealership very holistically. Every aspect of the dealership, whether it was glamorous or not, could make or break you. By running a service department, he could cater to not only his own customers, but also attract people who hadn't bought their cars from him."[2]

After graduating from high school, she worked as a bank teller and then as the office manager of a medical clinic. Says Marla, "I blindly entered the working world hoping to make money right away."[3] But after three years, she realized that to get where she wanted to go, she needed more education.

She entered Indiana University. Being slightly older and having already worked and lived independently in an apartment, she experienced college differently from most freshmen. She earned her tuition while attending school. "I ended up working at a restaurant and paid my way through college."[4] That restaurant was Butterfields, her first professional experience in a food-related business.

She received a bachelor's degree in accounting from the Kelley School of Business at Indiana University in 1984. Recognizing her as an outstanding alum, the school named her to the Kelley School of Business Academy of Alumni Fellows in 2007. The honor recognizes alumni who have earned the stature of business leaders and managers by their demonstrated successes in business organization and their contributions to management philosophies and practices.

Upon graduation, she took a job as a staff accountant with Peat, Marwick, and Mitchell accounting and auditing firm (later KPMG). Here, Marla gained valuable financial expertise and also learned something about herself. "It was a great opportunity to get a feel for different types of businesses at an entry-level position. I pushed myself to get a certified public accountant license, but I eventually realized that my focus was all backward-looking. It became clear to me that my interest was not about how a business performed historically, but how it should be operated going forward!"[5]

Moving Up the Food Chain

Marla's next employer was Kraft Foods, where she began in 1989. She advanced through increasingly responsible positions during her 14-year tenure. She had nine different job titles during that time, which kept her hopping back and forth, moving her office between the Kraft headquarters in Northfield, Illinois, and the Glenview, Illinois, office, a distance of less than three miles. (Berkshire Hathaway is Kraft's largest shareholder.)

Her first position was as senior financial analyst (Glenview). In this position, her responsibilities included overseeing the reporting and analysis of financial costs versus budget, comparing expense performance, and preparing budgets. She provided financial information to senior managers, impacting their decision making and project prioritization. In 1989, General Foods and Kraft merged to become "Kraft General Foods." During the 1990s the company expanded to Europe and Scandinavia through acquisition of other companies and now markets its brands in more than 170 countries.

The current CEO of Kraft, Irene Rosenfeld, was president of Kraft Foods, North America, while Marla was there. *Forbes* magazine has named Rosenfeld one of the world's "100 Most Powerful Women" and ranks her as second on its 50 Most Powerful Women in Business list.

Gottschalk started studying for her MBA in 1991 while still a full-time employee at Kraft. That year, she was named director of Financial and Business Analysis, and worked at the headquarters in Northfield. She graduated from J. L. Kellogg Graduate School of Management at Northwestern University in Evanston, Illinois, with a master of management degree in 1993.

For a year, from 1993 to 1994, Gottschalk was controller, sales (Glenview). Then in 1995, she became vice president of Finance for Sales and Customer Service (Northfield). In this position, she helped integrate four separate sales organizations necessitated by the General Foods–Kraft merger.

In 1996, she was named vice president of Strategy, Finance, and Systems, Kraft North American Foodservice (Glenview), and in 1997 she became vice president for Financial Planning and Analysis for Kraft Foods, North America (Northfield).

She decided to leave the realm of finance and took a job in marketing in 1999 when she was named vice president for Marketing and Strategy for the Kraft Cheese division (Glenview).

Of this transition to new ground, Gottschalk says, "Kraft wants you to be well-rounded. Even in finance, they expected we would be full business partners, making more input in decisions than just carrying the numbers. That's why I wanted marketing and strategy experience. When I talked to Bob Eckert, then Kraft's CEO of North America (now CEO of Mattel), he supported me. I moved over to the cheese division, Kraft's largest."[6]

From 2000 to 2002, Gottschalk was executive vice president and general manager of Post Cereals, the third largest cereal company in the United States behind Kellogg's and General Mills. In this position, her responsibilities included brand marketing, trade marketing, marketing research, finance, consumer promotion, and human resources. She also shared responsibility for five manufacturing plants and a research development facility.

Gottschalk was named senior vice president of Financial Planning and Investor Relations of Kraft Foods in February 2002. This required that she move to Rye Brook, New York. In this position, she led the global financial planning activities of a $30 billion business. She played a key role in establishing strategies as a member of the Kraft Operating Committee.

Of her time at Kraft Marla says, "We were encouraged to rotate through different departments and divisions to fully understand the company. I was fortunate to be given a lot of different experiences. I was constantly working hard and looking for the next opportunity. I was willing to take on less glamorous assignments if I thought I could learn from them and be recognized for my contributions. Taking on assignments in which things aren't working well is always an opportunity to shine if you get them running better."[7]

Her decision to take the position as president and chief operating officer of The Pampered Chef—already wildly popular—would present challenges of a different type. How can one improve upon something so successful?

The Pampered Chef Buyosphere

The Pampered Chef is located in Addison, Illinois, 25 miles southwest of the Kraft Foods headquarters in Northfield, Illinois, although Marla's final position with Kraft was located in New York. Relocation of her family back to Illinois was necessary prior to beginning her job with The Pampered Chef.

While the distance is short between the headquarters of the two companies, other differences are great. The Pampered Chef sells its products by direct selling, utilizing a network of 60,000 independent consultants. The company, itself, has about 750 employees. Kraft products are on store shelves worldwide and the company has approximately 127,000 employees.

At the time Berkshire Hathaway bought The Pampered Chef in 2002, annual revenues were approximately $740 million. Following acquisition, the company is no longer required to report its revenues, and widely ranging estimates are published. *Direct Selling News* reports The Pampered Chef revenues at $500 million, while Yahoo! Finance's company profile reports 2009 revenues at $700 million.[8]

The Pampered Chef may have experienced a decline in revenues in the past decade, but it would be wrong to make that assumption. In 2002, there were 70,000 consultants selling products and the company had 1,000 employees. It's possible that changes have made the company more efficient and able to achieve similar results with fewer resources.

Warren Buffett is pleased with Gottschalk's performance. As he said in 2010, "We had a number of companies at which profits improved even as sales contracted, always an exceptional managerial achievement."[9] For this achievement, Buffett recognized Marla and nine other subsidiary managers, including Susan Jacques, president and CEO of Borsheims Fine Jewelry.

When asked how the company was faring in the poor economy of 2009, Marla replied, "What's going on with the economy now is really helping our business. More consumers are staying at home and are budget conscious. Our consultants offer to come into your home and teach you and your friends how to make a meal for $2 a serving, much cheaper than eating out. Many consumers today are looking for easy meal solutions. Usually there's five to seven ingredients. You can make them in less than 30 minutes. It's terrific!"[10]

Direct selling is one of the few industries hiring right now. Unemployment fosters entrepreneurship. When jobs are unavailable, people often seek self-employment options. Scentsy is another home party direct seller founded in 2004, selling wickless candles. "Many consultants tell us Scentsy came at a critical time for their families," says Heidi Thompson, president of Scentsy Inc. "We had consultants whose husbands lost their jobs in the building industry. They started selling Scentsy to supplement their household income, but it soon became the sole source of family income. In some cases, their husbands now help them with their Scentsy business because they can make more working a Scentsy business with their spouse than by working outside the home."[11]

"We have long held that direct selling does well in poor economic times," says Amy Robinson, a spokesperson for the Direct Selling Association, the national trade association for 200 companies that distribute goods and services sold directly to consumers. "This is particularly true for products that are 'recession-proof,' such as cosmetics or kitchen utensils, which are things people won't give up regardless of the economy."[12]

Home party sales account for about 30 percent of the $30 billion in annual direct selling revenues.[13] Table 5.1 shows details of some companies ranked in the direct selling industry's top 100 globally.

The Pampered Chef has to stay current to retain its popularity. Says independent consultant Teresa Brown, "Marla has brought some extreme value to our company. For a while we were a day late and a dollar short, such as coming out with citrus colors. The rest of the world had it two years before. Now they're very current. They're very focused on being relevant and current with colors and products. Taupe is a hot color right now. And then in the spring, there will be a new color."

"Superior functionality and quality are our key criteria. That's what makes a Pampered Chef product unique," says Lisa Flynn, senior vice president of Product Development. "Our Product Development Team is composed of experienced specialists who have their finger on the pulse of the marketplace, and are trained to identify emerging trends and new opportunities," she says. "We add new products to our line based on the needs of our customers and our ability to improve upon what's currently in the marketplace. And we constantly reevaluate existing products to determine which need to be updated with improved features and technology."[14]

The Pampered Chef offers over 300 items for purchase at any given time. Most are exclusive products. Surprising (to me, anyway) is the

Table 5.1 Global 100 Direct Selling Companies

Company	CEO	Direct Selling Rank	Gross Revenues (approximate)	Number of Employees	Number of Independent Reps
Avon	Andrea Jung	1	10.9 billion	42,000	6.5 million
Natura Cosmeticos (Brazil)	Alessandro Giuseppe Carlucci	3	3 billion	5,000	1 million
Mary Kay	David B. Holl	6	2.5 billion	5,000	2 million
Tupperware	Rick Goings	7	2.3 billion	13,500	2.6 million
PartyLite	Anne Butler	21	545 million	1,200	63,556
The Pampered Chef	Marla Gottschalk	25	500 million	800	60,000
Scentsy	Orville Thompson	33	382 million	784	105,000
Longaberger Baskets	Tami Longaberger	62	200 million	900	35,000
Tastefully Simple	Jill Blashack Strahan	77	125 million	330	27,000
Creative Memories	(Mr.) Chris Veit	79	113 million	450	40,000

SOURCE: "Global 100," *Direct Selling News*, June 2011.

inclusion of edible items, such as 19 different sauces and 33 different spices, seasonings, and rubs.

Shop 'Til You Drop

Sociologists have actually studied the history and significance of shopping. It seems that there is a difference between buying and shopping. Buying is the simple act of exchanging money for services and/or goods. Shopping evolved once humanity gained leisure time. It's the act of perusing goods, making comparisons, handling items, and trialing them. There is an element of desire, as well as a "hunt and seek" challenge to the activity.

First came shopping. Then came fashion. Then came clearance sales. Further evolution has incorporated entertainment and education into the activity. Says Mark Moss, professor at Seneca College in Toronto, "Many people find it invigorating to go shopping. Just as it is uplifting to see a certain movie and, for many, inspiring to walk through a particular park, many people experience the same emotional states by going shopping. It is no secret that people acknowledge that shopping is a 'stress buster' and that the ritual of going out to a favorite store and purchasing something new is a very common way of getting out of a funk. Shopping brings about sensations that run the gamut from arousal to perceived freedom, as well as fantasy fulfillment."[15]

For some, shopping is a pleasure equal to anything life has to offer. Thomas Hine, a writer on history, culture, and design offers that shopping has a lot in common with sex. He says, "Just about everybody does it. Some people brag about how well they do it. Some keep it a secret. Most people worry, at least a little, about whether they do it right. Both sex and shopping provide ample opportunities to make really foolish choices. Some shopping is, like sex, an effort to fill fundamental biological needs. It is often playful, though the play is very serious. In sex we learn about ourselves in relationship to another person. Shopping defines us through our relationships to things, and to the meanings that our society attributes to them. We try things on, and as we do so, we try on identities."[16]

We commonly define ourselves by our ethnic culture, religion, and profession. But increasingly, we are defining ourselves largely by our tastes in things such as fashion, culinary choices, and entertainment—tangible objects that we consume. We are choosing lifestyle identities. Those who wish to be perceived as being good at golf, besides purchasing the essential golf equipment to play the game, also buy clothing from golf brands, buy golf-themed artwork and accessories for their homes and offices, and take golf-resort vacations. It may not help one's golf game, but it at least portrays the identity of a golfer.

The same scenario applies to persons who desire kitchen competence. Having the right tools in the kitchen can, indeed, make the task of food preparation easier, safer, and more efficient. Using unique, cleverly designed kitchen tools is fun and can even inspire one to create something they otherwise wouldn't attempt. In the process, they identify themselves and are perceived by others to be "chefs."

It's My Party and I'll Sell If I Want To

Sociologist Colin Campbell, professor emeritus at the University of York literally wrote the book on the relevance of shopping in our society. He says that "looking at many products offered for sale is an intensely stimulating exercise. It sparks fantasy and serves as a catalyst for the creation of daydreams. Many people together can experience the same heart-felt wants and needs and thus can participate in an approximate 'parallel experience.' "[17]

The home-shopping party concept fits perfectly into a parallel social and consumer experience. It's a shared occasion similar to what one has when attending a theater performance or sporting event. Having others around us sharing the same sensory stimulation heightens the experience for everyone.

Home parties take shopping a step further by including socializing and peer bonding. The social aspect is an important factor that is absent from e-commerce, which is conducted in an isolated environment online in one's home.

Home parties are not simply fun; they also provide ample opportunity for networking, forging new associations, and deepening existing friendships. Such relationships are a source of strength and empowerment for women.[18]

The Pampered Chef's kitchen shows provide an educational component. Attendees learn useful tips and facts about food preparation and nutrition. "Our consultants offer customers a unique advantage that they will not be able to find anywhere else," says Marla Gottschalk. "Retailers can't show every customer how to use the products they sell or allow them to try them out before they buy them. At a cooking show, our customers are encouraged to do exactly that. And they get to do it in a relaxed, friendly atmosphere."[19]

I was interested to learn how the independent consultants feel about working with the company, so I submitted the online form asking for a Pampered Chef consultant referral. Within 10 minutes, I had a phone call from Jennifer Sheldon, a local Omaha consultant. Jennifer's been with The Pampered Chef for four and half years. She says she started off "gung-ho" in Mississippi, doing six to eight shows per month. Then she moved back to Omaha, got busy with her family, and is now doing two to four shows per month. She's happy with the flexibility she has to devote as much time as she wants to it. "You will get out of it exactly what you put into it," she says.

Jennifer referred me to Teresa Brown, another Omaha consultant, to see what being a consultant is like from a different perspective. Teresa (Figure 5.2) is a full-time independent consultant and has been with The Pampered Chef since 1992. She's gone as far as you can up the nine-step independent consultant career ladder, having achieved the title of National Executive Director. She is one of only 25 independent consultants at this level and is making a six-figure income. Her business is so large that she even has an assistant helping her.

Teresa is a lovely, warm person. Her personalized Pampered Chef website states, "My mission is to help families get back around the dinner table where the real family magic happens and memories are made. Good times or not-so-good, you're still being a family. I want to help people save time and money by cooking at home more and make eating out more of a treat than the norm."

You're Invited!

Since I hadn't been to a home party (of any kind) for over 15 years, I attended one of Teresa's shows. (We called them *parties* back in the 1990s, but the terminology has changed since then—now they are

Figure 5.2   Left to Right: Doris Christopher, Teresa Brown, and Marla Gottschalk, 2011
SOURCE: The Pampered Chef.

shows). About 1 million Pampered Chef shows are held in the United States each year. Teresa warned me that shows are different now and that they're more interactive. "Are you going to make me cook?" I asked, with a grimace. I'm the first to admit that I'm not a great cook and not particularly good as a group activity participant. "Oh, we'll have you do something small . . . like squeeze a lime," she replied. Her intuition recognized my limitations.

At the show, hosted by Paulette Pentecost—another gracious lady—Teresa deftly demonstrated kitchen tools while making "Family Burrito Bake" (with packaged shredded cheese!) and chocolate lava cake (Figure 5.3). Everyone took turns trying out the gadgets and the food was delicious. I met some great women and bought $850 worth of kitchen supplies for myself and as gifts for my family. Well, I had 15 years to make up for, after all!

Typically, a person will volunteer to be the hostess and invite her friends to the show at her home, where a consultant will demonstrate

Figure 5.3   Teresa Brown Demonstrates Pampered Chef Tools
SOURCE: Karen Linder.

Pampered Chef tools by cooking an item that everyone will later enjoy eating. The hostess sets up the kitchen space with chairs for her guests and provides the necessary ingredients to prepare the food. The consultant brings crates containing various kitchen gadgets as samples for viewing and to use in the demonstration. Then the impressed guests will eat the prepared food, and complete order forms for items they select to purchase.

Teresa has set up her business in a unique, efficient, and entrepreneurial manner. She has converted her basement into a Pampered Chef kitchen showroom. "It's not the norm," she says. "So many people want to have a party, but don't want to have it at their house. This way, the hostess brings her ingredients the day before and we hold the show here. I do the invitations from her list of guests."

She adds, "I can have my team meetings here and do training. It's an expectation with the company that you meet once a month with your team. We do a recipe at each meeting as a demo to give them show ideas. They use tools that some of them don't have, so they can get their hands on them. We will pick a training topic and then we do individual recognition and prizes."

Teresa says of The Pampered Chef, "It's a culture in and of itself. If you're in it, you're really *in* it." She was recruited in St. Louis by Barb, who was recruited by Patty, who was recruited by Randy, who was recruited by Doris Christopher, herself. With 60,000 current consultants, the genealogy records in the home office form a many-limbed tree.

Multilevel marketing is a term used to describe businesses that compensate their sales force for sales made not only by themselves, but also by those whom they recruit. Who recruited whom is important when it comes to your earning power. Consultants who recruit others earn commissions on their recruit's sales. After you recruit one person, you become a Senior Consultant. If you recruit two people you become a Team Leader. The home office pays an "override" to consultants to train their recruits. That income is totally separate from and unrelated to sales.

"Bringing people into the business is an optional activity, but is the smart thing to do," says Teresa. "When you recruit one person, you get 1 percent commission, with two you get 2 percent, and it grows from there. The Director (fourth) level is where you start making significant money." These are people who have recruited someone who has in turn recruited another person (an in-direct recruit). It benefits team leaders to help their members get promoted to upper levels by recruiting others. "I could have a million people under me, but if I don't help any of them promote, I just stay at the same level. Payment wise, we only go down three levels. There's people that are way bigger than me and I've got some growing yet to do," says Teresa.

Teresa's team just won the Summer's Best Challenge by increasing their recruitment rate over the previous year. The reward was a party in St. Louis. The company ran another contest related to sales and five of Teresa's team members earned prizes in that one. I asked Teresa how large her team is. She replied, "I don't know exactly how many people are on my team. I'm going to say it's around 1,200 to 1,500, something like that." I was stunned.

Teresa left a full-time job as an administrative assistant at a school for children with learning disabilities and behavioral disorders. She says, "I loved that job, thought I'd never leave that job. It was great. I said I'd try this for three months, but it just really took off. I was enrolled in college, but never finished. I kick around going back to school every once in awhile. I might do that, but I know I couldn't get a job, even with a college degree, that pays me what I make now."

Teresa's first recruit was her sister-in-law, who was a stay-at-home mom with 15-month-old twins. Teresa felt it would be a perfect fit for her, but her sister-in-law was hesitant. Then, three months later, she asked Teresa to tell her more about the business. "Okay," said Teresa, "but why now?" Her sister-in-law replied, "I just found myself watching *Barney* and the kids aren't in the room."

The number of shows a consultant schedules varies widely. About 40 percent of Teresa's team work another job as well as their Pampered Chef endeavors. Typically, when you're at the leader level, you're doing 6 to 10 shows a month. "We have a lot of people that do, maybe, one show a month. And they're happy with that," says Teresa. "I'm trying to pare down to six a month. I want to invest more in my team, so I'm now down to five or six a month. Ideally, the magic number for people who are growing is two a week. That's the magic number for super success with the business. So, when you think about it, that's less than a part-time job. That's really a good number to shoot for. It keeps you in front of enough people to sell product and recruit other people to sell product."

Teresa adds, "Most other direct selling companies are *so* about recruitment. And we need to be more about recruitment, in my opinion, but we really do sell product that people love. That's our number-one thing."

Pink-Collar Jobs

Today, about 80 percent of the 15 million U.S. direct sellers are women. In 2010, the industry generated a total of $29.6 billion in annual sales.[20] The reasons women, or anyone for that matter, are attracted to direct selling careers are well recognized. It's a good fit for someone who wants to earn on their own terms. It's a solution for the difficult game of balancing work and personal lives.

New companies in the direct selling industry keep popping up. Perfectly Posh was founded in 2011. Alex+Von, AnyArt, and K&K

Designs were all started in 2010. "There are constantly new entrants in this industry, which proves that direct selling is still on the rise. This industry is going to continue to grow," says Elizabeth Thibaudeau, vice president of Opportunity and Brand Marketing at Nu Skin Enterprises. "People are looking for creative solutions to be in control of their financial and time freedom, and direct selling offers that. I truly believe it's going to be one of the biggest industries for the future."[21]

Cooking Up the Future

Few companies that have been in business for more than 30 years conduct their business as they did when the company was founded. The Pampered Chef headquarters has fully furnished test kitchens for research and development of new tools, tips, and recipes. A staff of home economists, food scientists, chefs, dieticians, and product developers edit, test, and develop more than 400 recipes per year. Not all kitchen conveniences have the lasting popularity of the Pizza Stone, a round, stoneware baking slab, one of the first items selected by Doris Christopher to include in her inventory. The Pampered Chef later added handles to it for convenience. The company is continually expanding its recipe and product collection to align with top flavor, ingredient, and lifestyle trends.

The Pampered Chef is also concerned about the environment. They now have a line of bamboo kitchen products. Bamboo is a grass that's naturally beautiful, extremely durable, and a renewable resource. As the fastest-growing plant on the planet, bamboo can be harvested every three to five years and naturally replenishes itself. And, because bamboo doesn't absorb moisture or conduct heat, it's perfect for kitchenware and serving pieces.

When The Pampered Chef was started in 1980, there was no computer system. The company's growth coincided with the growth in availability and improvement of information technology. "Technological change is occurring at an exponential rate that dwarfs all change in the past," said Doris Christopher. "With this in mind, no viable company can remain at a standstill. Great companies withstand the test of time by adapting to change. While the cooking show is the foundation on which The Pampered Chef does business, the Internet is a very important vehicle. It is another avenue through which The Pampered Chef and our consultants can communicate with customers. And it's an opportunity for new customers to discover Pampered Chef products, connect with a consultant, or learn about the business opportunity. But the same values must be as evident on the web as they are in the personal aspects of The Pampered Chef's business model."[22]

The company maintains a website for each consultant, but you must have achieved $1,250 in sales to qualify for a website. A consultant can't be solely an online seller. They also can't sell in a storefront or retail store, but can participate in one-time occasion events, such as craft fairs and farmer's markets.

"The Outlet website feature is an awesome tool," says Teresa Brown. "For discontinued products that we don't sell any more, they're really discounted. But they might only be there a couple of days. That drives some additional sales for our business."

Facebook and Twitter have given Pampered Chef a new way for consultants to communicate and also provide a method for the company to connect with their fans and customers. The Pampered Chef Facebook page has over 325,000 "likes" and the company's Twitter feed has nearly 1,000 followers.

Having a global presence is beneficial to direct selling companies. While cultures differ, many are even more receptive to direct selling than we are in the United States. Back in 1992, Rich DeVos, cofounder of Amway, optimistically envisioned his company as a $10 billion business, operating in 75 countries by the year 2000. At the time, it was a $3.9 billion company in 62 countries.[23] His prophecy was not far off. Amway's revenues for 2010 were $9.2 billion and it is present in over 80 countries.

The Pampered Chef expanded to Canada in 1996, the United Kingdom and much of Europe in 1999, Germany in 2000, and Mexico in 2009. Avon has representatives in 113 countries. Mary Kay Cosmetics now has more than 350,000 Chinese women who are selling American-style beauty products. They translated their sales books into Chinese, and the company song "That Mary Kay Enthusiasm" into Mandarin.[24]

Mentoring

The foundation of The Pampered Chef is its team structure. From the initial recruitment of individuals, mentoring and peer encouragement is a constant activity. Top performers meet with company executives, including Gottschalk, in the Chairman's Circle. Occasional incentive trips to headquarters are offered to participate in roundtable discussions. Over the summer of 2011, Pampered Chef flew in 100 of their consultants, 25 at a time. They paid for their travel and hotel and then picked their brains about what works, what doesn't, and asked for their ideas.

The 25 National Executive Directors get together once or twice each year with Marla and Jean Jonas, senior vice president of Sales. Says Teresa, "They ask us our opinion. They're thinking about rolling this out, what do we think? That's kind of cool. We love being heard by the company."

Chefsuccess.com is an online community for Pampered Chef consultants to ask and answer questions with each other. Over 25 discussion threads assist consultants with topics such as Increasing Sales, Recipe Tips, Fundraisers, and Business Tips.

The company holds an annual conference for its consultants at Chicago's McCormick Place each July. Any consultant can go, however, there is a fee to attend. Past attendees say that the fee is well worth it. Free admittance can be won by hitting certain goals as part of a conference promotion. Consultants can also sign up for the "conference club" to have the home office deduct a percent from their commission earnings to pay for the conference. Early-bird registration was $200 in 2010. The company provides breakfasts and lunches.

Teresa Brown has attended the annual meeting every single year since she joined the company. She teaches workshops there on a variety of topics. Workshops include live kitchen shows and lectures. Attendance is about 5,000. To increase their educational reach, the company plans to roll out local one-day programs in the spring and fall of 2012. Occurring at sites around the country, they hope to reach 10,000 to 20,000 consultants.

Earning Power

Direct selling is about having control of your lifestyle. Working when and where you want. Sacrificing a regular predictable paycheck is the tradeoff. The amount of effort expended is reflected in the financial

Table 5.2   Starter Kit Fees for Direct Selling
Companies

Company	Minimum Cost for Starter Kit
Scentsy	$99
Tupperware	$80
Mary Kay	$75
Creative Memories	$50
Avon	$10

gains. Many who participate in direct selling do it as a hobby on the side in addition to another job. The average income for a hobbyist is not impressive. But some simply derive enjoyment in the activity, getting a "rush" from doing demonstrations and socializing.

The initial buy-in for an independent consultant is relatively low at Pampered Chef. During special campaigns, the normal fee of $80 for the starter mini-kit is reduced to $40. An optional larger new consultant kit costs $159. A comparison of starter kit fees for various direct selling companies is shown in Table 5.2.

In 2010, Pampered Chef shows generated an average of $450 in sales per show. Commission rates for sales range from a minimum of 20 percent up to 31 percent after building a team.[25]

Linda Fears, editor-in-chief of *Family Circle* magazine, studied the direct sales industry as a potential career for women. Says Fears, "Median annual sales revenues in 2003 were $2,400 per person, but women who are serious about the venture can earn more. A few women we spoke with said they earn about $7,500 per year and one said she frequently made $1,800 a month. They need to be self-starters. Women need to take initiative to host parties at home, plan the parties, and recruit new consultants. Finally, they need to be persuasive. They need to show that they believe in the products they're selling, and know how to communicate the benefits of the products to their captive audience."[26]

Support and Giving

Pampered Chef supports charitable campaigns that are related to women's health, hunger, and family issues. The company also encourages wellness among its employees and consultants.

"At our corporate offices, we recently launched a Healthy Rewards Program that gives employees cash back for preventive cancer screenings, such as Pap smears, colonoscopies, and mammograms," says Gottschalk. "Additionally, we have provided free onsite mammograms. By taking care of our health, we are setting a positive example for the next generation and taking an active role in reducing the costs of health care. We consider it a victory when our consultants embrace the message behind our Help Whip Cancer campaign and participate in preventative screenings."[27]

Since 2000, The Pampered Chef has participated in the Help Whip Cancer campaign to fight breast cancer. Every May and October, the company offers limited-edition pink products, including pink paring knives, pink polka-dot kitchen towels, and pink latex dishwashing gloves. Every time a pink product is sold, $1 is donated to the American Cancer Society, with the proceeds supporting breast cancer education and early detection. So far, the company has donated $6.5 million to the cause. Grab these limited edition items while you can! The Pink Zebra High Heel Cake Server that I bought was available during the May 2011 promotion, but was not offered during the October campaign.

Also in October each year, The Pampered Chef participates in the American Cancer Society Making Strides Against Breast Cancer walks (Figure 5.4). The company offers team T-shirts for the walk to promote team spirit.

"This is something near to the hearts of so many people," Gottschalk says. "They really get behind the fundraising efforts. We provide the tools for consultants to use, but these programs are truly driven by them. Our consultants really get behind our charitable initiatives, making them bigger than you could in a corporate environment."[28]

Independent National Executive Director Dotti Shepherd, says, "My breast cancer experience has made me acutely aware of how important it is to make the most of every day and every moment. It gave me an even deeper appreciation for everything, including my Pampered Chef business, which allowed me to put my health first and schedule work around my treatments."[29]

The Pampered Chef is a Mission Partner with Feeding America. The hunger relief charity collects surplus food from growers, distributors, manufacturers, and retailers, and supports a network of over 200 food banks, food pantries, soup kitchens, women's shelters, Kid's Cafes,

Figure 5.4   Marla Gottschalk, CEO, and Jean Jonas, senior vice president of sales, at a Making Strides Against Breast Cancer Walk, 2011
SOURCE: The Pampered Chef.

and Community Kitchens. Founded in 1979, as America's Second Harvest, it is headquartered in Chicago, Illinois. Doris Christopher is a former member of Feeding America's board of directors. The Pampered Chef has collaborated with Feeding America for the past 20 years.

Round-Up from the Heart is another Pampered Chef campaign. This one fights hunger together with Feeding America. Customers round up their purchase totals. A collectible product to benefit Round-Up from the Heart is also introduced every year.

"Although each donation is rather small, all of those amounts add up to quite a bit of money," says Marla.[30] Round-Up from the Heart has raised more than $13 million.

Since 2000, The Pampered Chef has supported the University of Illinois College of Agricultural, Consumer, and Environmental Sciences in Urbana-Champaign. The department of Human and Community Development offers education in a Family Resiliency Program. "Our Family Resiliency Program really relates to The Pampered Chef mission of enhancing the quality of family life and bringing families together around the table," Gottschalk says.[31] Educational topics include parenting, managing stress, and balancing work and family commitments.

Marla joined CEOs Against Cancer in 2010, a program sponsored by the American Cancer Society. The group is an elite partnership among chief executives of leading businesses, representing millions of workers worldwide to enhance intellectual exchange, to develop future diverse cancer fighting solutions and to support the American Cancer Society mission nationally and globally. The group asks CEOs to ensure that their corporate culture includes four components: stay well, get well, find cures, and fight back. It assists human resources departments to enhance their employee benefits programs to include wellness incentives.

Rochelle Mangold, Direct of Corporate Communications for The Pampered Chef, says, "We want our consultants to know that we support them in their career, families and health, and that what is important to them is important to us."[32]

"The giving and support we get from our consultants is incredible—they are making it all happen, and they are amazing," Gottschalk says. "We're honored to support these programs."[33]

Outside Interests

Gottschalk serves on the Kelley School of Business Dean's Advisory Council. This 93-member council has extensive business knowledge and many years of service in their respective professions. They assist the University in the formulation and development of long-range plans, proposed new programs, fresh curriculum thrusts, research directions, and private sector funding.

Marla served on a number of boards in the past. Presently, her time is focused on running The Pampered Chef, but these board memberships gave her added insight in industries quite different from kitchen supplies and cooking.

She was a board member of Visteon Corporation, a Michigan supplier of automotive products, from March 2003 to December 14, 2006. She served as board member of GATX Corporation from July 21, 2006, to January 31, 2008. GATX, located in Chicago leases rail, marine, and industrial equipment. In the past, Marla also served on the boards of directors for Underwriter Laboratories and Potbelly Sandwich Works (founded in Chicago in 1977).

Marla married Andy Gottschalk in 1989. He is a partner at KPMG, LLP in Chicago. They have two daughters, Amanda and Laura. "My husband, Andy, is incredibly supportive. After we had children, we jointly decided we'd continue our careers. Both of us share household and family responsibilities. That means we both work smarter. Being a mom has had a positive impact on my career. You learn to do what's really important, what drives the business, and delegate more to the people who work for you to get the job done."[34]

She adds, "In life, I have two main focuses: my family and my work. I am not that complicated and I solely focus on those two aspects in life. After work, I go support my daughters at their swimming practice. During vacations, we love to go skiing."[35]

For others who struggle to balance work and life, Marla has advice. "My advice is work hard, play hard, and never give up on finding your passion. Your job is not jour life, but your life consists of your job. It is important to find a job that you enjoy doing."[36]

Although she was never a direct sales consultant, Marla's strengths in marketing, finance, and management are important skills in leading a company like The Pampered Chef. She has the great fortune of running a business that was built on strong values, enjoys continued popularity, and is equally beloved by its sales force and its customers.

Chapter 6

Beryl Raff—
Precious Mettle

Beryl Beth Raff, Chairman of the Board and Chief Executive Officer of Helzberg Diamond Shops, a wholly owned subsidiary of Berkshire Hathaway, is widely recognized within the retail industry as a strong multistore executive. Raff, 61 years old, is the most recent female addition to the Berkshire Hathaway "All-Star" manager roster, having joined Helzberg in 2009 (see Figure 6.1).

Helzberg Diamonds was founded in 1915 in Kansas City, and now has nearly 230 retail jewelry stores nationwide. Helzberg's headquarters are in North Kansas City, Missouri. While *diamonds* feature prominently in the store's name, it sells the same range of merchandise typically seen in jewelry chain stores, from engagement rings to watches.

The number of mall jewelry stores is staggering. Go to any mall, find the intersection of two hallways, and located at the four corners, are usually four jewelry stores. The brands vary a bit by geography, but the stores commonly seen throughout the country are Helzberg, Zales, Kay, and Jared.

Figure 6.1 Beryl Raff (left) with Barnett and Shirley Helzberg, 2010
Source: Cathryn Farley Photography.

Signet Jewelers is the parent company of both Kay Jewelers and Jared. In any mall, Claire's stores are ubiquitous. However, Claire's market and inventory do not overlap significantly with the others. It sells low-priced jewelry and accessories to the teenage set and younger. Its subsidiary, ICING, targets young women in their twenties. While Claire's Stores is an apple to these other oranges, it is worthwhile to include Claire's impact on the consumer in a comparison of the jewelry retail industry. Table 6.1 compares attributes of these stores.

The amount of sales per store illustrates several things. Performing well at each single location makes better use of fixed resources and overhead expense. Claire's low revenue per store is a reflection of its lower priced inventory. Though volume at Claire's may be comparable, it takes a far greater quantity of sales to equal the revenue levels of the other stores.

Utilizing fewer employees to achieve revenue targets cuts employee benefit expense for the company and increases sales commissions and bonuses for existing employees. The number of employees reported by

Table 6.1   Mall Jewelry Store Chains

	Helzberg	Zales	Signet Jewelers (Kay/Jared)	Claire's ICING
Number of Stores	230	1,800	1,852	3,400
Number of Brands	1	6	4	2
Annual Sales	$380 million	$1.74 billion	$3.27 billion	$1.43 billion
Sales per Store	$1.65 million	$966,666	$1.76 million	$420,588
Number of Employees	2,200	12,600	16,200	18,400

each company is subject to some inaccuracy, as companies report total number of employees, not total number of full-time equivalents. Many retail jewelry sales staff are part-time employees and most stores hire additional seasonal help during the holidays.

Interestingly, Raff's first name is the name of a gem available at her store. Beryl is a natural mineral, chemically composed of beryllium aluminum cyclosilicate. In its crystalline state, beryl is transparent, but may be colored green, blue, yellow, red, or white by impurities. In its green form, colored by chromium or vanadium, the beryl crystal is known as an *emerald*. How fitting it is that Beryl Raff would spend much of her career amidst gemstones and jewelry.

She graduated from Harriton High School in Rosemont, Pennsylvania, in 1968. Beryl received a Bachelor of Business Administration degree (magna cum laude) from Boston University School of Management in 1972. She earned her MBA from Drexel University in Philadelphia in 1976. The university inducted her into its honorary alumni society, The Drexel 100, in 2000. Established with just 100 individuals in 1992, the group has added new members every two years, and now has approximately 164 members. These alums have shown particular achievement by their professional accomplishment, public service, and philanthropic activities.

The Magic of Macy's

Beryl began her career with R. H. Macy & Company in 1975 as an executive trainee, starting in the housewares department in Deptford, New Jersey. During her 19 years with the Macy organization, Beryl moved steadily upward, holding positions as buyer, merchandise manager, and store manager.

She first started working amidst jewelry in 1983 when she became divisional merchandise manager for costume and bridge jewelry. After that, she held positions as vice president and divisional merchandise manager for fine jewelry; group vice president for costume, bridge, and fine jewelry; and finally, senior vice president and general merchandise manager for Macy's East (a 12-state division of R. H. Macy & Co.), bridge and fine jewelry, and lingerie.

I was stumped as to the meaning of "bridge" jewelry. It must be what one wears to plays cards, I decided. No, in fact, it is a term that fits into a classification scheme for jewelry, for example, "fine, bridge, and costume" in descending order of cost and value of precious metals and stones. Bridge *bridges* the gap between fine and costume. And "fashion" is a new alternative term for jewelry sometimes referred to as costume.

Raff gained skills in managing people, as well as numbers, in her time at Macy's. The general merchandise manager (GMM) leads the divisional merchandise managers to select inventory suited to customers of different store locations. The GMM plans promotional and sales strategies and manages the buying staff to respond to style trends and planned events. Responsibilities of the GMM include pricing the jewelry appropriately to achieve the financial goals for the organization.

Nineteen years at Macy's could reasonably be considered a full, complete career. Macy's was a relatively stable, conflict-free organization that supported Beryl's rise in management. But she would have many more years of interesting employment ahead when she decided to leave Macy's in 1994.

Platinum Setting

Former Macy's executive Robert DiNicola was a mentor and friend to Beryl Raff. DiNicola became CEO of Zale Corporation in April 1994 and he recruited Raff to join the company as president of the Zales Jewelry division in November of that year.

The first Zales Jewelers store was opened in 1924 in Wichita Falls, Texas. In addition to jewelry, the two Zale brothers, Morris B. and William, sold small appliances, cameras, and cookware. "M.B. really did a lot of wonderful things for retail and for the jewelry industry," says Beryl. "He was the originator of offering credit for jewelry, selling engagement rings to young couples and providing credit to help them get started."[1]

DiNicola left the CEO position of Bon Marché department store that he had held for two years and took over the Zale CEO position at a rough time in the company's history. Zale had just emerged from Chapter 11 bankruptcy in August 1993 as a newly restructured, independent, publicly traded company. Its $850 million in debt was settled.[2] Within one week of being released from bankruptcy, the company's CEO quit and a board member died. Zale Corporation was ready for a fresh start.

"I'm just happy that they have somebody up there," said Harold Glatstein, chief executive of Barre & Company, a Dallas investment firm, following DiNicola's acceptance. "It's certainly been a rickety, rockety type of board."[3]

The parent corporation, Zale, includes six retail brands: Zales Jewelers, Zales Outlet, Gordon's Jewelers, Peoples Jewellers (Canada), Mappins (Canada), and Piercing Pagoda. Zales Jewelers currently operates 650 stores. The other Zale Corporation jewelry brands are in an additional 500 stores, and there are over 670 kiosks from which Piercing Pagoda sells. Combined annual revenues are $1.7 billion.

Given her experience with Macy's jewelry enterprise, Beryl slid easily into the position of President of Zales Jewelers. During the backside of the 1990s, while the U.S. economy improved, Zales upgraded its stores and improved its purchasing, introducing a broader range of items.

In 1995, the company was on its way to recovery. With a "back-to-basics" approach, its revenues of that year, $1.04 billion, represented a 12.6 percent increase over the previous year. Net income grew by 36 percent, to $31.5 million. In 1996, Zales launched its eCommerce website.

Raff advanced to executive vice president and chief operating officer of the parent Zale Corporation in 1997, and then onward to president and COO in July 1998.

In 1998, a new division called Zales Outlet was formed, starting with 10 Zales Outlet stores. While not an early adopter of this new sales channel (the first multistore outlet mall opened in 1974) the division expanded in the outlet mall environment to 135 stores nationwide. In recent years, during a time of dismal retail sales, outlet malls are increasing in popularity.

In 1998, revenues hit $1.43 billion, a 43 percent increase in four years. Net income during the same period nearly tripled, from $23 million to $63 million. And, for the first time in the company's history Zale posted profits in all four quarters of the 1998 fiscal year.

Raff was promoted to CEO of Zale Corporation in 1999, the first woman to lead the company. Robert DiNicola stepped down as CEO at that time, but remained as Chairman of the Board. While Raff led Zales, the company acquired Peoples Jewellers of Canada. "Our strategy was very exportable to Canada," she said.[4]

Zale spent about $75.3 million to acquire Peoples Jewellers, with 176 Canadian stores. Together with Swarovski International, Peoples had earlier made a leveraged buyout of Zale for $650 million in 1988, then subsequently lost it when Zale was forced into involuntary bankruptcy in January 1992. By moving some of Peoples operations from Toronto to Dallas, the company gained efficiencies.

Raff directed increased resources into improved website development in 2000, but for that year, Internet sales were still only $6 million. The low Internet sales volume did not concern Raff. She said, "The objective is to position ourselves for the future. We want to understand the online environment, extend the brands appropriately on it, and make sure we can execute that well. Then when that foundation is well-placed, we can start to put on volume as the industry matures."[5]

A promotional strategy that Zale's attempted was offering a unique 0.5 carat diamond "Millennium" band that had the year "2000" set in diamonds in the shank. The next year, the owner could have the third diamond "0" replaced with a baguette to create "2001." That gave the concept "legs to continue into the future," said Raff.[6]

Hard Rocks

Sales in 2000 were strong, and Raff's appointment as Chairman of the Board was announced on August 31, 2000. She replaced Robert DiNicola upon his retirement. At this time, Zale operated about 1,400 stores and reported total sales of $1.79 billion in its fiscal year ending July 31, 2000.

"Bob DiNicola was really the person responsible for truly resurrecting the corporation and giving it definition and structure and a platform from which to move forward. Bob DiNicola is to be credited for saving the Zale Corporation and returning it to dominance," says Beryl.[7]

Though the deal was announced in August 2000 prior to Beryl's appointment as chairman, Zale acquired Piercing Pagoda for something over $200 million. The Piercing Pagoda's core business is ear piercing operated out of mall kiosks. The company markets itself primarily to teenage girls, offering free ear piercing with the purchase of earrings. (I remember begging my mother to let me get pierced ears at age 14. Had one of these kiosks been nearby, we could have avoided the visit to the doctor's office for the procedure.) As a Zale brand, Piercing Pagoda expanded the selection of items it sold and improved its physical appearance and now operates in more than 670 kiosks, down from 940 in 2000.

Acquisition of Piercing Pagoda "was on our radar screen for a long time," notes Raff. She cited a couple of reasons. "First, it operates within our core competency, the mall, in real estate, and an environment we understand. They complement our brands very well without any cannibalization or overlap. Second, the purchase extends Zale's reach in a dominant way into a consumer segment we didn't have: teens and young adults. It would've taken us a long time to build a presence in this market on our own; now, in one fell swoop, we're the major player. The real benefit is to capture jewelry consumers at the very beginning of their jewelry-buying life cycle and retain them through every important stage and jewelry buying event in their lives, from adolescent to adult."[8]

Holiday sales in 2000 went down 3.1 percent, considered a large blow to this company in an industry nearly completely dependent upon holiday sales for its livelihood. The second fiscal quarter, ending on January 31, 2001, showed a profit loss of 15 percent, though sales rose to $855 million for the quarter from $736 million the previous year. The company's results included a one-time charge of $25 million to reduce the value of the $150 million in overstock inventory that the company said failed to meet its standards.

In January 2001, Beryl said, "The last six years have been phenomenal and we want to continue that by focusing on our core brands, which are our more mature brands, and by growing our newer brands. Bob (DiNicola) and I are really of one mind when it comes to running the business. The flexibility to shift gears quickly to alternative strategies as business dictates, and our hands firmly on our expense structure, we feel well-prepared for fiscal 2001."[9]

In February 2001, after 18 months as CEO and six months as Chairman of the Board, the board forced Beryl out. "It's a long story," she says, "but six months later, in a political upheaval in the board room, I was ousted. And that was very, very difficult. But I'm not somebody who sits and says, 'Woe is me,' so I picked myself up, reflected on the situation, and tried to look at it as a learning experience. Then I started to figure out how to move forward."[10]

The company line was that Raff left to spend more time with her family. Phrases such as this, and "to pursue other interests" are rampant when executives depart. Wise women refuse to play that word game when their careers are on the line.

When Carleton S. Fiorina was fired as chief executive of Hewlett-Packard in 2005, board members asked her how she would like to position the news. The board suggested she say it was time for her to move on, or that she wanted to spend more time with her family. She refused. "I said, 'No, that's not the truth,' " Ms. Fiorina recalled. She had been fired and she wanted to make that clear to the public. "Telling the truth is about what's right and wrong," said Ms. Fiorina, who still walked away with a $21 million severance package. "It's pretty basic."

Scott Moss, a law professor at Marquette University who specializes in employment law, pointed out that as a woman, Ms. Fiorina might also have felt that giving such a reason could backfire. "It's a more dangerous reason for a woman to give than a man," he said. "It could be understood as, 'this is a woman not committed to the work force.' It's a double standard where working men spending time with their families is admirable, but when working women do it they're neglecting their jobs."[11]

During a conference call in March 2001, the Zale Corporations told Wall Street analysts that a strategy of sacrificing quality on lower-priced merchandise to lure shoppers who were spending less on luxury items had failed.[12] "Zale learned it wasn't a net gain in cheapening your product," said Lynn Detrick, a retail analyst at Sanders Morris Harris.[13]

When Raff left Zale Corporation, she was replaced as chairman and CEO by the returning DiNicola. Zales stock shares fell 14 percent on the news, but later rebounded. DiNicola retired, again, in the summer of 2002. Now age 62, he serves as senior retail advisor for Apollo Management, L.P., a private equity firm.

Raff spent six years working for the Zale Corporation. Her severance package was worth $2.5 million.[14] The six-year recovery that peaked in 2000 has not been seen again at Zale. The corporation continues to have unusually high executive turnover, particularly in the positions of CFO and CEO. There have been nine CEOs in the past 20 years (counting DiNicola only once, though he served on two separate occasions) and the company's stock share price is running at about $3 per share.

Raff has no hard feelings and doesn't gloat over the current sad state of Zale Corporation "The jewelry industry needs Zale," says Beryl, "It's not exactly a robust industry. When an important player struggles, it impacts everyone. It's bigger than Zale Corporation."[15]

A Penney Saves

Beryl went back into the department store environment in May 2001 when she took the position of senior vice president and merchandising manager for the fine jewelry division of J. C. Penney Company. The company is based in Plano, Texas, about 30 miles from the headquarters of Zale Corporation in Irving, Texas. Penney's COO, Vanessa Castagna, described Raff as "a retail industry leader who brings to J. C. Penney a blend of merchandising instinct and analytical sharpness."[16]

James Cash Penney founded J. C. Penney in Wyoming in 1902 as Golden Rule Store, a dry goods store, and the store celebrated its 100th anniversary in 2002, shortly after Beryl began working there.

Managing the jewelry division for Penney's meant managing jewelry counters in over 1,000 store locations nationwide. The jewelry division's annual sales were just under $1 billion. A significant portion of sales came from catalog, and later, the Internet.

After Sears discontinued its catalog sales in 1993, Penney's became the largest catalog retailer in the country. From this foundation, the company transitioned easily into eCommerce, launching its website in 1998. In 2005, the Penney's website surpassed $1 billion in sales.

In August 2005, Whitehall Jewellers announced that Beryl Raff was named chief executive officer (CEO) and would also join the company's board of directors. She was to replace Hugh Patinkin, the previous CEO, who had died of a heart attack at age 54 five months earlier.

Whitehall Jewelers, a shopping mall jewelry chain store, was founded in 1895 and headquartered in Chicago. It struggled in the mid-2000s. In 2005, Whitehall operated 388 stores in 38 states under the names Whitehall Co. Jewellers, Lundstrom Jewelers, and Marks Brothers Jewelers. Hoping to infuse some strong leadership, Whitehall recruited Beryl Raff as CEO.

Steven Pully, Chairman of the Board of Directors, commented, "Beryl Raff is one of the most accomplished merchants and senior executives in the jewelry industry. She has a long track record of demonstrated success and we are delighted that she is joining Whitehall Jewelers. The Board of Directors and the entire Whitehall family of employees welcomes her to our Company."[17]

Ms. Raff commented, "Joining Whitehall is an opportunity which I embrace with great energy and enthusiasm. Whitehall is a wonderful company with a great heritage and a very promising future. I am looking forward to working with Whitehall's management, employees, and vendors to drive Whitehall's business forward to greater successes in the future."[18]

"Beryl Raff gives Whitehall a fighting chance because she really knows jewelry," said jewelry industry analyst Kenneth Gassman. "This is what Whitehall needed two years ago."[19]

On September 7, a week before beginning her new job, Whitehall received a resignation letter from Raff. Neither Whitehall nor Raff provided an explanation. Leading Whitehall certainly would have been a challenging job. Whitehall's stock fell 69 percent after it announced that Beryl had resigned and that it was running short of cash.[20] In 2006, Whitehall became a subsidiary of WJ Holding Corporation.

While Beryl never really left Penney's, upon her official return in September 2005, she gained a newly elevated title of Executive Vice President and General Merchandise Manager of Fine Jewelry.

"She has done an outstanding job in growing our fine jewelry business," said J. C. Penney spokesman Tim Lyons. "From our viewpoint, we are pleased she is staying."[21] Beryl was Executive V.P. and general merchandise manager for three and a half years, during which time she became the first general merchandise manager to receive the J. C. Penney Chairman's Award, the highest tribute to managerial excellence—an honor she received three times.

Beryl's career path could not have been evident when she started selling housewares at Macy's. But she was able to adapt to her jobs and to her employers, learning important skills and lessons along the way. In exploring diverse employers within the jewelry retail industry, she was able to become an expert in multistore management.

"Wherever you start, get a solid foundation and experience," she says. "Being a 'job hopper' is not a good thing, but reasonable multiple experiences broaden your background and can often be beneficial to a career. I really believe that hard, smart work is recognized. Be patient. Take the extra steps. Learn it, study it, be curious. Pick yourself a mentor. It's really, really important. Create a network as you're going along. Understand how important your network is to you."[22]

Cut and Polish

In April 2009, Raff left Penney's to become chairman and chief executive officer of Helzberg Diamond Shops, a subsidiary of Berkshire Hathaway. At that time, Helzberg was a 270-store chain. There are now about 230 stores, and sales in 2010 totaled $380 million.

The founder of the store was a Russian immigrant, Morris Helzberg. He arrived in the United States in 1885 and married Miss Lena Cohen, the daughter of a tailor, in Kansas City in 1891. By 1900, he was a saloonkeeper in the bustling cow town. The Helzbergs had five children, two girls and three boys. The family of seven rented several homes in the center of town, including one at 2809 Olive Street.

Morris Helzberg opened a small jewelry and housewares shop in 1915 in a 12-foot-wide building at 529 Minnesota Avenue. But within a couple of years he suffered a disabling stroke and his son Barnett, the youngest child at age 14, had to take over running the business. Barnett attended school with Walt Disney in Kansas City, where Disney lived from age 10 to 16.

The two older Helzberg brothers were unable to help out with the store because Morton was attending dental school and Gilbert was shipping out to serve in World War I. His sisters, Elsa and Bernice had been recently married in 1916 and 1917, respectively. The family asked an uncle to watch the store while Barnett went to school during the day. The young Barnett would then return to work at the store each day after school at 3:00.

Morris died in 1922 and when Gilbert returned from the war, he became partners with Barnett. Barnett was ambitious, and a big fan of advertising. He spent thousands of dollars on newspaper ads, some of which featured the two brothers' portraits, with the slogan "Meet the Helzberg Boys, Wear Diamonds." The phrase was later copied and used in the 1930s and 1940s as "Meet the Brodkey Boys, Wear Diamonds" by a Nebraska jewelry store, and there may well have been other stores dotting the Midwest landscape that used it during that era.

Barnett was ambitious and opened new store locations in other towns. He lived at home alone with his mother until age 27, when he married the daughter of another prominent Kansas City jeweler in 1930. He even doubled the size of the downtown Kansas City store during the Great Depression in 1932, the only major business expansion in Kansas City that year. Gilbert Helzberg died in 1934, in an automobile accident, and Barnett took over Gilbert's share of the company.

Throughout the 1940s, the business expanded its chain of five stores to 11 in the Midwest. Barnett founded the Diamond Council of America in 1944. The organization is still thriving as a nonprofit association providing training and education to jewelry sales professionals.

Barnett's son, Barnett Jr., started working at the store when he was 15. He formally joined the family company in 1956, after getting a degree in business from the University of Michigan.

"The feeling that you are our own boss, that your future is in your hands, is a frightening and thrilling prospect," says Barnett Jr. "I became president of Helzberg Diamonds in 1962 at age 29, when my father became ill and asked me to take over. I was nervous and definitely not ready, but I did so with absolute backing from Dad and the entire family. It wasn't always smooth, but it was always interesting. I made mistakes and had my share of failures, but my enthusiasm and the backing of my family never wavered."[23] Barnett Sr. committed suicide in 1973 by jumping from his apartment.[24]

When Barnett, Jr. became president of the company, Helzberg Diamonds had 39 stores, mostly in downtown locations. But the growth of suburban shopping malls in the 1960s hurt revenue in downtown business districts. Helzberg chose to lease space within other existing stores, such as Kmart, rather than go with the flow to the malls. Kmart was first opened in 1962 by the S. S. Kresge Corporation (founder of five-and-dime store fame).

In 1965, Kmart discontinued leasing space to Helzberg's, who had set up jewelry counters within 24 (out of 150) Kmart stores. With the dwindling downtown business and Kmart's abandonment, Helzberg had to close 38 of the store's 39 locations. These happened to be fortuitous events, or as Barnett Jr. comments, it was a case of *when bad news is good news*. It forced Barnett Jr. to finally consider shopping mall locations, which would be the company's most successful business decision.

Says Barnett Jr., "Oddly, with the advent of the covered malls we went to sleep and were very late into the game. We nearly destroyed the company by our tardiness but were lucky enough, with tremendous effort, to recover the fumble and run it to the end zone. We had one mall-based jewelry store in Overland park, and sales at that store were growing stronger all the time. So we forged ahead with multiple mall locations in our markets."[25]

I Am Loved

Helzberg's *I Am Loved* campaign began with a newspaper ad in the *Kansas City Star* in November 1967. The slogan was the inspiration of Barnett Helzberg, Jr., who thought of it after his girlfriend, Shirley Bush, accepted his marriage proposal. He drew the words on a piece of paper and attempted to develop an advertising concept around his idea. He looked at it, embarrassed, and threw it away.

The next morning, he retrieved his doodling from the wastebasket and showed it to the store's advertising artist. The artist liked the concept and came up with a lapel button design. Buttons were printed with the *I Am Loved* slogan and given away for free. The newspaper ad resulted in an overwhelming response. The buttons became a pop culture hit. They were sent to hospitals, to servicemen in Vietnam and celebrities of the time, including Frank Sinatra, Joe Namath, and President Lyndon Johnson. More than 18 million buttons have been distributed, and they are still offered free at any Helzberg store.

In the 1970s, Helzberg opened more stores and redesigned their appearance. The outside walls with display windows were removed. They often positioned themselves on a corner and designed an open floor plan, making it easy for customers to walk right into the store, or pass through without entering a doorway. At Helzberg's, gone were the days of "window" shopping.

The chain increased its pace in the 1980s, opening many more stores. By the end of the decade, Helzberg Diamonds had 81 stores in 19 states. Annual sales for the company were estimated at around $70 million for 1986, and some Helzberg stores were bringing in $2 million each.

In 1988, Helzberg's hired a new president, Jeffrey Comment. Formerly an executive with Wanamaker's department store in Philadelphia, Comment was the first to hold that top managerial spot outside the Helzberg family.

Comment successfully led Helzberg's in continued growth and again redesigned the stores' physical layout. Stores opened after 1988 were larger than their predecessors, averaging 1,500 to 1,600 square feet. Comment also introduced a new, larger store called Jewelry3, so named because it offered three times the selection of most jewelry stores. Jewelry3 stores opened in strip malls, with a 4,000-square-foot floor plan.

Diamond Studs

In 1994, Helzberg Diamond stores averaged sales of more than $1.7 million per store, nearly double the average for jewelry chain stores. Total sales were $282 million. Barnett Jr. was in New York City in May of that year to visit with his financial advisors at Morgan Stanley about possibly taking the family business public. By chance, as he walked past the Plaza Hotel, he saw Warren Buffett on the sidewalk. He stepped forward, held out his hand in greeting, and introduced himself.

Barnett remembers, "Then, right there on the sidewalk, as busy New Yorkers rushed past us and street traffic buzzed around us, I told one of the most astute businessmen in America why he ought to consider buying our family's 79-year-old jewelry business. 'I believe that our company matches your criteria for investment,' I said. To which he replied, simply, 'Send me the information. It will be confidential.' My conversation with Buffett lasted no more than half a minute."[26]

Barnett owned four shares of Berkshire Hathaway, the first purchased in 1985, and had just attended the company's annual meeting in Omaha days before. His dream buyer for the family business was Warren Buffett because he would keep the headquarters in Kansas City, wouldn't change the company's character, and would keep all of the employees. He was thrilled to think Buffett might actually be interested in buying Helzberg's, but he put off sending out the requested financial information for several months, worrying over confidentiality issues. Finally, he scolded himself for procrastinating and sent the information and was invited to visit with Buffett in Omaha.

In his annual letter to shareholders, Buffett said,

Barnett, then 60, loved the business but also wanted to feel free of it. In 1988, as a step in that direction, he had brought in Jeff Comment, formerly President of Wanamaker's, to help him run things. The hiring of Jeff turned out to be a homerun, but Barnett still found that he couldn't shake a feeling of ultimate responsibility. Additionally, he owned a valuable asset that was subject to the vagaries of a single, very competitive industry, and he thought it prudent to diversify his family's holdings.

Berkshire was made to order for him. It took us awhile to get together on price, but there was never any question in my mind that, first, Helzberg's was the kind of business that we wanted to own, and second, Jeff was our kind of manager. In fact, we would not have bought the business if Jeff had not been there to run it. Buying a retailer without good management is like buying the Eiffel Tower without an elevator.

We completed the Helzberg purchase in 1995 by means of a tax-free exchange of stock, the only kind of transaction that interested Barnett. Though he was certainly under no obligation to do so, Barnett shared a meaningful part of his proceeds from the sale with a large number of his associates. When someone behaves that generously, you know you are going to be treated right as a buyer.

Helzberg's, it should be added, is an entirely different sort of operation from Borsheim's, our Omaha jewelry business, and the two companies will operate independently of each other.[27]

"Basically, the way to negotiate with Warren Buffett—you don't negotiate. He tells you the deal and that's the deal," says Barnett Jr. Buffett's deal included retaining the employees and keeping the business intact. "I did not want a lot of people spitting on my grave," adds Barnett.[28]

Upon Berkshire's purchase, Comment became chairman and CEO of the company. Barnett Jr. retired completely from the company, but founded the Helzberg Entrepreneurial Mentoring Program (HEMP) and serves to this day as the program's Chairman of the Board of Directors. HEMP matches seasoned, successful entrepreneur mentors with less-experienced entrepreneur mentees. Considerable mentoring is also fostered through peer-to-peer relationships derived from involvement through HEMP.

Helzberg's had grown to be the third-largest jewelry retailer in 1995 with 148 retail outlets. After it became a subsidiary of Berkshire Hathaway, it continued growing. Store openings were increased from 20 to 30 a year, with more of the Jewelry3 large-format stores.

The company also worked to continue to raise comparable store earnings. In early 1996 the sales average per store was over $2 million. The company aimed to bring the sales average up to $3 million over the next few years. By 2001 it had over 200 stores, and was one of the largest jewelry retailers in the nation. Stores were located in nearly all 50 states.

Jeff Comment led Helzberg Diamonds during a time of huge growth. Comment was very active in his professional societies and civic and philanthropic organizations. For one week every holiday season for nine consecutive years, Jeff dressed up like Santa Claus and traveled to visit more than 15,000 sick children all around the country. In his book *Santa's Gift*, he shared his experiences and thoughts on one-on-one philanthropy. Story contributions were included from Elton John, Warren Buffett, and others. All author proceeds from sales of the book are donated to the Elizabeth Glaser Pediatric AIDS Foundation.

Comment worked for Helzberg Diamonds for 16 years until October 30, 2004, when he died unexpectedly at age 60, after collapsing at a private party. Said Comment, "Everyone dies. The choice and the challenge are in how we choose to live. And the more meaning you find in your life, the more reason you have to live."[29] Buffett appointed H. Marvin Beasley, Helzberg President and COO, as the new chairman and CEO.

"You'd have to describe us currently as a company with associates who have a lot of broken hearts," said Beasley. "At the end of that grieving process, we'll do all the things that Jeffrey would have wanted us to do. Most of our goals for 2005 are being worked on and finalized, and Jeffrey certainly had his fingerprint on all of those. One thing about Jeffrey was that he let all of his executives and people in management do their jobs. He didn't look over their shoulders, he just let people do their jobs. And that's what we're going to do now."[30]

Marvin Beasley served as CEO for five years and chose to retire at age 65, in 2009. That's when Beryl Raff first heard about the vacancy and opportunity to run Helzberg Diamonds.

Raff Riffs

As Beryl recalls, "Out of the clear blue, an acquaintance called and said, 'Do you have an interest in running Helzberg Diamonds? If you do, Warren Buffett would be interested in talking to you.' Three days later, on a Sunday morning, I was on a plane to Omaha, where Warren lives. He picked me up at the airport himself and it was an extraordinary day, ending with an offer for the job. Two days later I called back and accepted the position. I believe I am still the happiest, luckiest person in America."[31]

Buffett said Raff is "widely recognized throughout the retail industry as an outstanding merchant and strong multistore retail executive. She will bring a finely balanced blend of merchandising instinct and analytical sharpness to her new position."[32]

"Warren's an amazing person in every way," says Beryl. "He does not create complexity. He wants his businesses run properly, for the long-term, to be sustainable and profitable. He is also very realistic."[33]

Less than a month after the announcement of her new job, she attended the 2009 annual shareholder's meeting of Berkshire Hathaway. While there, she hosted a dinner for the Helzberg team, visited the Nebraska Furniture Mart, and met Bill Gates, a Berkshire Hathaway Director.

Of her experience at the meeting, Raff said, "There were so many moments when I pinched myself and thought, 'Is this real?' I asked my husband, 'Do you believe we're so fortunate to be part of this whole thing?' It really felt like a family to me."[34]

Helzberg's executive committee includes two females out of seven. The other woman, besides Raff, is Becky Higgins, Senior Vice President of Marketing. There were very few women in top management positions of retail corporations prior to 2000, even though women dominate the market as retail consumers, making 80 percent of purchase decisions.

"We had role models in the late 1970s and early 1980s, but it wasn't 50-50," says Beryl. "Over time, though, females have slowly crept up." Professor Leonard Berry, founder of the Center for Retailing Studies at Texas A&M, says, "It should have happened earlier. Talent isn't gender specific, but the number of women participating should have led more women into the executive suites."[35]

Beryl, a widow for the past year, has one son, Edward. She was able to balance her career with the needs of her husband and son. At times, family needs require attention. Raff addressed a luncheon of professional women in 2006, saying "Every hour you have to make a choice. Never apologize for having to take care of your family."[36] (see Figure 6.2.)

Helzberg is evolving to become more upscale and offer increasingly finer quality items. Its application to the American Gem Society (AGS) was a first for any of the so-called mall jewelry chain stores. In 2010, Helzberg gained membership. Only about 5 percent of all jewelers, designers, appraisers, and suppliers meet the standards for membership in the Society. Other Berkshire Hathaway subsidiaries with AGS membership are Ben Bridge and Borsheim's Fine Jewelry.

Figure 6.2 Beryl Raff Presenting Lecture "Rising to the Top, Managing It All"
SOURCE: Jewish Federation of Greater Dallas.

"We are proud and excited to see Helzberg Diamonds become a member of AGS," says Beryl. "Our culture and philosophy dating back to the Helzberg family is in total alignment to that of the AGS—the protection of the consumer; ensuring a well-trained, educated, and professional staff; and demonstrating the highest integrity in everything we do. Helzberg has always catered to the upper middle market with an average household income consumer considerably higher than most other mall-based jewelers. Our vision is to continue to focus on the consumer base we serve, giving our guests the best customer experience possible."[37]

Raff serves on the Advisory Board of Jewelers Circular Keystone, a trade publication and industry authority. She also serves on the Advisory Board of Jewelers of America and on the Executive Board of the Jewelers Vigilance Committee, both nonprofit organizations dedicated to social responsibility, education, legal, and regulatory issues facing the jewelry industry.

Raff is a Director of the National Association of Corporate Directors Heartland Chapter, a nonprofit organization for corporate board members. She is also a member of Women's Corporate Directors, an organization of women who serve on corporate boards to provide networking and education.

Though leading Helzberg keeps her busy, she still finds time to serve on two corporate boards of directors. Since 2001, she has served on the board of Jo-Ann Stores, Inc., a national specialty retailer of crafting, decorating, and sewing products. Jo-Ann's home office is in Hudson, Ohio. On this board, she is a member of the Corporate Governance Committee and is Chairman of the Compensation Committee.

She has also been a member of the board of directors of Group 1 Automotive since June 2007. This company is a Houston-based auto retailer, owning and operating over 100 auto dealerships. Raff's combined compensation for these two boards in 2009 was $376,163.

She is a past executive board member and vice chairman of the North Texas Chapter of the Make-A-Wish Foundation, and a member of the National Board of Make-A-Wish, a nonprofit organization that grants the wishes of children with life-threatening medical conditions. Helzberg collaborates with Make-A-Wish by donating proceeds of sales from the "I Am Loved" stuffed bear to the Foundation.

Beryl's ties to Dallas are still strong. She is a member of the Dallas chapter of The International Women's Forum (IWF). The IWF is an organization of women that furthers dynamic leadership, leverages global access, and maximizes opportunities for women to exert their influence. Membership in the IWF Dallas Forum is by invitation only. Raff also serves on the Advisory Board of Dallas Summer Musicals, a not-for-profit theater company.

In 2001, Beryl received the Community Achievement Award from the ORT America Jewelry Industry Chapter. ORT America promotes the understanding and appreciation of Jewish values through a global network of schools and training programs in 55 countries. The ORT America Outstanding Community Achievement Award honors professionals who have substantially improved the quality of life for their fellow individuals, created role models that could be emulated, and/or established new directions for society.

Raff is also the 1999 and 2006 recipient of the United Jewish Appeal (UJA) Federation of New York Diamond, Jewelry, and Watch Division's "Leadership Award of Excellence." In 1999, the Women's Jewelry Association named her to its Lifetime Hall of Fame, and she was inducted into National Jeweler's Retailer Hall of Fame in the Majors category in 2009.

Cruel Jewels

Pursuing a career in jewelry retailing is not for the faint of heart. Along with security and insurance issues, and keeping pace with fashion trends, Beryl Raff faces significant competition from numerous sources. Retail jewelry stores fight among each other to capture the dollars spent by consumers on a product purchased with relative infrequency. Retail jewelry is a $64 billion industry. The largest jewelry retailer in the combined U.S. and Canadian markets is believed to be Wal-Mart.

The business model for jewelry retailing has and will continue to evolve. Finding and adapting to new sales channels is more important than selection of the product, because to the average shopper, mall jewelry stores basically sell the same stuff. Increasingly, jewelry purchases are made outside of the mall environment, and even outside of brick and mortar stores. The Internet and QVC television sales are growing.

In times of economic recession, the jewelry business is hit hard, along with other luxury items, as shoppers put off discretionary spending. Even those with plenty of money would rather not *appear* to live extravagantly. Outward expressions of wealth, such as large gems and glittering jewelry, are not popular when strolling through parks inhabited by the "Occupy" movement.

Beryl faces challenges in the very nature of jewelry buying habits. The jewelry business suffers from severe seasonal extremes. The vast majority of sales are made in November and December for holiday purchases. One can simply acknowledge this and attempt to have a wildly successful hit for a particular holiday year, or one can plan strategies that pay off during other seasons. Beware of quick profits, however, if they detour a better long-term strategy.

Beryl Raff has bravely faced numerous challenges during her career. She is a problem solver and lifelong learner. Her leadership of Helzberg Diamond Shops, Inc. will allow the company to distinguish itself from the competition and survive to serve future generations of romantics who feel "I am loved."

Chapter 7

Charlotte Guyman— Impact Creator

Charlotte Guyman, former Microsoft manager, is a director of Berkshire Hathaway, serving since 2003. She was the first female non-Buffett family member of the Board of Directors. Guyman was invited to join the board by Warren Buffett himself, with whom she had become acquainted through Bill and Melinda Gates. Charlotte and her husband, shareholders of Berkshire, grew to know Buffett well in 1995 when they traveled together to China.

"Warren called me up one day and said 'I'd like you to be a board member,' so that was pretty exciting," she says. "It's such an incredible honor. He is truly such a high-integrity person, just the finest human being. The people that he has attracted to Berkshire, in terms of managers and board members, are all like that too. I was completely flattered to be asked." Bill Gates joined the Berkshire board two years after Guyman.

I first met Charlotte Guyman (Figure 7.1) at the 13th Annual Fortune Most Powerful Women Summit in Laguna, California, in

Figure 7.1   Berkshire Hathaway Director Charlotte Guyman
SOURCE: Charlotte Guyman.

October 2011. The summit featured 83 prominent women and one prominent man—Warren Buffett—discussing issues such as leadership, global business, innovation, and social good. Charlotte has attended the annual event off and on for several years.

Guyman, age 55, has shoulder-length light brown hair and bright turquoise eyes. On this day, she's wearing a black shift dress with white trim and pearl drop earrings. I was captivated by her soft voice, intelligence, and charm as she and I chatted in a St. Regis Hotel restaurant over hot tea and Diet Coke, respectively.

Adding Value

The year 2003 saw a significant change in board composition at Berkshire Hathaway. Four new directors were invited to join that year. Chairman Warren Buffett sought self-nominations from the shareholders. As he explained in that year's annual Letter to Shareholders, "Last year, as we moved to change our board, I asked for self-nominations from shareholders who believed they had the requisite qualities to be a Berkshire director. Despite the lack of either liability insurance or meaningful compensation, we received more than twenty applications. Most were good, coming from owner-oriented individuals having family holdings of Berkshire worth well over $1 million. After considering them, Charlie and I—with the concurrence of our incumbent directors—asked four shareholders who did not nominate themselves to join the board: David Gottesman, Charlotte Guyman, Don Keough, and Tom Murphy. These four people are all friends of mine, and I know their strengths well. They bring an extraordinary amount of business talent to Berkshire's board."[1]

With 79 subsidiary companies, Berkshire Hathaway is a complex organization to oversee. Charlotte understands her director's role and how important the board is to Berkshire.

"I think of the board as being accountable to the major constituents of the organization. I believe that I work for the shareholders of Berkshire Hathaway, and also our customers, and of course, government entities. But a board isn't the management. The board is in support of management, and is the conscience of an organization," she says. "The board needs to be very careful to understand strategy, the regulatory environment, and succession planning and most of the major issues that a company or an organization is facing."

With Charlotte's computer technology and Internet expertise, she adds valuable knowledge in areas that the Berkshire board previously lacked. Shortly after joining the board she traveled with Sharon Osberg, former Wells Fargo Executive and Buffett's friend and bridge partner, to GEICO headquarters to help improve the company's website.

In November 2011, she traveled with Warren Buffett and Cathy Baron Tamraz to Japan (Figure 7.2). They attended the opening of a Berkshire subsidiary carbon tool plant in the Fukushima Prefecture, hit by an earthquake less than a year earlier, and visited with Business Wire's Tokyo staff.

Charlotte is a member of the board's audit committee. There are three other board members that serve with her in this capacity: Susan Decker, Donald Keough, and Thomas Murphy. Murphy is chair of the committee. The purpose of the Audit Committee is oversight of corporate financial statements, and legal and regulatory filings.

Serving on the audit committee of any corporate board is easily the most time-consuming and intensive task of board governance. Audit

Figure 7.2   Left to Right: Charlotte Guyman, Warren Buffett, and Cathy Baron Tamraz during a Visit to Japan, 2011
SOURCE: Business Wire.

committee activities are subject to firm regulatory requirements. The Securities and Exchange Commission (SEC) even has a definition of the position of audit committee financial expert.[2] The rules define an expert as a person who has the following attributes:

- An understanding of generally accepted accounting principles and financial statements.
- The ability to assess the general application of such principles in connection with the accounting for estimates, accruals, and reserves.
- Experience preparing, auditing, analyzing, or evaluating financial statements that present a breadth and level of complexity of accounting issues that are generally comparable to the breadth and complexity of issues that can reasonably be expected to be raised by the registrant's financial statements, or experience actively supervising one or more persons engaged in such activities.
- An understanding of internal controls and procedures for financial reporting.
- An understanding of audit committee functions.

The Sarbanes-Oxley Act of 2002 requires a company to disclose whether it has at least one audit committee financial expert serving on its audit committee, and if so, the name of the expert and whether the expert is independent of management. A company that does not have an audit committee financial expert must disclose this fact and explain why it has no such expert.[3] For the purposes of reporting this information, Berkshire Hathaway states that Murphy, age 85, is an audit committee financial expert.[4]

Regarding the Audit Committee, Charlotte says, "So much fun! I like it a lot because it's a really great look at the business. We get to work closely with our accountants. There are so many interesting regulatory requirements around industries like insurance, energy, and railroads. And the CFOs of the businesses are brilliant just like the CEOs."

The Berkshire Audit Committee's most widely reported recent activity is likely the David Sokol incident. Sokol, a longtime friend and colleague of Warren Buffett and CEO of NetJets, a Berkshire subsidiary, made some personal stock purchases of Lubrizol Corporation prior to advising Buffett to purchase the company in early 2011. When Berkshire announced the deal, Sokol's shares gained $3 million in value.

The audit committee was charged with investigating and reporting to the board their findings of Sokol's actions. The committee determined that Sokol violated company business ethics standards in his personal purchase of Lubrizol stock and Sokol resigned from his position. Buffett said Sokol's actions were "inexplicable and inexcusable."[5]

With Berkshire's diversity of holdings, it would be difficult for any board member to have industry knowledge in all of the areas in which Berkshire is involved. But that's what Charlotte loves about the company. "It makes it really fun because there are so many different industries. It feels like being in business school all over again getting case studies. One can always keep learning about the company and getting to know the different businesses."

She advises that anyone wanting to serve on a board be certain that there is good company management. "Make sure you understand the company really well and continue to learn. A board member has to be able to add some value somewhere. If it was never clear where I would add value, I wouldn't want to be on a board, and I'm always looking at how I can add value," she says.

Get *Into* It

Charlotte was born in 1956, in Renton, Washington, located about 12 miles south of downtown Seattle. She was the youngest of four children and the only daughter. Charlotte's grandmother also lived with the family of six in a two-bedroom home. When Charlotte was eight, they moved to a four-bedroom home in a middle-class neighborhood of Seattle.

Charlotte's parents both grew up in western Pennsylvania. Her maternal grandfather was a lay minister, working at a YMCA. Her mother completed one year of college at the University of Pittsburgh, but had to leave school to get a job to help her family during the Depression.

Charlotte's parents married following World War II and moved to Brazil, where her father taught aeronautical engineering. They moved back to the United States after their first child was born and Boeing hired Charlotte's father as an aerospace engineer.

Boeing's two major production facilities are in Renton and Everett, Washington. The Renton factory, built on land that was formerly the marshy shores of Lake Washington, began building planes in 1941. The facility's first project was a reconnaissance aircraft for the U.S. Navy: the XPPB-1 Sea Ranger, an experimental flying boat. The extremely successful Boeing 737 commercial airplane has been built in Renton since 1965.

Charlotte's mother was a homemaker who kept busy with volunteer activities and raising her four children. When Charlotte was in middle school, her mother returned to the local community college and obtained her Associate's degree.

Charlotte began working at an early age. "I had my first paid job at age 14 working with autistic children—at about $1 an hour, as I recall!" she says. "And my second job at age 17 was working in a pie shop as a cashier and baker."

Following high school graduation, Charlotte entered the University of Washington. She remembers, "My parents paid for my first year of college and I paid for the rest of my education as I worked multiple jobs during college." She worked in the dormitory cafeteria during the evenings of her freshman year.

Charlotte had the good fortune to work for two Seattle icons. "I got a great job as an elevator operator at the Space Needle in Seattle the summer after my freshman year," she says. The Space Needle is 605 feet tall and has three elevators. Two of the elevators are high-speed and can travel at a rate of 10 mph, or 800 feet per minute. The third elevator is slower and used primarily for freight. (Coincidentally, a decade earlier Charlotte's future colleague Bill Gates, age 11, won a dinner at the Space Needle restaurant offered by his pastor. Gates had to memorize Chapters 5, 6, and 7 of the Gospel of Matthew, better known as the Sermon on the Mount, and he recited the sermon flawlessly.)

Charlotte learned some useful lessons in her early work life. Required to talk about the Space Needle to visitors as they rode in the elevator, she discovered, "If I ever came to work kind of draggy or tired, and I got all these tourists in the elevator, they would also be draggy. But if I was really into it and energetic, then they were really energetic. If you can't get out of it—get *into* it. Because it is what you make of it."

"I really enjoyed working with tourists. I kept that job all the way through college, working full-time in the summer and part-time in the winter. It enabled me to live independently and pay for most of my college education. So, I've been financially independent since I was 19 years old and I consider myself very lucky for that," she said.

Charlotte graduated in 1978 with a Bachelor of Science in Zoology and planned to work in the field of animal behavior. After college, she did some traveling and then moved to California.

"I moved to San Diego to work at SeaWorld, hoping to be a cetacean [whales and dolphins] trainer, but started out working in the education department as a tour guide." Coincidently, Southwest Airlines has three custom Boeing 737 planes (likely built in Renton, Washington) painted to look like Shamu the killer whale, as advertisements for SeaWorld.

She was a science educator, posted at specific exhibits to talk about the animals and their environments. It was a natural fit with her prior tourist experience at the Space Needle and her zoology degree. Even so, some on-the-job training was required to learn about the numerous species of animals.

"I have always loved a job where you learn. Hopefully one goes to bed each night knowing more than one knew in the morning. And that constant learning and growth is fun, and that's what makes jobs really fun."

Her experience teaching and guiding tour groups would benefit her later in managing work teams. Working with tourists taught her to see her own world through their eyes. "One thing that's nice about tourists is the freshness they bring," she says. "Because everything is new, it's exciting. So that was a really good lesson to me when I was young. So they're not from here, but look at all the people who are, and are just bored. When in fact, wherever you are is really great."

Ever the hard worker, she simultaneously held a job teaching sailing. Within a short period of time, she became the assistant manager at a sailboat rental business while still working at SeaWorld.

The HP Way

After less than a year in San Diego she decided that she wanted to work in the nascent computer industry. She moved back to Seattle and signed up for a Fortran computer programming language course at a community college.

For income while attending school, she returned to work at the Space Needle. "They were very flexible and when I came back from San Diego and I was going to school and looking for a job for those four months, they hired me back. It's really nice when you do a good job; people will be accommodating. I learned that when you work hard, people want to retain you."

She began an extensive job hunt and in April 1980 was hired as a Field Marketing Representative for Hewlett Packard (HP) in the Bellevue, Washington, office. Hewlett Packard, founded in 1938 in Palo Alto, California, was a well-established successful company. It had $3 billion in revenues at that time and over 57,000 employees. In 1980, the company debuted its first personal computer, the HP-85. Charlotte says,

> With HP, I had a year-long training program for becoming a technical computer sales representative. After a year, I was given the sales territory of Alaska, which is the territory I most wanted, and for more than two years, I traveled from Washington to Alaska every other week. I sold HP's real-time processing

computer, the HP 1000 series, and desktop computers 9800 series to engineers and scientists working at the University of Alaska, Alyeska Pipeline Service Company, ARCO, the U.S. Army cold-weather test station, and the State of Alaska.

After a few years, I was asked to manage the Systems Engineering team for Western Washington and Alaska, about 10 people, opening up the Alaska office for HP from Seattle. I did this job for two years and in the process I decided that I needed to know more about business, as I didn't understand basic things like why a customer cared about managing their inventory or receivables. I also realized that I didn't want a lifetime in sales and sales support as I really enjoyed business strategy and management. Consequently I applied to business school at the University of Washington and HP was kind enough to allow me to attend full time by giving me an educational leave of absence.

Think It, Build It

Armed with her new MBA, Charlotte set out to find a management position. "Upon graduation, I had eight job offers," she says. "I had spent the last quarter doing a very hardy job search and I chose to go to a relatively small company in Redmond, Washington—Microsoft—as a channel marketing manager. I began in April of 1987 and recall that I was employee number 1,187." Thus began her association with the second Seattle icon.

From 1987 until 1999 she was an employee of Microsoft—a Microsoftie or *Softie*, as they call themselves—where she held several marketing and general management positions, including general manager of MSN Internet Sales and Marketing, general manager of Kids and Games Software, director of Consumer Division Marketing, and director of International Marketing.

Microsoft was founded in New Mexico in 1975, moved to Bellevue, Washington, in 1979 and then finally settled in Redmond, Washington, in 1986. It was a time of huge growth for the company. Windows 2.0 was released in 1987. By the end of that year, Microsoft had 1,816 employees and revenues of nearly $346 million, a significant increase over the previous year's revenues of $197 million. At the time Charlotte retired from Microsoft in 1999, the company would have 31,575 employees and revenues of $19.75 billion. Today, annual revenues are approximately $70 billion.

To manage creative people and technical skills, Microsoft follows a strategy that can be described as the organization of small teams of overlapping functional specialists. The company is unusual in the degree to which it empowers people in these specialties to define their jobs, hire new people, and train new hires. Microsoft employees are oriented toward self-critiquing, learning, and improving.[6]

There's a company-wide commitment to accepting mistakes as part of the process because so many new areas are being explored. Allowing people to fail with impunity (on the right occasions) paves the way for those people to take risks again in the future. They'll be more free with their ideas. They won't shy away from a project that has a chance of going under. The freedom to fail helps move the company forward.[7]

In 1987, Microsoft was selling largely through retail stores like Egghead and CompUSA. "It was a challenge to pitch all these different products to the retailers. Then, we had the idea that we could be more like a retail company and roll out programs with focused products to make it easier for the retailer and more efficient for Microsoft," says Charlotte.

One of the first big promotions that Charlotte worked on was Microsoft Works, launching one of the new versions during demonstration days in stores all over the country. MS Works is a home productivity office software suite. It's smaller, less expensive, and has fewer features than Microsoft Office.

Guyman next became Director of International Marketing. "That was a fantastic job for a career learning experience," she says. "I worked as a staff assistant to the senior vice president who ran all of international, plus product support and our international product group. It was the first time that I was really close to and understood what executives think about, like pricing strategy and marketing, because my boss worked directly for Bill Gates, and the company was still pretty small. I saw what you really think about in the boardroom, the strategic issues and the trade-offs."

Microsoft was creating products that were tailored for and marketed to each country by the international division. They were customized because individual countries had specific features that they wanted. Customers didn't understand why they had to pay a different amount for MS Word in France than they did in the United States, but it was because the products were different. This was a problem that Charlotte had to address. She explains, "As our customer base was becoming more global, we also needed to become more global."

Many U.S. companies had to transition to thinking and acting globally as they entered the early 1990s. "I got to be right in the middle of that at Microsoft, which was really a fantastic experience," says Charlotte. "I was part of the meetings where we visited the different country managers, and they really ran their own businesses. So, it was like visiting individual CEOs. I got to see they had control over all kinds of things. I learned *so* much."

Charlotte's Web

Employees at Microsoft work on numerous projects, some successful, some not. But everyone has the opportunity to impact the world by influencing how Microsoft's products are built and subsequently utilized. Each work task is a big responsibility for the employee and can make or lose significant revenues for the company. This responsibility is balanced by a huge opportunity to create something of significance that will positively impact millions of users.

Microsoft evolved when it decided to enter the consumer market. As Charlotte said in 1993, "It used to be home computers sold to hobbyists and people who did work at home, and software was personal productivity and games. Now the market is expanding to spouses, kids, an aging parent—people who basically aren't computer literate, or who may be technical but never got a home computer."[8] Things obviously changed rapidly and Charlotte was there at the beginning to witness the explosion of the information age.

When Guyman took a consumer marketing job with the product groups, the challenge was to promote consumer products from a company that wasn't necessarily seen as a consumer developer since a lot of the original customers were corporate-based. It was difficult to get the attention of customers with a lot of small products.

One of the basic marketing questions that the Consumer Division faced as its growth accelerated was whether to create a separate brand identity for the consumer titles, lest the Microsoft name, with its association with dull operating system or office software, hurt its appeal to consumers.

Charlotte was among the contingent that advocated a name wholly separate from Microsoft, such as "Lifeware," that would provide as much distance as possible from what Guyman saw as the company's "techno-nerdy" image. She and other managers were convinced otherwise, however, by research indicating that Microsoft's name was in fact an asset. "Microsoft Home" was the subbrand that was introduced in 1993.[9]

"We felt we needed a subbrand within Microsoft, because targeting the home market is so different than targeting the business market," said Charlotte. "Microsoft Home products are friendlier than our image of someone who's a real techie company. We see the consumer market really changing and taking off. The computer is finally actually competing with other forms of learning and entertainment like books or movies or other types of computer games."[10]

At times, Charlotte's division was threatened by outside companies. One can only imagine how competitive this newly emerging industry was at that time. Compton's, the encyclopedia company, announced that they held coding patents that covered methods for searching and accessing multimedia in November of 1993, at the same time that Microsoft was unveiling new CD-ROMs and multimedia software, such as the Encarta encyclopedia and the Dinosaurs "edutainment" CD-ROM.

Software developers complained that the patent would deter innovation and that the U.S. patent office was ill-equipped to evaluate complicated code in software applications. Charlotte was readying her products for the holiday sales season and said in response to the possible patent threat, "It's full steam ahead for us. We've been enthusiastic promoters of CD-ROM and multimedia technology since hosting the first CD-ROM conference in Seattle in 1986, and we're not about to change now."[11] The Compton patent application made

41 claims, but was rejected in March 1994 by the U.S. Patent and Trademark office, stating the claims were obvious and not novel.

Top managers took bets on the amount of holiday sales for 1993. Charlotte guessed 20,000 units. Everyone, even the most optimistic, underestimated sales, which turned out to be over 120,000 units, representing more than 65 percent of market share.[12]

By mid-1994, Microsoft had 54 consumer CD-ROM products in 27 languages. In 1995, it had over 100. Guyman's responsibilities included development of learning software for adults and children, including the titles Flight Simulator, Dinosaurs, Julia Child, Musical Instruments, Microsoft Money, and Microsoft Project. "We were a very small part of the Microsoft revenue stream, but we got to do a lot of innovative things," she says.

While Microsoft was able to create a lot of products, they were not all able to gain a significant market share. For example, MS Money, introduced in 1991, was outsold by Quicken seven to one.[13] Part of the reason for this was that Quicken was released by Intuit, in 1984 and was already used by thousands of people. In September 1988, it was the number-one best-selling consumer software product.

In 1993, Charlotte admitted that, "Intuit has done a really fine job establishing the category. They have huge name recognition. We're realistic about how long it takes (to gain a foothold), but we're definitely committed."[14] Microsoft Money remained a viable product, though it was a distant second in the personal finance market for several years before losing more market share and was eventually discontinued in 2009.

Davidow's Law (named for Bill Davidow, senior vice president of marketing and sales at Intel in the 1980s) states that the company that releases a product first will dominate the market, especially if it is the first to obsolesce its own product.[15] Being first to market is an important advantage, even if your product is inferior to products released subsequently. It's much easier to sell a new tool for a specific task to a user than it is to convince a user to alter their behavior and use a different tool for a task they already perform by a familiar method.

Davidow's Law rewards speed. Slow innovators are left behind. New software products cannot simply replace old ones because software products do not wear out. They die when they become obsolete. Many successful products are winners because their manufacturers value market share more than quick money. Customers acquire the software at a reasonable purchase price and then become committed and loyal to the product.

Quicken's success cannot be attributed to Davidow's Law. In fact, there were 46 personal finance products on the market at the time of Quicken's release. Those products, however, were extraordinarily complicated and users were anxious for a product that didn't make them feel like an idiot.

Of competition in the consumer products division, Guyman said, "Microsoft's greatest competition in the consumer market may come not from other software companies but from other creative interests. We're competing with people going to a movie or reading a book. Our software has to be fun."[16]

Microsoft was even able to partially conquer that competition. In a relatively short period of time people would watch those movies and read books at a computer with the assistance of Microsoft products.

Perhaps the most successful consumer product that Charlotte worked on was the Internet travel application, Expedia. Melinda French, who started at Microsoft the same year as Charlotte and later married Bill Gates (in 1994), also worked on the Expedia project.

"Expedia started out as an idea to do a travel CD-ROM," explains Charlotte. "So, we talked to major travel publications about putting travel books on it. In the process, there was one guy who was working with me who said, 'We could actually make this a travel agent, ultimately, because of the Internet.' So, this person and I went to a meeting with Bill Gates to pitch the idea. A really great program manager, Greg Slyngstad, came over to work on it and really helped pull it together and Rich Barton was the marketing manager, and that's how Expedia was born."

Expedia was founded as a division of Microsoft in 1996, was spun off in 1999, and was purchased by Ticketmaster in 2001. In 2008, Expedia was ranked third by CNNMoney in America's Most Admired Companies in the industry of Internet Services, Retailing.

Slyngstad would work for Microsoft for 15 years, then leave to found VacationSpot.com, which was sold to Expedia in 2000, whereupon he rejoined Expedia. He then left Expedia in 2002 and has served on the boards of Roost.com and Kayak.com. He is now CEO of TravelPost.com.

Guyman also worked on the partnership that was formed between Microsoft and DreamWorks studio in March 1995. David Geffen, Steven Spielberg, and Jeffrey Katzenberg came to Microsoft because they wanted to have a software developer partner for their new movie studio.

"I was the junior executive who helped put together a plan with Dreamworks," she says. "One of my colleagues, Bruce Jacobsen, worked with me on it and he moved to California and started running Dreamworks Interactive. I took over his job, then, which was Kids and Games."

Guyman's final position with Microsoft before retiring from the company was general manager of MSN Internet Sales and Marketing. Microsoft had realigned the company to focus on the Internet in 1995. An Internet Division was formed and nearly every product plan contained an Internet component. "Bill Gates has likened the Internet to the Gold Rush," said former Director of Business Development for Internet Commerce Jeff Thiel. "It's hard to know if the real winner will be a guy who strikes a vein or the people selling the pans to the miners. But when it happens, we'll be there."[17]

In Charlotte's new position with MSN, she managed a sales force challenged with selling advertising space on MSN's web channel. MSN was developed as a project with the code name Marvel and when it debuted was originally called the Microsoft Network. It debuted as an online service in 1995, originally conceived to be a dial-up service provider like America Online with a file system of topic folders. Open access to the Internet was not included in the initial launch. Over a half-million users signed up for the service within its first three months of existence. MSN 2.0, launched shortly thereafter in 1996, offered Internet connectivity.

Eventually, the MSN Web channel became a portal for travel, finance, real estate, and MSNBC news. Success in selling ads is directly related to the quantity of web site viewers. Advertisers look for the best investment for their marketing budgets and that is determined by the number of people visiting each web page. "Being able to reach a lot of people is critical to getting in the door," said Charlotte, "but it's not just content—it's how good a partner can we be?"[18]

Negotiating win-win partnerships pays off in the long run since clients are able to track online visits and purchases related to online advertising, even more so than they can from other forms of marketing.

The Interactive Advertising Bureau was founded in 1996 and for the first time online advertising revenues were reported. The new online advertising industry made approximately $267 million that year. By 2009, there was nearly $23 billion in revenues reported for online advertising.

The Big Switcheroo

Microsoft, like other early tech start-ups, has a reputation for being a casual, fun place to work. Employees wear jeans, arrive and leave whenever they choose, and can drink as many free beverages as they want. Over 23 million drinks are consumed annually at the home office.

As Robert Slater wrote, "Bill Gates treated employees as if they mattered, giving them their own offices (for entry-level programmers that was no small perk), their own computers (no small perk either), and free Coke (a very big perk!). They were made to feel as if they were making significant contributions to society. This was all heady stuff for the young employees at Microsoft."[19]

Microsoft employees work hard and play hard. And often, they play *at* work. As Microsoft's 25th anniversary book states, "Pranks and practical jokes sprout like mushrooms everywhere around here, and there is nothing predictable about them, from their timing to their execution. Some of them are incredibly dumb and sophomoric; others are as brilliant and quirky as the people who dream them up. Only one thing is certain: If you leave your office for more than an hour—even if it's to do something as innocent as taking a few leisurely laps in 'Lake Bill'—you may not recognize it when you return."[20]

Charlotte says, "I've been really lucky every place I worked, that the style has matched me pretty well, which is to work hard and to have fun. Microsoft, at the time I joined, had a lot of young people. In fact, I might have been one of the older ones. I remember I was the first of the product-marketing people who even was married or had a baby. I was 30 when I went to Microsoft. We had a lot of fun."

"I remember one prank," she says. "I really like M&Ms. I don't eat them anymore. My administrative assistant, Linda, used to always have M&Ms on her desk in a gumball machine. If I was working really late, trying to do a presentation, I would somehow end up eating so many of them. And then the next day, I'd have to bring her a bag to replace it. So I was rather embarrassed about this and I'd always be ashamed."

"And one time I went on vacation and when I came back, my team had taken all the files out of all my drawers of my desk. And when I opened it, it was full of M&Ms. You could literally stick your arm in up to the elbow. I was told Mike Metzger was behind it but that it was a team effort."

Hoppers

When Microsoft began, Bill Gates and Paul Allen hired people who were similar to themselves in knowledge, behavior, and personality. Many brilliant and enthusiastic people started as new graduates fresh out of the best colleges and universities in the country and others came from the rapidly evolving computer industry. They were, for the most part, single men in their 20s with no outside interests.

"At the first company picnic I went to, I looked around and realized that there were no kids," remembers Mike Maples, former executive vice president. "It struck me then just how young this company really was. The average age was about 26, and most of them were still single. That's why they were able and willing to work such incredibly long hours. One developer worked on a project for six weeks once without leaving his office. He slept, ate, and lived there. I also remember walking past offices and finding people with their hands on the keyboard, just asleep. They kept going until they just stopped thinking."[21]

In 1984, Ida Cole was the first senior female executive hired at Microsoft, after leaving her job at Apple. She was different. She was a woman and she was 37 years old. She took over as vice president of applications directly from Gates.

"In my career," Ida says, "I have never tried to be one of the boys. I am who I am and I take all of me into everything I do. I believe in recognizing and nurturing talent in young people, regardless of their gender. I don't ever single out just women. Never! It separates women rather than integrates them. Competence to do a job is not a gender-related issue."[22]

Back in the 1980s, there were very few women—especially women programmers—working at Microsoft, and they were not particularly happy with their treatment by their male colleagues. In 1990, a few of the female employees started an organization to support the women of Microsoft called "Hoppers." The group was named for Rear Admiral Grace Hopper, the inventor in 1952 of COBOL computer programming language. The first Computer Science *Man* of the Year Award presented in 1969 was, in fact, given to a woman—Grace Hopper.

Charlotte was not a member of Hoppers, as it was initiated in the software developer area and she was in marketing. She says, "With HP and Microsoft both being technical companies, unfortunately, there's a paucity of females in the operating and line jobs. But I felt like both companies really wanted to rectify that. And if a person was willing to take risks and *be technical* either from training or through aptitude, it was quite equitable."

Teri Schiele, former Group Program Manager at Microsoft, wrote the Hoppers charter. The group has three goals:

1. To improve the lives of the women at Microsoft.
2. To get more women into the company.
3. To help women move up in the ranks.

Says Teri, "When I was in the Windows group, I'd be the only woman at major conferences where there were 200 people. We established the Hoppers board of directors, and I was the chairperson. None of this was company sponsored. It was all volunteer work. We did it out of our desire to change the situation. Today, Hoppers is a great success. It went from hundreds of members to thousands in just a short period of time."[23]

In just one year, Microsoft officially recognized the organization. Hoppers runs a summer computer camp for young girls to expose them to computers and science. They sponsor college scholarships for girls to study computer science, provide workshops to employees, sponsor a Take Our Daughters to Work Day, and sponsor corporate networking and marketing events.

As former vice president of human resources at Microsoft, Deborah Willingham knew exactly how many qualified female job applicants existed. Throughout the 1980s and 1990s, the number was very small.

"Being a woman in a traditionally male environment is not always fun. For me, school was hard, and I was picked on by some professors who said, 'No woman can get better than a C in my classroom.' There weren't many mentors or any role models. I figure the best thing I can do for women is to be successful at this level so that it becomes more accepted and expected."[24]

She adds, "Let's just say this: No one has the right percentage of women in senior jobs," Willingham blames, in part, the paucity of technically trained women graduating from college today. "People need the right experience to be successful," she says. "You can't say, 'I want more women at the top, so put more women at the top.' It has to start on the bench."[25]

Under Willingham's leadership, Microsoft expanded the pool of candidates for senior jobs by opening them up to women on staff who had less managerial experience than male applicants. "We ask whether we'd be willing to take a risk on someone to grow the diversity of the team," she says.[26] Charlotte adds, "I had a really good core group of women who worked with me at Microsoft and we still stay in touch."

Servant Leadership

When Microsoft was small, it was a collection of highly technical people. As it grew, the company needed to recruit and/or develop people with management skills.

"Anyone who has people reporting to them has the word *manager* in their title," says Mike Murray, another former vice president of human resources. "We expect them to get more out of their people. We have found that there are three key drivers of a successful manager at Microsoft:

1. They make sure the group and every member in it have clear goals and objectives and performance measures.
2. They must be very good at planning the sometimes tedious process of figuring out the details of how to get there.
3. They give continual feedback."[27]

As a manager, Charlotte was in the so-called trenches. "I was pretty engaged," she says. "I feel like you have to be in there. So, when there's product shipping times, you show up on the weekend with everyone else because people respect that. And my big view is that everybody is only as successful as the people who are doing all the work."

"I'm a high-relationship, high-task person," she adds. "I think situations might dictate different kinds of leadership styles. So for example, if there's a new employee and they don't know how to do their job, they're going to need much more hands-on leadership if they're working directly for me. One of the biggest problems when people don't do their job is that no one told them exactly what was expected. So, I like to set pretty clear expectations about what needs to be done. But then be there to either train or help if a person gets in trouble. Success comes from the things that are achieved in the business. It's not about any one of us in particular."

"I strive always to be a *servant leader*," says Charlotte. This means that as a manager, Guyman focuses on the needs of her team, promotes personal development, and assists them to solve problems. She is thereby able to lead content and motivated people to perform according to the company's culture and mission and fulfill expectations.

Her management success gained national attention when Charlotte was featured in a *New York Times* article that discussed employee rewards and retention. At that time, in 1997, she was managing over 100 employees. She was looking for a way to recognize and continually motivate her team, so she created a unique award in her department: the *Char-Latte Award*.

She says, "It was an incentive given to employees for producing great results, showing teamwork, or removing barriers to doing the right thing. People thought it was very fun. They'd get a gift certificate to go get a latte, attached to a bunch of helium balloons in a meeting. It was very public."[28]

It's a bit surprising, but perhaps not unique at a company like Microsoft, that Charlotte had the opportunity to work in five different divisions over the course of 12 years. These experiences gave her a broad education and the chance to meet and interact with a diverse collection of colleagues and clients. She says, "I had a fantastic learning experience and career at Microsoft and loved it!"

A Catalyst

Microsoft has a long-standing reputation and tradition for philanthropy and social responsibility. The company integrates economic, social, and environmental considerations into its operations. Microsoft ranks 23rd on *Corporate Responsibility Magazine's* 2011 Top 100 Best Corporate Citizens list. The rankings are compiled based on seven factors:

1. Environment
2. Climate change
3. Human rights
4. Employee relations
5. Corporate governance
6. Philanthropy
7. Financial

The number-one company listed as Best Corporate Citizen for 2011 is Johnson Controls, followed by Campbell Soup Company and IBM.

Employee giving and company matching funds totaled almost $90 million in 2009. It's certainly a unique accomplishment that this company could make so many people so rich and at the same time guide them to be socially responsible and instill the desire to give with a passion to improve the world. While Microsoft's employees create software products because that's their job, they do it with the belief it will genuinely improve lives.

The company's legacy of philanthropy took inspiration from Mary Gates, the mother of Bill Gates and a leader of United Way. "It spread starting from Bill and his family to the company and it sort of became part of our culture," said Pamela Passman, corporate vice president and deputy general counsel.[29]

Microsoft also encourages art appreciation in its employees. The company's art collection has almost 5,000 pieces of contemporary art in every type of media installed at more than 180 Microsoft buildings. The art collection even has its own mission: to create an inspiring work environment that fosters creativity and innovation. Current employees and their guests have the opportunity to attend a monthly artist lecture series at the Redmond campus conference center.

Guyman is a founding member of the Microsoft Alumni Foundation and member of the Founder's Circle. There are over 85,000 Microsoft alumni worldwide. The purpose of the foundation is to "Catalyze the collective power of the Microsoft Alumni Family and leverage our resources to make a difference for others." Microsoft alumni have founded and supported more than 150 nonprofit organizations and social ventures working around the world.

The 2011 Forbes 400 list of the richest people in America includes three billionaires whose wealth came from Microsoft: Bill Gates ($59 billion), Steve Ballmer ($13.9 billion), and Paul Allen ($13.2 billion). Thousands of millionaires were created from within the company's employee ranks via the employee stock option plan. Options were first issued to employees in 1981.

"At Microsoft, there was a little application program you could use to follow your stock options value during the day," says Jeff Reifman, former group program manager. "It was part of the cult of the company. I remember this very clearly one day, sitting across from my hall mate, when we realized our stock was worth about $100,000, and laughing and saying how unreal that was." When Reifman left Microsoft in 1999, he left with $6 million in stock options.[30]

Timing is everything. Those who were unable to cash in prior to December 31, 1999, saw their option values dwindle. Microsoft's stock price fell 65 percent in the dot-com crash of 2000.

"While the exact number is not known, it is reasonable to assume that there were approximately 10,000 Microsoft millionaires created by the year 2000," says Richard S. Conway Jr., a Seattle economist whom Microsoft hired to study its impact on Washington State. "The wealth that has come to this area is staggering."[31]

"No one," said CFO John Connors, "could have foreseen the unnatural phenomenon that stock options became an incredible short-term lottery win. No one could have foreseen how well we would do. What was designed as a long-term program became a short-term payout program."[32] In 2003, the company discontinued its stock option benefit and switched to a stock purchase plan.

Many, many former Microsoft employees are now philanthropists and others have started new businesses that address social issues. Microsoft cultivated a social consciousness. And while anyone can be charitable, the business lessons and skills employees learned during their years at the company have helped their charities and ventures to succeed.

"The line that people draw between 'it's for-profit' or 'it's not for-profit' is not such a big one in my mind," says Charlotte. "I mean, we do important things that change the world and sometimes money is exchanged and sometimes you make money from doing some of those things. But it's not the main thing in my mind. I look at Bill Gates and what he did with Microsoft. He really had a vision to bring people technology. He didn't just do all that to be this rich guy. It's not what drives him."

A Purposeful Life

Charlotte retired from Microsoft in 1999 to spend more time with her children who were, at the time, ages 3, 8, and 11. Since then, she has participated in philanthropic and governance board activities. When asked how much of her current time is divided between family, board activities, and philanthropy, there was not a quick and simple answer. "It adds up to more than 100 percent," she replies.

Charlotte and her husband, Doug, live in Medina, Washington, a town on the eastern shore of Lake Washington, opposite Seattle and about seven miles west of the Redmond Microsoft home campus. Bill and Melinda Gates, as well as several other Microsoft employees and alums, also live in the town of about 3,000 inhabitants. Charlotte enjoys sailing, skiing, bicycling, hiking, yoga, pilates, and playing the piano.

Guyman joined the board of University of Washington Medicine in 2000 and served 10 years, chairing the finance and UWMC hospital committee and later served as Chairman of the Board. She currently is a member of the UW Medicine's Strategic Initiatives Committee.

"It is truly a great institution winning more medical research grants than any public institution and second only to Harvard Medical School," she says. Currently, there are 152 medical schools in the United States. The UW medical school serves five states: Washington, Wyoming, Alaska, Montana, and Idaho. She adds, "It's one of few medical schools that also directly manages clinical operations with four hospitals, including Seattle's Harborview, which is a level 1 trauma hospital, and primary care clinics as well as providing the faculty for the Seattle Cancer Care Alliance partnership and Children's Hospital in Seattle."

Since 2007, Charlotte has been a trustee for the humanitarian organization Save the Children, where she has served on the finance, audit, compensation, and executive committees. Save the Children focuses on two primary areas: enabling economic sufficiency for young people and families and providing education.

She is also a member of the advisory board of Soccer Saves, a division of Save the Children. Soccer Saves helps create healthy lifestyles for disadvantaged youth by partnering with global humanitarian organizations that work to provide HIV/AIDS education, nutrition, gender equity, and reproductive health using the power of soccer.

Charlotte is a compassionate idealist with the confidence of someone who knows without a doubt that she can accomplish whatever she sets her mind to. She says, "I have always really wanted to make a difference in the world. One wishes that they have made some life a bit better. I felt this way even when I was at HP and the Space Needle. I really believe that each person touches many people and many more than any of us have any idea that we could touch. It's a little bit like throwing a pebble into a glassy pond, and the ripples just go on for such a long, long way."

Visiting countries where Save the Children has programs provides Charlotte the opportunity to give personal attention to her philanthropic goals. Looking at statistics on paper does nothing to convey the reality of living conditions in parts of the world not found on typical tourist itineraries. In May 2011, she was in the African country Malawi, where village programs are reducing childhood mortality, reducing maternal childbirth deaths, educating pregnant women, and supplying community health products, such as rehydration kits.

In November 2010, Charlotte and her husband, Doug, visited some of Save the Children's humanitarian programs in the Gaza Strip and the West Bank. They visited schools and vocational training programs. Traveling from Israel to the Gaza Strip required them to pass through a series of gates followed by a long walk in an open metal cage (Figure 7.3).

"We had been coached to make no sudden movements so as not to risk getting shot at by the guards in the towers who watch the crossing," she recalls. "Although it is illegal and risky, people—including

Figure 7.3 Long Walking Tunnel Connection between Israel and the Gaza Strip
SOURCE: Charlotte Guyman.

children—were in the no-man's land called the *buffer zone* gathering stones from rubble for building materials. They loaded donkey carts and drove them back to building sites. We were told that occasionally someone is shot doing this work."

"The perseverance of the people of the West Bank and Gaza—and of our team and our partners and others who are helping to better this tumultuous part of our world—is truly inspiring."[33]

Experiences like this cause a wide range of emotion. There is surprise and amazement at how different conditions are from what we take for granted in our country. There is hopefulness in seeing how people make small improvements to their lives. And there is anxiety about the fragility of life when human actions can cause great harm or great support.

During a trip to Calcutta in 2004, Guyman recalled spending part of a day at Mother Teresa's Home for the Dying. There, she was captivated by one young woman suffering from AIDS and tuberculosis who was "just bones," as Guyman says. No one could break the woman's zombie-like stare.

The next day she went back with Melinda Gates. "Melinda walks in, pauses, and goes right over to this young woman," Guyman recalls. "She pulls up a chair, puts the woman's hand in her hands. The woman won't look at her. Then Melinda says, 'You have AIDS. It's not your fault.' She says it again, 'It's not your fault.' Tears stream down the woman's face, and she looks at Melinda." Guyman can't forget the connection. "Melinda sat with her. It seemed like forever."[34]

Even back in her home state, Save the Children is solving health and nutrition problems for children in poverty on the Quinault Indian reservation. Efforts are also being made in the rural Mississippi Delta region. "We hope to be in all 50 states by 2014," says Charlotte.

In the United States, Save the Children is utilizing state health metrics, supporting prekindergarten learning and emergency preparedness. Charlotte's optimism is inspiring. It's a quality that is valuable in all areas of life whether as an employee, board member, or wife and mother.

Charlotte Guyman is appreciative and thankful for her opportunities to contribute to the success of her business and personal relationships. Throughout her life, she actively sought out new knowledge and career challenges. Nothing happened to her passively because she was in the right place at the right time. She put herself there, in a position to make a positive impact and gain personal benefits in the process. She keeps a low profile and does not flaunt her achievements in business and philanthropy. A desire to learn more and make things better continues to drive her as she quietly gets things done.

She acknowledges that, "I've been unbelievably lucky just to have stuff I like to work on. So, you get out of it what you put into it. On the one hand, it's really great to be driven and ambitious, but on the other hand, it's great to really love what you do. So do what you love and love what you do. And that's more fun for you because you do a better job. I never forget that I am very, very lucky."

Chapter 8

Susan Decker— Desire to Inspire

S usan L. Decker is one of two female members of the 12-member Board of Directors of Berkshire Hathaway and is also the youngest director, at 49 years old. She's been a member of the board since May 2007, and is also a member of the Governance, Compensation, and Nominating Committee and the Audit Committee.

At the time of her recruitment to the board, Sue was president of Yahoo!. Berkshire Hathaway Vice-Chairman Charles Munger, Chairman of the The Washington Post Company Donald Graham, and David Gottesman, a fellow Berkshire board member, recommended her for board membership.

"She passed some pretty tough tests when she got A-pluses from all three," Warren Buffett, Chairman of Berkshire Hathaway recalls. He describes Decker as a "home run" for a Berkshire board seat. "We made the right choice. She's young, so she's going to be there a long time.

When we next have to find a director, I'd be very happy if we find someone like Sue."[1]

Buffett adds, "In selecting a new director, we were guided by our long-standing criteria, which are that board members be owner-oriented, business-savvy, interested and truly independent. That's exactly what we've found in Susan Decker. We are lucky to have her: She scores very high on our four criteria and additionally, at 44, is young—an attribute, as you may have noticed, that your chairman has long lacked. We will seek more young directors in the future, but never by slighting the four qualities that we insist upon."[2]

Serving with Sue on the Governance, Compensation, and Nominating Committee are Walter Scott, Jr., and David Gottesman. Their role is to assist the board by:

- Recommending corporate governance guidelines.
- Identifying, reviewing, and evaluating individuals qualified to become members of the board.
- Setting the compensation of the Chief Executive Officer and performing other compensation oversight.

Perhaps the easiest task in the above list is determining the CEO's salary. Warren Buffett has received a salary of $100,000 each year for the past 30 years and that, likely, will never change. Although Buffett is responsible for Berkshire Hathaway beating the S&P in 24 of the past 32 years,[3] he does not ask for a bonus and he receives no stock options. He also pays back the company for postage, personal phone calls, and use of staff for personal tasks, amounting to about $50,000 annually.

"Considering that far-more-mortal executives have been paid far more for delivering far less, the standards of comparisons would warrant a monumental increase," said Tom Russo, partner at Gardner Russo & Gardner in Lancaster, Pennsylvania, which holds Berkshire stock. "He could say, 'I'm worth a billion a year,' but that's not Buffett."[4]

While Warren Buffett's salary is lower than most CEOs, his net worth increases by millions each year. His wealth accumulates from dividend income and long-term capital gains from his ownership of Berkshire Hathaway. Controlling 33.3 percent of the voting Class A shares and 8.4 percent of the Class B shares, he "earned" about $62.8 million in 2010.[5]

In 2011, Sue also joined the board's Audit Committee with Charlotte Guyman, Donald Keough, and Thomas Murphy. The purpose of the Audit Committee is oversight of corporate financial statements, and legal and regulatory filings.

After a 23-year career in business, Decker is now a private investor and advisor. She was born November 17, 1962, and raised in Denver, Colorado. She obtained a Bachelor of Science degree in Computer Science and Economics from Tufts University in Medford, Massachusetts, in 1984.

Sue began working in the computer industry while still a student. "My summer jobs in college involved programming computers," says Sue. "One year I worked for a subsidiary of General Electric, specializing in the creation of a fourth-generation programming language. It helped pay for school, and I enjoyed the discipline. It also taught me early on that you can often add more value quickly and have a greater impact as a specialist than as a generalist."[6]

Decker entered Harvard Business School straightaway following graduation at a time when female students at HBS were a distinct minority. In 1975, just 11 percent of the class was composed of women. By 1995, the number had increased to 28 percent. The numbers continue to approach parity with women accounting for 39 percent of the incoming class at HBS in the fall of 2011.

Sue absorbed everything and recalls a valuable lesson that she learned there: "Richard Tedlow, an outstanding professor, taught me that the teacher is more important to the students than the course material. The same applies in business. Leadership is more about the passion, humor, and sense of purpose conveyed than with the task itself; I've used that knowledge again and again."[7]

Sue obtained a Master's in Business Administration from HBS in 1986. On September 30, 2010, Decker received the school's most important alumni honor, the Alumni Achievement Award. Presented annually since 1968, the award recognizes individuals who have contributed immeasurably to their professions, industries, and communities.

The HBS Alumni Achievement Award has been given to 165 individuals since 1968, 23 (14 percent) of whom are women. Other notable recipients of the award include Robert S. McNamara (1968), Berkshire Hathaway Director Thomas S. Murphy (1990), Meg Whitman (2008), James A. Lovell (2010), and Robert K. Kraft (2011).

Decker made the list of *Forbes* The 100 Most Powerful Women in 2008 at number 50. She was also listed at number two on *Fortune* magazine's Highest Paid Women list in 2006 at $25 million. In 2007, she slipped to number 19, with compensation of just over $10 million in income.

Wall Street Wonder

Sue went to work at Donaldson, Lufkin & Jenrette (DLJ) directly following graduation from Harvard and was there for 14 years. No longer in existence, DLJ was an investment bank founded by William H. Donaldson, Richard Jenrette, and Dan Lufkin in 1959. Headquartered in New York City, its businesses included securities underwriting; sales and trading; investment and merchant banking; financial advisory services; investment research; venture capital; correspondent brokerage services; online, interactive brokerage services; and asset management.

Sue started as an equity research analyst covering the newspaper industry. She provided coverage to institutional investors on more than 30 media, publishing, and advertising securities. She immersed herself in industry and company details and had a knack for distilling bits and pieces of information gathered through dozens of meetings and understanding the bigger picture, often better than the companies themselves. "[Executives] didn't always like her opinions of their company or industry, but they respected her," says Jill Greenthal, who worked with Decker at DLJ.[8]

In this capacity, she received recognition by *Institutional Investor* magazine as a top rated analyst and qualified for its All America Research Team for 10 consecutive years. "When I was an analyst, Warren Buffett was the big influence. And that's the way I look at businesses and think about value," says Susan.[9]

As an analyst at DLJ, Sue covered Yahoo! for a year and a half after it went public. In 1996 she reported that up to 75 percent of Yahoo!'s ad space was going unsold.[10] Her in-depth analysis of Yahoo! would prove to be beneficial when she left DLJ for a job in California with Yahoo! in June 2000.

In 1998, Sue became the Managing Director of Global Equity Research where she helped design and build DLJ's global equity research business, a $300 million operation. Among other things, she was responsible for building and staffing a non-U.S. research product based on global sector teams.

Her performance at DLJ was acknowledged and appreciated by her superiors. "She was one of the top 10 talents I've ever worked with," says Stu Robbins, Sue's former boss at DLJ.[11] Within two months of Sue's departure, DLJ announced that it was being bought by Credit Suisse. The firm employed 11,300 people at that time.

Bean Advisor

Decker received the designation of Chartered Financial Analyst in 1989 and served on the Financial Accounting Standards Advisory Council (FASAC) for a four-year term, from 2000 to 2004. The group, created in 1973, serves to advise the Financial Accounting Standards Board (FASB). It is the job of the FASB to establish the "generally accepted accounting principles," to which public financial reporting by U.S. corporations must conform and to keep those principles current.

As a member, Sue met quarterly with the Council at the FASB's offices in Norwalk, Connecticut, to provide input and participate as a sounding board of diverse voices to the seven full-time members of the FASB.

The approximately 35 members of FASAC are drawn from the ranks of CEOs, CFOs, senior partners of public accounting firms, executive directors of professional organizations, and senior members of the academic and analyst communities, all with an interest in the integrity of full and complete financial reporting and disclosure. The 2011 Advisory Council has 37 members, of which 11 (29.7 percent) are women.

During Sue's tenure at the FASAC, the Sarbanes-Oxley Act of 2002 was passed and became federal law. Arguably, it is the most controversial accounting law passed in the history of the FASB. The goal of the act was to make corporate accounting more transparent. In practice, some would say the law's requirements have had the opposite effect.

The Act also provided for funding of the FASB from public company fees. Previously, the FASB was a subsidiary of the Financial Accounting Foundation, a nonprofit organization. The FASB is now a quasi-governmental agency, whose accounting standards are law, carrying punishments in the millions of dollars and up to 20 years in prison. The enforcer of these laws, the Public Company Accounting Oversight Board (PCAOB), was created specifically by the Sarbanes-Oxley Act. This board also sets federal auditing standards.

Yahooville

Sue Decker was hired by Yahoo! of Sunnyvale, California, in June 2000 to replace the retiring Chief Financial Officer (CFO), Gary Valenzuela. Competition for the CFO job was fierce. When Valenzuela told Tim Koogle, then CEO, he planned to step down, Koogle was incredulous.

"He said, 'Don't you realize most CFOs would cut off their right arm to get this position?'" says Valenzuela, who was Yahoo!'s first CFO and played a role in naming his successor. "There was some concern given her lack of CFO experience," Valenzuela said of Decker, but she had strong knowledge of the company's business model. "I'd always kid her that her questions were the toughest and her financial model the most involved," says Valenzuela.[12]

Upon her appointment Koogle, said, "We are extremely pleased to welcome Sue to Yahoo!'s management team. She brings a broad base of financial experience and global expertise to Yahoo!, as well as a solid reputation among the financial community and a deep understanding of Yahoo!'s business. I am confident that Sue will drive our unrelenting focus on building value for Yahoo! shareholders and will maintain our track record of financial excellence and fiscal conservatism established under Gary's leadership."[13] Decker served as CFO for the next seven years.

Yahoo! got its start when two bored PhD candidates at Stanford, Jerry Yang and David Filo, hacked together a system that helped them win a fantasy basketball league. "The prospects of finishing and getting on with life were pretty grim," Yang recalls. "The real story is that we were bored with our PhDs and we did everything we could to avoid writing our thesis."[14]

Yahoo! had gone public just four years before Sue joined the company. In that short time, it grew from a start-up company to having a billion dollars in revenue in 2000. However, the company's success appeared to have already peaked and it was beginning to experience a difficult period.

The stock price of Yahoo! reached an all-time high of $120 per share on January 3, 2000. By June of that year, its value had dropped by half. Shortly after the 9/11 attacks, on September 26, 2001, Yahoo!'s stock hit its all-time low of $8.11. Today, it trades around $15 per share. In April 2001 and then again in November of that year, the company was forced to cut more than 800 jobs from its workforce. Decker said the cuts saved the company approximately $30 million annually.

As executive vice president and chief financial officer, Decker managed all aspects of the company's financial and administrative departments including finance, facilities, investor relations, human resources, and legal.

"I spend a lot of time setting the tone and the vision, finding the people, and rethinking the priorities and accountabilities," said Sue. "I sort of view my role, and the role of my peers, as steward of something that's going to be here in 20 years, we hope in 50 years. I hope that when I leave, we'll all have created a place for the next generation of leaders."[15]

Sue recognized early the problems that were coming to the dot-com industry. Others were in denial, but using her analytic skills, she based her opinions on facts. The numbers didn't lie. She calculated exactly how much of Yahoo!'s revenues came from other dot-coms, revealing her company's weakness. If an Internet company sells its services primarily to other Internet companies, it makes the service provider company extremely vulnerable to Internet industry fluctuations. As dot-com companies folded, Yahoo! lost a substantial source of revenue.

"For six quarters in a row, she provided that metric," says Mark Mahaney, a Citigroup Internet analyst. "She was there as the stock plummeted, providing a very material piece of information that the prior management team didn't give out. She was the first one to talk about the dot-com problem."[16]

Decker adapted her work process from one of an analyst to a strategic leader. "As an analyst, I tended to be very focused on value and free cash flow. When I came in as CFO, I was probably less focused on the value implications of day-to-day accounting," says Decker. "But I don't want to say accounting isn't critically important. I lean toward conservative choices. We've made choices that were dilutive to GAAP EPS [generally accepted accounting principles earnings per share], but were value-creating."

Sue had to be careful when communicating so that analysts would not overreact and hurt Yahoo!'s stock price. It isn't beneficial to anyone if they are too grim or too excited. Sue preferred to err on the conservative side when she communicated *guidance*, or future expectations, in earnings reports.

"On Wall Street, you need to think about what the market already expects about a particular company. Here we ask, what is the market saying right now? For example, back in the days when the Internet sector was melting down, we were pretty proactive about making sure the market knew how much of our revenue might be exposed. Finally, I see it as my role to have very transparent communications and to reduce volatility where we can."[17]

Sue was far more involved in strategic planning and decision-making, than the typical CFO. "She plays a critical strategic role in running [Yahoo!]," Mahaney said, adding that her role is "a stark night-and-day contrast" with that of counterparts at other large Internet companies.[18]

Double-Decker Job Title

In December 2006, the company restructured itself into three major business groups. While still CFO, Sue was appointed to head the Advertiser and Publisher Group. The other two major groups were the Audience Group and the Technology Group.

A Yahoo! press release addressed Sue's new role and the purpose of the new group: "Decker has been an important contributor to the company's business strategy, has set and managed all aspects of financial and administrative direction, and has recently overseen the Yahoo! Marketplaces business unit, which she will continue to oversee as part of the Advertiser and Publisher Group. This group will lead the transformation of how advertisers connect with their target customers across the Internet, with the goal of driving more value for more advertisers and publishers. The goal is to create a full-fledged global advertising network on and off Yahoo!."[19]

Terry Semel was Yahoo!'s CEO from 2001 to 2007. Semel wrote, "An expert on far more than financials, Sue has been a terrific contributor to our business strategy. She's one of the best executives around and the ideal person to fill this critical new role."[20]

"Sue Decker is absolutely brilliant," said Rob Solomon, a former Yahoo! senior vice president and now president of Groupon. "I think it's wonderful to have her brainpower thinking about more than finances."[21]

In her advertising leadership role, Sue sealed several high-profile deals, including an ad deal with eBay, and Yahoo!'s purchase of ad-technology company Right Media. She led the launch of Yahoo!'s newspaper consortium and new ad platforms.

In June 2007, Semel resigned as CEO, but he stayed on as a nonexecutive chairman until January 2008. Jerry Yang, cofounder of Yahoo!, took over the CEO job and Decker was appointed President (Figure 8.1).

Some were surprised by the move and others felt that it was a sign that Decker was on the road to becoming the company's CEO. "She was extremely well thought of as a CFO," said Christa Quarles, a former

Figure 8.1 Yahoo! President Sue Decker Addresses Employees, April 2008

SOURCE: "El Presidente," © 2008 Yodel Anecdotal, used under a Creative Commons Attribution 2.0 Generic license: http://creativecommons.org/licenses/by/2.0/legalcode.

analyst at investment bank Thomas Weisel Partners. "But it's one thing to manage the results and another thing to manage an organization."[22]

"She nicely explained Yahoo!'s business," said Charlene Li of Forrester Research. "Even when the news was bad, she explained why it was bad and what Yahoo! was doing about it," Li said. "The question is can she run a business? This is where she has to prove her chops."[23]

Despite these concerns, being a very active member of the Yahoo! executive team made her transition into the president's position go fairly smoothly. In the announcement, Semel called Decker "one of the most talented executives in the industry," adding, "Sue has played a broad and important role in driving our strategy over the years, and has shown even greater skills and leadership with the success she's had in taking on more operating responsibilities." He also credited her with being "an outstanding CFO" in her seven years holding that job.[24]

Colleagues described Decker as intense and hard-driving. As president, Sue helped guide Yahoo!'s business strategy and vision and was responsible for all of the global business operations, including sales, product marketing, product, and distribution across the three major customer groups of audience, advertisers, and publishers.

Gender Studies

In the years when Sue was an executive, there were very few women in her professional position. In 1995, *CFO* magazine conducted a survey that revealed there were 10 women holding the title of CFO in the Fortune 500. By 2007, the number had risen to 38 (7.6 percent). In many respects, the women who ascended to large-company CFO posts got there the same way that men do: half were promoted internally, and half were outside hires. But the numbers of women will likely increase since the number of female controllers, a key position in the CFO pipeline, increased from 16 percent to 21 percent during 2007,[25] and the trend continues.

Decker says she hasn't run into any glass ceilings that have hindered her aspirations. While working at Yahoo! she said, "I don't think of it in that way. I just come in each morning and think about how we're going to try to succeed."[26]

She further suggests that Yahoo! exemplifies the fact that the glass ceiling she was spared is a thing of the past. "I think that's more based on history, that there weren't as many women engaged in business. But I think all of the numbers are moving in the right direction. Certainly, at Yahoo!, we have a workforce that's about evenly split."[27] At the time of this statement in 2008, the company employed 32 percent women and 45 percent minorities. That was the most recent year Yahoo! was ranked in the Fortune Top 100 Best Companies to Work For. Yahoo! currently has approximately 13,700 full-time employees.

There's definitely room for improvement at Yahoo! in parity at the executive level of the company. Yahoo!'s board of directors currently has two female members out of nine and the management team has one woman in the group of eleven executives.

Heir Apparent

Negotiating partnerships, collaborations, and acquisitions occupied Sue's attention soon after she began as president. In January 2008, Yahoo! itself became the target of a takeover by Microsoft who made a $45 billion bid. Yahoo! rejected the bid as too low. Yang, Decker, and other Yahoo! board members were widely seen as resistant to selling to Microsoft, though shareholders were hoping to profit from the proposed deal.

On May 3, 2008, Decker and Bill Gates, Chairman of Microsoft, both attended the 2008 Berkshire Hathaway annual meeting in Omaha. Their two companies were still negotiating the acquisition, but on that very day company representatives met elsewhere to discuss a purchase price.

"I was in Omaha at the Berkshire Hathaway annual meeting, sitting next to Bill Gates, who's also on the board of Berkshire," says Sue. "I got there and reached over to whisper in his ear saying, 'Should I kiss you hello, or will people think we're getting married?' He said, 'Don't' and stood up stiffly to shake my hand. Thirty thousand people at the Qwest stadium were watching us on the floor."[28]

When no agreement could be reached, Microsoft pulled its bid for Yahoo!, sending Yahoo!'s shares tumbling lower. Decker was faced with answering difficult questions regarding the failed deal in subsequent public appearances (Figure 8.2).

Figure 8.2 Susan Decker during Q&A at Web 2.0 Conference, May 28, 2008
SOURCE: Renee Blodgett, Magic Sauce Photography.

On May 7 Decker said of the negotiations, "I don't know if I can tell you anything that's not been in the paper because our company leaks like a sieve . . . as does Microsoft and everyone else involved. It really just came down to price. Microsoft's timing was really good. It was at a low point, we were $19 per share. We hadn't gotten out to the Street to tell them what we were doing and the stock was reflecting a lack of understanding in that. There was a bid and an ask of about $4. I thought Ballmer would take it. They made a choice that that was too much."[29]

She also explained Yahoo!'s decision-making process and its positive impact on the company saying, "Our board is very focused on maximizing shareholder value. Price is the first variable that the board has to entertain. There's a whole series of issues that didn't get discussed because we didn't get through the price door. [The publicity] was a galvanizing force for our employees. There's a level of excitement in our employees in showing what we're going to do."[30]

Unhappy shareholder, Carl Icahn, who had built up a big stake in the company, announced his campaign to replace the Yahoo! board. The company faces shareholder lawsuits over its handling of Microsoft's acquisition offer that continue to this day.

A proposed search deal with Google that Decker drove as an alternative to a transaction with Microsoft was blocked by the U.S. Justice Department to preserve competition in Internet advertising.

On Nov. 17, 2008, Yahoo! announced they were commencing a search to replace CEO Jerry Yang. Decker was an internal candidate for the job. With Sue's increased responsibility and higher profile, many had been speculating for the previous two years, both verbally and in writing, that she would be the next CEO of Yahoo!. If others repeatedly say this about you, it's natural to eventually believe it yourself. Thus, when the CEO position did not come through for Sue, it was a surprise to everyone, and possibly to Decker herself.

Carol Bartz was hired as CEO and Decker announced her intention to resign. In Sue's farewell email to employees (about half of which is reproduced below), she announces her departure with grace.[31]

From: Sue Decker
Sent: Tuesday, January 13, 2009 2:32 PM
To: all-worldwide@yahoo-inc.com
Subject: The next chapter

Yahoos

After almost nine incredibly rewarding years with this terrific company, I have decided that it is time for me to pursue my next chapter, just as Yahoo! is charting the next phase of its path-breaking journey.

I have not made this decision lightly. I have been with this company for nearly a decade, and together we have been through a period of amazing change during this time. In particular, I want to thank the Board and especially Jerry, who has been my partner and friend from the very beginning, for affording me the opportunity to contribute to Yahoo!'s success.

The Yahoo! of today is a radically different company than the one I joined in 2000, as befits a major franchise in one of the world's fastest-evolving industries. Financially, the company has grown its revenue base from a little over $1 billion in 2000 to more than $7 billion, and has more than quadrupled its operating cash flow from around $400 million to close to $2 billion. Over that period, working together, we have reshaped one of the world's most vital Internet brands and transformed the company in ways the outside world is only just beginning to

(continued)

see. We did this by anticipating customer needs and evolving our business model ahead of dynamic changes to the online marketplace. While it is true that competition has never been fiercer, it is equally true that Yahoo! has moved decisively and creatively forward.

I am extremely grateful for the time I have had at Yahoo! This has been a profoundly enriching experience for me, both personally and professionally. As I set off on for my next mission, I want to extend my sincerest wishes to all of you for continued success.

Sue

It was not immediately clear where Decker intended to go next. With her industry experience and accumulated resources, she is a valuable consultant and knowledgeable private investor. She keeps very busy with her family and various board activities.

Boarding School

Decker's success and skills have drawn praise from other well-known business leaders, who have invited her to join their boards of directors. Steve Jobs named her to the board of Pixar Animation Studios, where she served from June 2004 to May 2006, until its sale to Disney.

In October 2004, Sue joined the board of Costco Wholesale Corporation, based in Seattle. She serves there with fellow board member Charlie Munger, Vice Chairman of Berkshire Hathaway. Sue serves on Costco's Audit Committee, where Munger is chair. As an independent director, Sue receives $30,000 annually in compensation from Costco and an additional $1,000 per board and committee meeting attended. Directors also receive 3,000 restricted stock units every October. Sue's 2010 total compensation from serving on the Costco board was $205,879.

Craig R. Barrett asked her to join the Intel Corporation board where she has served since November 2006. The company is located in

Santa Clara, California, and designs and builds components for computing devices. In addition to her director role at Intel, she is Chairman of the Audit Committee and member of the Finance Committee. Her total director compensation for the Intel board in 2009 was $265,600.

Sue has been a member of the board of directors of LegalZoom.com, Inc. since October 20, 2010. LegalZoom.com of Glendale, California, is a private company providing online legal documents.

The compensation Sue receives for serving on the Berkshire board of directors is miniscule by comparison with the other boards at $2,700 annually. Her time commitment is just as great, however, especially since she recently also joined Berkshire's Audit Committee (increasing her annual compensation by $4,000).

Sue's board memberships consume a fairly large portion of her time. The audit committee of a corporate board is the most intense and time-consuming committee assignment. Being a member of two audit committees and chair of another requires considerable attention.

While still at Yahoo!, the time she spent on board memberships did not sit well with shareholders. At a shareholders' meeting in August 2008, investor Eric Jackson, founder of Ironfire Capital, asked Decker, "How are these extra 187 hours a year best serving our company?" Decker replied that she had learned a lot from all these companies, citing how she had applied supply-chain knowledge from Costco to Yahoo![32]

Ivy Mentor

During the 2009 to 2010 school year, Decker served as Entrepreneur-in-Residence (EiR) at her alma mater, the Harvard Business School. In this role, she worked with students interested in entrepreneurship. She helped the Harvard faculty develop and deliver curriculum, was involved in case development activities, worked with students, and helped develop and deliver portions of the January 2010 Silicon Valley Immersion Experience Program. The program provides field studies for faculty and students who want to do something productive with the time off between first and second terms.[33]

"The EiR program seemed like a good fit, in that it's an advisory role that keeps me focused on an institution I care about while also

Table 8.1 Harvard Business School
Female Faculty

Professor Level	Percent Female
Full	18%
Associate	24%
Assistant	37%

allowing a bit more time flexibility than I could have when I was running Yahoo!'s operations," says Sue.[34]

Sue's greatest impact at HBS could be her presence as a role model and mentor to female students. Despite HBS's increase in the female student population, there is still an extreme shortage of female professors. Table 8.1 illustrates the percent of women at different faculty levels.

A lack of female mentors may be a reason that a lower proportion of women at HBS graduate with honors. The top 5 percent of each graduating class are known as "Baker Scholars." In 2010, only 20 percent of the Baker Scholars were women and in 2009, only 11 percent were women, though 35 percent of the total class was female.[35]

Webster's dictionary defines an entrepreneur as one who organizes, manages, and assumes the risks of a business or enterprise. Most often, we think of it as someone who starts a business from scratch. To my knowledge, Sue Decker has not done that. Assumption of the risk of company *ownership* is a key component of the definition. Decker does, however, have experience working at an innovative tech company and innovation is essential for any entrepreneur.

Sue's experience in the tech industry gives her valuable insight that she is able to share with budding entrepreneurs. "When it comes to technology, we all have the same core desires to do things smarter, faster, and simpler, and to stay connected to each other," she says. "Entrepreneurs who find better ways to address these needs will add value through new companies and services."[36]

Earlier, while still at Yahoo!, Decker addressed a group at Stanford University on the topic of entrepreneurship. She told them, "Focus on the customer as the guiding light in everything you do. It's difficult to do and it's super hard to change if you don't start out that way, but it has a lot of power in how successful you are."[37]

Pausing

Since leaving Yahoo! in 2009, Decker has taken time out from the corporate world to focus on what she feels matters most—her family and giving back to society. She is divorced with three children and makes her home in Marin County, California.

"In every musical composition, there are notes and pauses," she says, "and the pauses are as important as the notes in the production of the entire piece. Now that I'm in a pause, I realize how much I really wanted and needed it. If the right opportunity came along sometime in the next few years, and it worked with my life, I'd love to do it. But I'm not spending any time thinking about it now. The thing I feel so blessed to have is time to spend in the moment."[38]

It's doubtful that Sue's pause will be permanent. She is not lying low. She still participates in professional conferences and seminars, though her schedule of invited presentations and lectures has slowed. I saw her at the 2011 Fortune Most Powerful Women Summit where she was networking with other women and lunching with Warren Buffett.

"She would like being a CEO but there are other things in life she likes, too," said Warren Buffett. He added that he doesn't plan to hire her into Berkshire because he likes her work as a board member too much.[39]

Says Patty Sellers, an editor-at-large of *Fortune* magazine, "She's a finance ace and could get a job as a CFO at another Fortune 500 company. But she's already done the CFO job at Yahoo!. I know from talking with Decker that she prefers running a business, and probably a big one. No question she'll tap one of her fans, Warren Buffett, to help her get her career back on track. Especially in this job market, that's a fine fan to have."[40]

Sue enjoys physical activities. She's run a couple of marathons and likes to ski and hike. Being in good physical condition enabled her to work long hours in her previous jobs.

Decker is a Trustee of independent organization Save the Children and member of its Finance and Administration Committee. Save the Children serves impoverished, marginalized, and vulnerable children and families in more than 120 countries.

She also served as a board member of the Stanford Institute for Economic Policy Research from March 2005 to May 2007. The institute's goal is to improve long-term economic policy by connecting Stanford's researchers and scholars with the private sector.

Her colleagues and friends describe Sue as unpretentious and fun-loving. At a Clinton Global Initiative party in New York that she attended with Margie Fox, a college friend, Decker appeared surprised to be surrounded by so many celebrities. "She was unaware of how much of that world she is," said Fox, who runs a marketing firm, Maloney & Fox.[41]

Leading Lessons

On leadership, Decker says, "Great leaders don't limit the actions of their followers; rather than telling them to jump three feet to finish a task, they motivate them to see just how high they can jump by believing in them and giving them the freedom to perform."[42]

"One of the themes we talked about a lot at Yahoo! is fast failure. You want to create a culture that encourages taking risks and trying new things. If they don't work out or fail, which many of them will, you want to do that quickly, so you can regroup and go on to the next new idea or product or opportunity within the organization."

"I was at back-to-school night for my first-grader a little while ago. The teacher said that they're trying to encourage the kids not to fear failure by having a mistake jar in the classroom. Every time someone makes a mistake, they put a little note in the jar about it. And when it's full, everybody celebrates. I thought that was great."[43]

"People trust her," Lisa Nash, a former Yahoo! marketing executive, said of Decker. "They trust her when times are good, and they trust her when times are bad."[15] This trust combined with her financial and management skills could once again be put to use as a corporate executive in the future.

Susan Decker's career can be described in a single word: intense. The fast-paced New York investment banking business where she started was a calm and placid environment compared to the frenzy associated with the Silicon Valley tech industry. The issues of Internet advertising, branding, search engine services, and numerous other strategies and projects at Yahoo! required an unfocused approach to conducting business. Multitasking in one's kitchen is difficult enough, but making decisions for a multibillion-dollar company has a much larger impact on numerous lives.

Susan Decker already appears in the tech industry's history books, but we haven't seen the last of her yet. She is a shooting star, blazing with tech-world celebrity, not yet close to fizzling out.

Chapter 9

Katharine Graham—
Capital Publisher

Katharine "Kay" Graham was the first-ever female CEO of a Fortune 500 company and for many years, she was the only one. From 1963 to 1991, she served as publisher, and then chairman of the board of The Washington Post Company. The Washington Post Company is not a Berkshire Hathaway subsidiary, but Berkshire is the largest minority shareholder of the Post, and Kay Graham and Warren Buffett, Chairman of Berkshire Hathaway, had strong and lasting business and personal relationships.

There is at least one significant difference between Kay Graham (Figure 9.1), and the other CEOs profiled in this book: Warren Buffett was not Graham's boss, as he is with CEOs who run wholly owned subsidiary companies. Nonetheless, a short profile of Kay Graham is essential to this book as she was a strong female leading a major corporation affiliated with Berkshire Hathaway. The relationship between

Figure 9.1   Katharine Graham
SOURCE: Library of Congress, permission PD-USGOV, www.loc.gov/about/awardshonors/
livinglegends/images/Katharine_Graham.jpg.

Buffett and Graham was unique and she serves as a treasured role model for women in business.

Katharine Graham lived the first half of her life as a traditional daughter, wife, and mother to four children. But unforeseen circumstances changed everything and at age 46 she became, as *Fortune* magazine called her, "one of the greatest chief executives in American business history." The magazine ranked Graham as ninth in an impressive list of the 10 Greatest CEOs of All Time.[1] She was also on World Almanac's annual list of the 25 Most Influential Women for many years, beginning with the first year of the list's inception in 1976. In 1993, she was named to *Fortune*'s National Business Hall of Fame.

The *Washington Post* newspaper was founded in 1877 and is owned by The Washington Post Company. The company owns more than just the newspaper of the same name. The Post Company also owns Kaplan (education), Cable One (cable/Internet provider), the Slate Group (online publishing), and several other newspapers and television stations. The company owned *Newsweek* magazine for nearly 50 years, but sold it in 2010 to Sidney Harman. Harman, 92 years old at the time of the sale, was founder of Harman International, maker of audio equipment. He died eight months later.

Figure 9.2 Katharine Graham Receiving the Pulitzer Prize for Her Memoir
SOURCE: Eileen Barroso/Columbia University.

Berkshire Hathaway purchased shares of The Washington Post Company between 1973 and 2004, owning about 25 percent of the Class B shares, resulting in approximately 18 percent ownership of the company. Katharine Graham's heirs own the Class A shares. The company's 2010 revenues were $4.7 billion and it has approximately 20,000 employees.

There are several very good biographies of Katharine Graham, and her own autobiography, *Personal History*, won a Pulitzer Prize in 1998 (Figure 9.2). These resources provide in-depth personal accounts of the amazing life of Kay Graham.

Family Business

Katharine was born on June 16, 1917, into the wealthy family of Eugene and Agnes Meyer. She was the fourth of five children. Her father was ambitious and very strict. Her mother was critical of Katharine and self-absorbed. A nanny raised the children. In fact, four months after Katharine's birth, Agnes moved to Washington, D.C., to join Eugene, who had been living there since earlier in the year, while the children stayed with a nanny in a Fifth Avenue apartment in Manhattan. The family was finally reunited in a mansion in Washington, D.C., four years later.

Eugene bought the *Washington Post* newspaper in a bankruptcy auction in 1933, held on the steps of the run-down newspaper office building, for the price of $825,000. At the time, D.C. had five newspapers. Upon Katharine's graduation from the University of Chicago in 1938, her father encouraged her to pursue newspaper reporting and she worked for the *San Francisco News* as a reporter for a year. She joined the staff of the *Post* in 1939, where she edited the letters to the editor. None of Katharine's siblings were interested in journalism.

Kay married Philip Graham, a Harvard Law School graduate, in 1940 and didn't work again until 1947, when she started writing a column for the paper called "The Magazine Rack." The Grahams had four children between 1943 and 1952: Elizabeth (or "Lally"), Donald, William, and Stephen.

Eugene Meyer didn't believe that a woman should run the paper and his only son was a physician, so he invited his son-in-law Philip Graham to join the *Post*. After serving in the military, Philip began as associate publisher in January 1946 and became publisher six months later. In 1948, Eugene Meyer sold 70 percent of the Class A shares of voting stock to Philip and 30 percent to Katharine.

Kay's marriage was difficult, but perhaps more so for outside observers than for herself. Philip Graham was a charming, brilliant man, but criticized and demeaned Kay both privately and publicly. The pain of her husband's insults was compounded by the burden of his manic-depressive disorder, which began in 1957, and his eventual descent into insanity. There were many public embarrassments, most notably an incident at the 1963 annual meeting of newspaper owners and publishers where Philip took the podium, called the audience names, and stripped off his clothes.

Kay had intelligence and ambition, but lived in a time and in a stratum of society that demanded that she be a forgiving, dutiful wife and mother. She described herself as a "doormat wife." Philip left Kay for another woman, asked for a divorce, and told her he was taking the newspaper business with him. She was willing to proceed with a divorce (though it never happened), but refused to let go of her family's company.

Their disagreements became moot when, in late 1963, Philip Graham committed suicide with a .28-gauge shotgun while staying with Kay for a weekend at their country home, a 350-acre Virginia cattle farm called Glen Welby. He had been hospitalized for psychiatric care, but convinced his doctors and his wife that he was well enough to spend the weekend away. Katharine realized later that he had other intentions.

"He deceived me into thinking that he was better than he was," says Katharine. "He went down there to kill himself."[2] Phil Graham's *New York Times* obituary included the following charming froth: "He played golf in the 90s, appeared regularly on the dinner circuit, took his vermouth on the rocks, and avoided mass receptions. He was known as a staunch member of Athletics Anonymous, an informal group dedicated to avoiding strenuous exercise."[3]

Philip was buried in Oak Hill Cemetery, directly across the street from the Graham's Georgetown home. The grave, near the fence, was visible from Katharine's bedroom window.

One month later, Kay assumed the position of President and Publisher of the *Post*. "I wanted to go to work and I was determined to keep the paper," she says. "I viewed it as a holding place until my son grew up. I didn't view myself as running anything. I did take Phil's title, but I didn't think I had that power, that I would run anything."[4]

She also said, "Selling what I had seen my father and my husband create with such agony and devotion was unthinkable."[5] Kay decided that she needed to learn more about the business of publishing a newspaper now that she had controlling ownership of the company. She performed many tasks, including answering phones in the circulation, complaint, and classified advertising departments.

"You sort of are formed by what you are engaged in," said Kay. "And so just gradually you get some confidence, and what that means is not that you're going to be something else, but it means you can forget yourself and become engaged in what you are doing."[6] "I didn't understand the enormity of what I had to learn," she says, "and it was very painful for the people around me."[7]

Graham could have chosen to be a passive business owner, letting others do the actual tasks of running the paper. But by taking an active role in the company, she found the strength within herself to lead. She knew her limitations and she wisely hired Benjamin Bradlee to be Executive Editor of the paper. "What I essentially did," she said, "was to put one foot in front of the other, shut my eyes, and step off the ledge. The surprise was that I landed on my feet."[8]

Graham created a well-defined role for herself. She did not write. She did not tell others what to write. And, she stated, "I never killed a story in my life."[9] Famed *Post* reporter, Bob Woodward says, "It is true that Katharine Graham kept her hands off the news reporting and editing. But as important, she kept her mind on it—ferociously. At times, she was a secret source passing on a tip from her celebrated off-the-record dinners. I always protected her but joked with her and others that we observed the Graham rule—off-the-record meant it would not be used unless it was really good."[10]

Donald Graham, Kay's oldest son, joined the *Post* in 1970, after serving in Vietnam with the First Air Cavalry and working for 15 months as a D.C. policeman. He worked in several different departments: news, sports, and editing—even as a *Post* truck driver—before joining the business side of the company.

Of Donald's decision to join the police force, Kay said it was a "darn good and original idea. He decided it would make him aware of people's lives in a way he'd never be as a reporter, even a police reporter."[11]

In 1979, Kay stepped down as publisher of the *Post*, but remained as chair of the board and CEO of The Washington Post Company until she stepped down as CEO in 1991 and retired as chairwoman at age 76 in 1993. Donald assumed the positions of publisher, CEO, and chair in succession, following his mother. Donald is the current CEO and chairman of The Washington Post Company.

The Dawn of Female Leadership

Agnes Meyer was still alive when Katharine took over the Post Company and seems to have been proud of her daughter. In her own time, Agnes spent more time as an activist for women's rights than did

Katharine. She supported the women's suffrage movement that won the right for women to vote in the United States in 1920, and during World War II she criticized the government for failing to provide childcare to working women. However, she later wrote that, "the only vocation for a woman is motherhood."[12] Agnes also addressed the problems confronting veterans and migrant workers, education reform, and racial discrimination. She died of cancer at the age of 83 in 1970.

The second wave of the feminist movement, also known as the women's liberation movement, began in the early 1960s and fought for reproductive rights, equal pay, support for maternity leave, and the elimination of domestic violence and sexual harassment.

It took some years for Kay to gain confidence in herself. She did not believe herself capable of running the company and was truly fearful of causing harm to the business through her actions. "I grew up in a society in which most women considered themselves unequal citizens and were considered unequal citizens," Graham said, "and I had grown up with some pretty dominant individuals and I didn't consider myself equal to them and I wasn't. And so, if you start there, it was an agony."[13]

Kay's method of adapting to the world of business—a man's world—was to behave more like a man. But some of her feminine personality characteristics would prove to be beneficial. Many of her colleagues felt that she was a very good listener, a trait that serves leaders well. She often collected opinions of others when confronted with the need to make a decision. While this was frustrating to those waiting for an answer, it frequently resulted in a well-researched plan of action.

Commenting on his mother's autobiography, Donald had one suggestion: "I think that I would go back and try to expand on what it was like to be a woman CEO of a corporation in 1963, because it colored everything."[14]

Being a female CEO of a corporation in 1963 was extremely rare and there were none in the country's largest companies. Kay was the only female CEO of a company large enough to be included in the Fortune 500. Following the brief surge of female employment during World War II, married working women were not common in the United States in the 1950s and 1960s. Secretary, teacher, and nurse were among the rare professions pursued by women in those decades. But the year 1963 was a turning point for professional women in several ways.

The Equal Pay Act of 1963 was a result of recommendations from the President's Commission on the Status of Women, initiated by President John F. Kennedy in 1961 and chaired by Eleanor Roosevelt. Harvard first began accepting women into its graduate school of business in 1963.

The book *The Feminine Mystique* by Betty Friedan was published in 1963. This book objected to the mainstream role of women in the home, stating that they were wasting their talent and potential.

1963 was the year that Mary Kay Ash, at age 44, was passed over for a promotion while working for Stanley Home Products. The promotion was given to a man she had trained. She quit her job and wrote a book to assist women in business. That book became the business plan for her store, Mary Kay Cosmetics, which opened later that same year.

There were no high-ranking women in business to serve as role models and Katharine Graham had no leadership aspirations. "I adopted the assumption of many of my generation that women were intellectually inferior to men, that we were not capable of governing, leading, managing anything but our homes and our children," said Graham.[15]

Says Warren Buffett, "She had been taught all her life—wrongly—that only men possessed a managerial gene. But she also understood completely—and correctly—that independent and first-class journalistic institutions are key to creating and preserving a great society. When the obligation to manage such an institution was thrust upon her by her husband's death, she felt she had no choice but to march forward—however loudly her knees might be knocking."[16]

Allen H. Neuharth, founder of *USA Today*, remembers that when Graham began attending meetings of the American Newspaper Publishers Association, "she was looked on with distaste by most of the good old boys, but she was a tough competitor and an unhappy loser and had ways of expressing herself that the guys understood."[17]

There was obvious inequality in gender status at *Newsweek* magazine, owned by the Post Company, and Kay attempted to set things right. She complained at the *Post* in the late 1960s that she "couldn't get those goddamned people at *Newsweek* to hire some women."[18]

At a *Newsweek* sales meeting once, Graham wanted to know why they didn't have more women in the meeting. She was told by a male executive that there was enough trouble without adding more women.

The only woman there, Graham reached for an ashtray and threw it across the room. She cried, "Sexist!" (and other words) as the ashtray crashed. After that incident, more women came to the sales meetings.[19]

"As a former *Newsweek* mail girl who was told when I applied for a job that women did not become writers at the magazine, I was even more fascinated by Katharine Graham's recounting of her own gradual coming to terms with feminism," said Nora Ephron. "Two factors she cites as crucial: her dawning sense of condescension from male colleagues (many of them her employees) and her long talks with Gloria Steinem."[20]

Kay's attempts to improve conditions at *Newsweek* didn't fix the problem. The magazine's female employees filed a federal sex discrimination complaint in 1970. The suit was settled, but another complaint was filed two years later charging that *Newsweek* editors had not kept their promises. This time, they won specific commitments from management. A similar suit was filed and settled at the *Post* in 1980.

When asked if she faced special problems due to her gender, Graham replied, "I think more than I realized. I thought all my troubles were newness, the fact I had everything to learn. I didn't see that some of it might have been less difficult if I had been a man."[21]

Kay Graham was an unintentional feminist. She did not set out to blaze a trail for women journalists and publishers, but that's just what she did. When she was honored by *Ms.* magazine, Graham told them that she preferred Mrs. to Ms. and she disliked being called the most powerful woman in America. Graham had earlier given $20,000 in seed money to help the magazine get started.

During her tenure, Graham greatly increased the number of women working at the *Post*. Robert Kaiser, *Post* staff writer said, "The women who worked for her had special feelings about Mrs. Graham. Partly this was because she let them see her as both the grand and imposing boss and as a woman, and would also take them seriously."[22]

While hiring practices gradually changed, a glass ceiling preventing women from entering executive positions was still firmly in place above their heads. The rare women who broke through were instrumental in creating parity among employees. But it would take several more decades for women to mentor other women to enter the C-suite and join boards of directors. Mark Edmiston, former president of *Newsweek* said of Graham, "She was pressured to put a woman on the board—highest-ranking woman CEO in the world, and for years she never had a woman on the board."[23]

The Washington Post Company board of directors currently has 11 members, of which two (18 percent) are female. Of those two directors, Katharine Weymouth is Kay's granddaughter (and Lally's daughter). The other female director is Anne Mulcahy, retired CEO of Xerox Corporation. Katharine Weymouth was named publisher of the *Post* in 2008, and Lally Graham Weymouth is a journalist and senior associate editor of the *Post*.

Kay's personal and work lives were thickly intertwined from 1963 onward. She worked during the day and entertained in her home or attended social events in the evening and on weekends. Her social acquaintances were often the day's newsmakers.

Kay realized that with her corporate responsibilities she had to make personal sacrifices. When she took over the paper, her two youngest sons were 10 and 14 and she was no longer able to devote herself entirely to her family. Lally and Donald were already away at college. She wrote that Bill and Steve "lost both parents at once."[24] Still, she attended the boy's sports matches and took them along to events when she was able.

Kay did not pressure her children to join the *Post*, but she would not bar them from it either. Her only requirement was that they earn their spot. As she said when asked about having her children work for the *Post*, "there is probably room for one or two, if they are totally professional and prove themselves somewhere else. I just don't think you can make your child the movie reviewer because you like him. That louses up people's advancement. I feel very strongly that they have their own dough, that there's no need for them to do this unless they're obsessed. And able. And serious. If they are, then I think that families in newspapers can be constructive. On the other hand if they can't pull their weight it's a bad show. It kills the newspaper."[25]

Rather than do it all, Kay chose to focus her energy and attention on running the business. As a single mother of three children, Katharine Weymouth now faces her own challenges of balancing her career and family. Said Graham, "I very much worry about women these days who are trying to do it all."[26]

Following your passion is always a good idea. If your work and passion are the same thing, you will live a purposeful, rewarding life. Katharine loved the newspaper business. As she said, "To me, involvement with news is absolutely inebriating. It's what makes my life exciting."[27]

Challenges

Running a newspaper is a responsibility laden with risk, controversy, and challenges. In pursuing the best reporting, risks must be tolerated and controversy accepted as a natural aspect of practice. Not everyone will be pleased with all the content printed, nor will any reader support a particular newspaper all the time. The goal is to seek the truth and print it. The public is entitled to accurate, timely information.

Says Donald Graham, "Over the years, the company's leaders—my predecessors—have taken great risks to ensure that citizens have unfettered access to the news. The decision by my mother, Katharine Graham, to publish the Pentagon Papers and her support of the *Post*'s Watergate reporting were the two most famous examples."[28]

It was a controversial time for the *Post* in June 1971, when it began publishing excerpts from the Pentagon Papers. The papers were a history of the U.S. Department of Defense's political and military involvement in Vietnam since the end of World War II. The government fought to forbid publication of the Pentagon Papers by both the *Post* and the *New York Times*, saying that the papers held secret information. The Supreme Court ruled in favor of the newspapers.

The following year, the *Post* broke the Watergate story, earning a Pulitzer Prize for the paper. It began on June 17, 1972, when five men were caught breaking into the Democratic National Committee headquarters at the Watergate Hotel. *Post* managing editor Howard Simon called Kay Graham at home and said, "You will not believe what is going on."[29]

At one point during the investigation, President Nixon's reelection committee subpoenaed some of the *Post*'s employees, including Bob Woodward and Carl Bernstein, to try to ascertain how they were getting their information. Says Bernstein, "I went to [Ben] Bradlee and I said, 'I just got a call from the guard downstairs that there's a subpoena with a piece of paper with my name on it.' And he said, 'Look, go see a movie while we figure out what to do.' I went to see a movie, in fact, the movie I saw was *Deep Throat*. I came back to the office. Our notes were transferred to the custody of Katharine Graham. Therefore, if anybody was going to go to jail, she was going to go, also.

"Bradlee said, 'Wouldn't that be something? Every photographer in town would be down at the courthouse to look at our girl going off to the slam.' And Mrs. Graham was ready to go to jail because she understood the principle. I accepted the subpoena, and they backed off. They didn't want to take on Katharine Graham."[30]

Graham said that in her most difficult moments during the Watergate investigation and the recriminations, she drew on something her father had told her. "When you think you're right," he had said, "you must be willing to stand alone."[31]

Bob Woodward recalls the early days of investigative reporting during the Watergate incident when he called former Attorney General John Mitchell to get his response to allegations of wrongdoing: "This was a time when you could call the attorney general at home and you could get him. And he felt so confident he could say, 'Katie Graham's gonna get her tit caught in a ringer.' Imagine Eric Holder saying that. They would never let him speak that freely, unsupervised, unattended, to a reporter."[32]

Following Watergate, Kay was the recipient of many awards, as well as a visit from Robert Redford, who wanted to make a movie from Woodward and Bernstein's book about the experience. Although the producers of *All the President's Men* hired an actress to portray Katharine Graham, her scenes were cut and not included in the film.

The whole affair was a bit too much attention on her and her paper for Kay to handle. She urged the press to not insert themselves into the news. At a breakfast given in her honor in 1974 she said, "The press as a chronicler of events, not a participant, is essential to the functioning of a democratic society. I hope and pray all of us will be able to lower our profiles and mirror society and all its complexities for our readers and viewers."[33]

Graham understood the proper role of the press. Neutral reporting leaves interpretation of the news with the reader. And newspapers cannot set out with an agenda in mind. "It's not our responsibility," she said, "to reform the world. I really feel very strongly that the press has no damn business doing good or doing evil. We're here to bring information. We're not, goddamn it, do-gooders."[34]

She tried to downplay her role and did not accept any credit for the Watergate story, but she backed up what her reporters had discovered. "I don't mean to be corny or coy," Kay said, "but there was nothing really heroic about the whole thing. I mean my only decision was whether to back my editorial staff and my reporters. Well, I have great faith in their judgment and ability. I knew we had to go ahead with the story. That's really what our business is all about. Heroism is when you have a choice. As the story unfolded I knew we were on sound ground. You can't shut your eyes to it. Besides, we had the full backing of the corporate group. They felt as I do that excellence on the news side and profits go hand-in-hand. It was that simple. But well, sure, I had sleepless nights."[35]

Another challenge arose when Kay took on the worker's unions during a pressmen strike in 1975. The fight became violent when members of the union vandalized the pressroom, tried to set it on fire, and beat up a night foreman. Katharine was burned in effigy. The vice president of the union, Charles Davis, carried a sign reading, "Phil shot the wrong Graham."[36]

Kay worked in the trenches to ensure that the paper got out during the strike, which lasted 139 days. The union rejected the *Post*'s final offer and the paper hired replacement workers, including—for the first time—women and minorities.

Of Kay's handling of the strike, Warren Buffett says, "During that period I watched Kay suffer, tormented by the thought that she was destroying what her family had spent more than forty years building. Some of her most trusted advisers urged her to cave. But with her knees knocking louder than ever before, she persevered."[37]

Former *Post* writers J. Y. Smith and Noel Epstein said, "As a manager, her strengths were intelligence, toughness, a willingness to listen and learn, and an ability to judge character. She gave her executives great autonomy, but it was always clear that she was in charge. Mrs. Graham also insisted that she never be surprised by what she read in the paper, although she believed in leaving most journalistic decisions to her editors."[38]

"Here is what is so great about the institution of the *Washington Post*," says Bob Woodward. "I say it about Politico. I say it about most news organizations in America. They know what their job is. When it gets hard, they actually do their best."[39]

Kay thrived on the ever-present crises and controversial political issues that are a part of life when living in the nation's capital. She said, "In the very first entry in my mother's diary, back in 1917, she wrote 'The march of events has been much too rapid.' That simple sentence holds true for the entirety of my life as well. I believe that the fast pace was exacerbated by living in Washington, and by all the drama that that involved."[40] When times got tough, Kay found the strength to survive. These challenges are what transformed Graham from a timid newspaper heiress into a self-confident leader.

Kay and Warren

Warren Buffett enjoys saying that he first became associated with the *Washington Post* when he was a newspaper delivery boy in Washington, D.C., at age 13. His father was then a member of Congress. But it would be 1971 before he would personally meet Katharine Graham.

Charles Peters, founding editor of the magazine, the *Washington Monthly*, made the introduction of Warren Buffett, an investor in Peters's magazine, to Graham. Buffett asked for the introduction so that he could talk to Graham about whether she would like to buy the *New Yorker* magazine, another publication in which Buffett owned stock.

"Warren asked me to introduce him to Kay Graham, which I did," says Peters. "And it turned out to be a very good thing for both of them. He became her principal financial advisor and the leading minority holder of *Washington Post* stock. They have made each other a lot richer than either was before they met. I should have asked for 10 percent."[41]

Graham was not interested in buying the *New Yorker*, but after they met, Buffett was impressed with Kay and became interested in The Washington Post Company. Enticingly, the company had decided to issue stock shares to the public for the first time in June 1971. Class B common stock was issued for the price of $26 per share ($6.50 per share when adjusted for a subsequent 4-for-1 split).

The B share class is now valued at just over $2.5 billion. They traded near $1,000 each in 2004, but have since slipped back to about $350 per share today. The Grahams and the Sulzbergers, who have owned the *New York Times* since 1896, are the only two remaining private families who still control major media companies in the United States.

"Warren Buffett later told me he didn't think we really had to go public but was glad we had," said Graham. "In fact, I was glad we had, too, although I still dislike some of the responsibilities being public entails."[42]

In the years 1973 and 1974, Berkshire Hathaway purchased $10.6 million worth of shares in The Washington Post Company. The shares were bought at a time when the markets were down over several months.

Says Charlie Munger, Berkshire Hathaway vice chairman, "We bought in at about 20 percent of the value to a private owner. So we bought it on a Ben Graham–style basis at one-fifth of obvious value and, in addition, we faced a situation where you had both the top hand in a game that was clearly going to end up with one winner and a management with a lot of integrity and intelligence. That one was a real dream. They're very high-class people—the Katharine Graham family. That's why it was a dream—an absolute, damn dream."[43]

Kay said, "Warren bought into the company without my knowing him. He wrote me a letter when he owned 5 percent of the company and he said, 'Dear Mrs. Graham. I just bought 5 percent of your company and I mean you no harm. I think it's a great company. I know it's Graham owned and Graham run and that's fine with me.' So, I asked to meet him. And I thought 'Whoa this guy's really terrific.'"[44]

When Buffett came to visit the *Post* in person for the first time, he again wanted to assure Kay that he did not wish to take over the paper. After lunch, they spent an hour together, during which he offered to stop buying Post stock because he perceived it was worrying Graham. Says Kay, "He described his bite of the company as *baby teeth*, but added, 'If they look like wolf's fangs, I'll take them out.' I agreed I would like that."[45]

"I invited him on the board," says Graham. "People thought he was manipulating me, trying to run the company through me. Actually, I was just asking for advice because I realized how brilliant he was.

He taught me so much about business. He realized how ignorant I was. He used to come to our board meetings with 20 annual reports from different businesses and take me through these annual reports. It was like going to business school."[46]

Buffett was chair of the finance committee of the board of directors. He left the board in 2011, after nearly 26 years of service. (He joined the board in 1974, but left from 1986 to 1996). Buffett said that he was leaving the Washington Post board because of other travel commitments linked to Berkshire Hathaway acquisitions abroad.

"Warren was sending me a constant flow of helpful memos with advice, and occasionally alerting me to problems of which I was unaware," says Graham. "In the beginning I didn't realize how fortunate I was to have this mentor, but I grew very dependent on his advice, and liked it. In effect, he was beginning to teach me the fundamentals of thinking about business, for which I had so longed."[47]

Donald Graham said, "No important decision at The Post Company has been taken for all those years without asking for Warren's input. What he nudged us into is easily described: the purchase of what is now Cable One, the Houston and San Antonio TV acquisitions, our active stock repurchasing, the selection of our pension advisers."

"What he kept us out of was still more important: Kay Graham described in *Personal History* the advice Warren gave when she was eager to buy newspapers and TV stations. She bid, but followed Warren's ideas of value and didn't bid crazy prices. Likewise, he talked me out of a couple of ill-conceived acquisition ideas that would have created serious problems."[48]

"Warren is incomparable. For 37 years, we've been privileged to have the single best adviser a corporation could have had in those years. He says he'll still be willing to advise us as before; there will be a lot more D.C.-to-Omaha phone calls and plane travel coming up."[49]

Buffett served as Kay's financial advisor and provided valuable guidance and assistance in running the *Post*. Learning business fundamentals was a boost to Kay's confidence. While he was teaching her about business, she improved his eating habits and attire.

They also became very good friends very quickly. In June 1974, she visited Buffett and his family at their Laguna, California, home. Afterward, she wrote him a letter saying, ". . . your intensity, concentration and drive almost scare me, but are luckily and happily relieved by those other things you also possess—decency, gaiety, enjoyment and warmth."[50]

Early in their friendship, Buffett wrote a letter to Graham saying, "When you can obtain total participation by talented and intellectually diverse people without diluting authority—and at the same time enjoy yourself immensely—you are achieving something." With the note he sent a box of See's candy.[51]

Kay said, "I've had two great professors. One is Warren Buffett, and the other is experience."[52] Buffett advised Graham in 1985 on a significant business strategy when her company acquired 53 cable television systems owned by Capital Cities Communications for $350 million. The large deal paid off in future years as the cable stations showed profits when noncable stations were in decline.

Now, the value of Berkshire's Post Company stock—including what was purchased after 1984—is at $600 million. Still, that is less than 1 percent of all of Berkshire's common stock investments, valued at over $64 billion. Table 9.1 shows the five largest Berkshire Hathaway stock holdings in December 2011. Other large holdings include Bank of America ($5 billion), Kraft Foods ($3.3 billion), Johnson & Johnson ($2.4 billion), Wal-Mart ($2.2 billion), and ConocoPhillips ($2 billion).

Buffett summarized the financial impact of Berkshire's investment in the *Post* when he wrote to Katharine Graham in 1984: "Berkshire Hathaway bought its shares in the *Washington Post* in the spring and summer of 1973. The cost of these shares was $10.6 million, and the present market value is about $140 million. . . . If we had spent this same $10.6 million at the same time in the shares of . . . other (media

Table 9.1 Berkshire Hathaway's Five Largest Common Stock Holdings (December 2011)

Company	Percentage of Company Owned	Market Value
Coca-Cola	8.8	13.5 billion
IBM	5.4	12.4 billion
Wells Fargo	6.8	9.7 billion
American Express	13.0	7.4 billion
Procter & Gamble	2.8	5.0 billion

companies) . . . we now would have either $50 million worth of Dow Jones, $30 million worth of Gannett, $75 million worth of Knight-Ridder, $60 million worth of the *New York Times*, or $40 million of *Times Mirror*. So, instead of thanks a million, make it thanks anywhere from $65 to $110 million."[53]

Katharine Graham died at age 84 in July 2001 while attending the Allen & Company business conference in Sun Valley, Idaho. Allen & Company is a boutique investment bank in the media and entertainment sector. The annual conference takes place for one week each July. Graham attended every year. Donald Keough, a member of the Berkshire Hathaway board of directors, is chairman of Allen & Company and Warren Buffett and his family also attend the conference each year.

Kay Graham was found on the floor of her condo unconscious, but it is unknown whether she fell and hit her head, or if she had a stroke. She was airlifted to Boise, but never regained consciousness and died three days later. Warren Buffett served as an usher at her funeral, held at Washington National Cathedral.

Fortunately, Kay was spared witnessing her hometown being attacked two months after her death. She loved Washington, D.C., and was planning to publish an anthology of stories about the city. At the time of her death, the book was structured, but unfinished. Her assistant, Evelyn Small, and editor Robert Gottlieb pieced it together and published *Katharine Graham's Washington* in 2002.

In the book's foreword, Katharine states, "For more than eight decades, Washington has been my hometown. My whole orientation is toward this place. It is a city that offers me more people—more different *kinds* of people—than I could otherwise possibly have come to know in a lifetime. It is a city whose geography is embedded in my mind. It is a city whose industry—first and foremost politics, both local and national—got into my blood early and stayed there. In short, in Washington, I've always found people to see, places to go, things to do."[54]

Legacy

The *Post* newspaper continues to be controlled and led by the Graham family. Some shareholders wouldn't miss it, though. Therein lies one of the most common negative aspects of taking a family business public—a responsibility to the shareholder.

"The reason we own the stock isn't because of its newspaper business, it's in spite of it," says Charles de Vaulx at International Value Advisers, whose 7.4 percent stake in the company is the second-largest external holding after Berkshire Hathaway's. "If they ever reach the conclusion that one of their businesses, for instance, the newspaper business, is hopeless, I wish they'll be willing to cut the cord and not feel any emotional attachment."[55]

The Graham family's personal ties to the newspaper are strong, however. "The Graham family is a newspaper family, and I cannot envision any future scenario that would involve them spinning off the *Washington Post*," said industry analyst John Morton.[56]

Buffett acknowledges that, "the newspaper business will be tougher and tougher and tougher, and it is already plenty tough." While he said that the newspaper was "the centerpiece of the Post Company, that doesn't mean that it will earn the most money."[57]

Buffett has been pessimistic about the state of the newspaper industry for some time. Although Berkshire Hathaway purchased the *Omaha World Herald* newspaper in December 2011, it was seen as a sentimental purchase unaligned with Berkshire's typical purchase criteria.

"Fundamentals are definitely eroding in the newspaper industry," said Buffett. "When Charlie and I were young, the newspaper business was as easy a way to make huge returns as existed in America. As one not-too-bright publisher famously said, 'I owe my fortune to two great American institutions: monopoly and nepotism.' No paper in a one-paper city, however bad the product or however inept the management, could avoid gushing profits. Now, however, almost all newspaper owners realize that they are constantly losing ground in the battle for eyeballs. Simply put, if cable and satellite broadcasting, as well as the Internet, had come along first, newspapers as we know them probably would never have existed."[58]

Warren Buffett and Kay Graham shared the same philosophy of business practice. As he says, "Kay understood the two most basic rules of business: First, surround yourself with talented people and then nourish them with responsibilities and your gratitude; second, consistently deliver a superior, ever-improving product to your customer. Among journalistic leaders, no one carried out either task better than she. The consequence was outsized profits. Indeed, if we look at newspaper and television profit margins on what I would term a 'quality-adjusted' basis, she took The Washington Post Company from near the bottom straight to the top."

"Kay brought brains, character, guts, and, not to be omitted, the deepest sort of patriotism to her job as CEO of The Washington Post Company. She always said that what she most wished for was a Pulitzer in management. In my book, she earned one."[59]

Now, Kay's descendants are making their mark at the *Washington Post*. In the newsroom, Katharine Weymouth is referred to as "KW" or "K-Wey." Weymouth is likely to fill Donald Graham's leadership position in the future, but when asked about succession, Donald Graham said, "I'm going to be in my job for a while longer."[60] There are no other Graham descendants in Katharine Weymouth's generation that work for the company.

Lally gave Katharine and her younger sister, Pamela, a clear view of reality. "She told us the world didn't owe us anything. Success is 90 percent hard work and 10 percent talent," says Katharine. "I'm very grateful to my mom for that."[61]

Of her responsibilities as publisher of the newspaper, Weymouth says, "I'm very clear-eyed about the task ahead of us. It's going to be really hard. But I think that we're well positioned. We have incredible penetration, a great newspaper, a great web site, and great people."[62]

Weymouth is less inclined to get involved in public policy than her grandmother. "That's not my world," she says. "I don't pretend to have any ambitions in that way. My grandmother knew JFK and LBJ. That was her world. I enjoy meeting interesting people, but that's not my world."[63]

Katharine Graham's memoir vividly recounts her life, and earned her a Pulitzer Prize. *Washington Post* reporter David Broder said, "There have been many days in my 35 years at the *Post* when I felt privileged just to be part of the paper. But the best, bar none, was the day Kay Graham received her Pulitzer. She had earned many honors for the work of the paper, but this was for the book she had written herself, a story only she could have told. The news of her Pulitzer had leaked inside the building. But custom decrees there be no celebration until the official word crosses the Associated Press wires.

"She had come down to the newsroom that afternoon and was waiting in Executive Editor Len Downie's office, along with Bradlee and Meg Greenfield, the editorial page editor. The newsroom staff gathered at the desks closest to that office. When she came out, the applause began—and just did not stop. Without a word being said, all of us realized in the same instant that this was the time we could express our thanks to the woman who had provided us such unstinting support and such unlimited freedom to do our jobs—the greatest gift any publisher could give. As the applause went on, she began to weep, and so did we."[64]

Kay Graham said, "I've been very privileged. Working at something you love is the greatest privilege in life. And to have the opportunity that I had was unbelievable."[65] Kay Graham's legacy is a multibillion-dollar company with diverse media holdings. She grew The Washington Post Company by more than either her father or husband did. Kay Graham is preserved in our memories as an early female role model, not just for those in the newspaper industry, but for women in all of corporate America.

Chapter 10

Women at the Top and at the Table

Female representation in corporate management is a topic that has been discussed and debated for at least the past four decades. Some view it as an issue of "fairness." But it is more important to study the topic in light of its impact on the culture of various societies and on the economic strength and success of a company.

In comparing the top executives of today with those of two decades ago, today's Fortune 100 executives are younger, more of them are female, and fewer were educated at elite institutions.[1] The Fortune 100 itself has changed over time. Only 20 of the companies on the list in 1980 are still in the Fortune 100 in 2011, most notably due to a decrease in manufacturing and a shift to a service economy.

Berkshire Hathaway currently has women running four of 79 subsidiary companies, up from just one in 2001. The company has two female directors, out of twelve, on its board of directors and two female corporate officers. Though the Berkshire Hathaway conglomerate has about 260,000 employees, only 21 of these work at the corporate headquarters in Omaha. Included in these are two key individuals who also happen to be women: Sharon Heck, vice president of taxes, and Rebecca Amick, director of internal auditing. It can truly be said that there has been a surge of female leadership in corporate America in the past decade simply because female executives were practically non-existent in the past.

Gender Diversity

Countless studies show that gender and ethnic diversity in the workplace enhances overall productivity and effectiveness. McKinsey & Company, an international management consulting firm, evaluated organizational excellence, including operating margins and market capitalization. The rankings showed a positive correlation with having three or more women in top management functions and the highest level of financial outcomes.[2,3,4]

Female leaders have distinctive abilities to communicate, relate to the public, and provide strategic insights and competitive advantages. Including women in executive management has invigorated businesses with a different type of energy and unique insight.

It's not that women are better than men, or that men are better than women as corporate leaders. More minds are generally a good thing. Tapping talent from both genders doubles the life experiences that can provide expanded knowledge and wisdom. Diversity drives growth and innovation. It not only encourages new concepts and ways of doing things but also expands points of view and relationships.

Women may not be willing to admit that they are using their brains differently from men. The facts and research prove, however, that women *do* use their brains differently, and those differences can, in fact, be an asset. Men and women make decisions and solve problems in different ways. There are situations that occur in every company that could best be handled by a man and those best handled by a woman. But that doesn't mean that men and women are *unable* to perform all tasks required. Ideally, teams are composed of both sexes and leaders possess attributes of both.

Some of the disparity at the top may be due to family obligations. Balancing family and work is a real challenge. Women still carry an unequal share of the burden. It's not that women can't necessarily do it all, but in some cases they just can't do it all at once.

In a 2002 study, there was an inverse relationship found between the level of job position women held and the number of children they had, while there was no such relationship for men. Indeed, the more successful the man, the more likely he was to have a spouse and children.[5]

Mentoring experiences differ between men and women. It's very rare for a man to mentor a woman due to the potential for perceived indiscretions. Therefore, if women must rely on mentoring and advice from primarily other women, it's difficult to find a mentor at high levels of the corporate structure. Mentoring practices appear to be improving for younger generations of women. Two-thirds of women aged 45 to 66 report that they are not or have never been mentored by women, whereas more than half of women between the ages of 18 and 29 say that they are or have been mentored by women.[6]

If these mentoring connections are strong factors in promotion, then the cycle of male advancement over women is perpetuated. Women who are corporate officers should consciously invest more time in mentoring other women. As Madeline Albright said at the TEDWomen conference of 2010, "There's a special place in hell for women who don't help other women."

There are misconceptions about what it takes to become a female executive. Many of the stereotypes of strong women are off-putting and not the way women leaders want to be perceived. This may contribute to hesitation on the part of young women setting the goal of becoming a CEO. No one dreams of being labeled a "bitch" when they grow up.

Women graduates from 12 of the nation's top business schools cite the following barriers to women pursuing MBA degrees:[7]

- Lack of female role models: 56 percent
- Incompatibility of careers in business with work/life balance: 47 percent
- Lack of confidence in math skills: 45 percent
- Lack of encouragement by employer: 42 percent

Women may also be making a conscious choice not to pursue executive management positions. One study showed that 27 percent of women in the business sector list "a powerful position" as an important career goal, the lowest ranking (eighth) of any goal in the survey.[8]

Far more important to these women was:

- The ability to associate with people they respect: 82 percent
- The freedom to "be themselves" at work: 79 percent
- The opportunity to be flexible with their schedules: 64 percent

When women first began occupying the executive suite, they were advised to behave like men to succeed. Later, it was recognized that there are leadership styles women possess that are different, but equally effective.

Climbing the career ladder may require a woman to adopt behaviors that are not inherently her nature, such as self-promotion. Women must be comfortable talking about themselves and articulating their strengths. Women tend to understate their abilities to others, even if they acknowledge to themselves that they are capable. Men take responsibility for their success, while women generally thank others for their achievements.

CEOs

As of January 2012, 18 (3.6 percent) women hold the CEO position at a Fortune 500 company, up from just one in 1996, and 15 in 2010. In Europe the number of female executives varies greatly from country to country. In general, gender diversity is stronger in northern and eastern Europe than in southern Europe and Germany. Norway is a leader, with women holding more than 32 percent of the top executive jobs.[9]

When studying CEO positions, there are very large cultural differences, as shown in Table 10.1.[10,11,12] Rapid growth in emerging markets appears to be conducive for women. This could be due to the absence of a long-standing tradition of male leadership, thus allowing the strongest leaders of both genders to achieve success.

A so-called Gender Gap Index study performed by the World Economic Forum ranks the United States at 17 out of 135 countries. First place went to Iceland, having the smallest gap between genders.[13]

Table 10.1 Percent of Women in CEO Position by Country

Country	Percentage of Female CEOs
Thailand	30%
China (mainland)	19
Finland	13
Norway	12
Turkey	12
Brazil	11
Italy	11
European Union	9
Japan (all registered companies)	5.4
United States (public companies)	5
FTSE 350 (United Kingdom)	4
U.S. Fortune 500	3.6
ASX200 (Australia)	2
Japan Nikkei (listed companies)	0.8

Globally, one study found that there are industry sectors where female CEOs are found more frequently and some where they are completely absent, as shown in Table 10.2.

According to statistics released in 2011 by Catalyst (a nonprofit organization expanding opportunities for women and business), women still lag far behind men in attaining the higher levels of executive status, especially considering that they comprise close to half of the working population.[14]

- Women in the U.S. labor force: 46.7 percent
- Women in management, professional and related occupations: 51.5 percent
- Female Fortune 500 corporate officers: 14.4 percent
- Female Fortune 500 board seats: 15.7 percent
- Female Fortune 500 top earners: 7.6 percent
- Female Fortune 500 CEOs: 3.6 percent

Regarding compensation, the median salary for new female business school graduates in 2010 was $78,254, compared to $78,820 for the newly graduated men.[15] A study of 1,500 publicly traded U.S. corporations

Table 10.2   Global Female CEOs by Industry

Industry	Percentage of Female CEOs
Agriculture	18%
Media and Entertainment	14
Health	12
Travel & Tourism	11
Professional Services	10
Food and Beverage	9
Energy	8
IT and Telecom	4
Engineering and Construction	3
Financial Services and Insurance	2
Logistics and Transport	0
Mining	0
Automotive	0
Real Estate	0
Textiles	0
Chemical	0

SOURCE: World Economic Forum, 2010.

found that women are not as well compensated as men before becoming CEO. But, the few who do reach the CEO position receive compensation comparable to their male counterparts.[16]

Business Education

Having female representation at the top executive level requires recruitment of women into business careers at the entry level. It took many years for women to approach parity with males in obtaining undergraduate and graduate business degrees. Fortunately, it now appears that women are pursuing and obtaining nearly equivalent levels of education as men. Figure 10.1 shows a steady, but very slow increase—over almost 40 years— in the number of degrees awarded to women.[17]

In 2010, females received:

- 48.9 percent of Bachelor's degrees in business
- 45.4 percent of Master's degrees in business
- 38.7 percent of Doctoral degrees in business

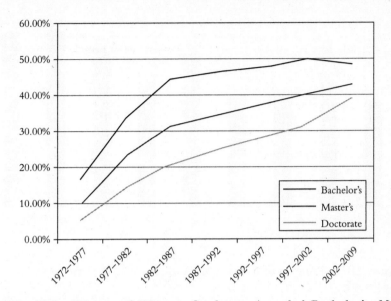

Figure 10.1 Percent of Women Graduates Awarded Bachelor's, Master's, and Doctoral Business Degrees, 1972 to 2009
SOURCE: U.S. Department of Education, 2010.

Does the increase in women students translate into more female executives and entrepreneurs? How many years will it take for new female MBA graduates to make an impact in the proportion of female CEOs?

Gender disparity in graduate level education is narrowing. More women (105,900) took the GMAT business school entrance exam in the 2009–2010 test cycle than in any other year since the exam was created more than 50 years ago, comprising 40.1 percent of all GMAT exams taken worldwide.[18]

While law and medical schools have nearly reached gender parity, MBA programs still lag behind with only 30 percent females entering. One factor contributing to the difference may be the issue of *timing*. Most, but not all, medical students enroll straight from undergraduate school. Law schools are seeing a trend of increasing delayed enrollment of about two years post undergraduate degree. But it's common for business graduate students to enter business school after four to six years of work experience. This puts female business students at a critical decision point in many of their lives—the choice to start a family or perhaps stay home to raise their young children.

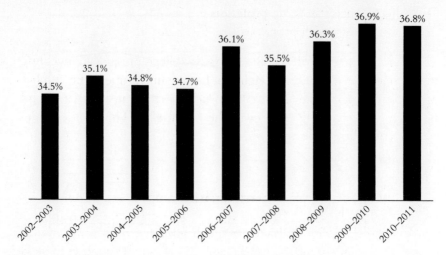

Figure 10.2 Percent of Female MBA Graduates by Year
SOURCE: Catalyst, 2011.

In the United States, 36.8 percent of 2011 MBA graduates were female (Figure 10.2). The change in the past nine years shows a steady climb at low incline and glacial pace.

Educational resources are needed for female business students that specifically address the unique challenges faced by women in the corporate world.

Graduate educational institutions can set an example by employing more women in upper level administrative and faculty positions. Female faculty and school administrators serve as role models to female students and provide diverse interactions with the male students. This adds to the educational experience graduate schools can provide.

There are more women teaching at business schools now than ever before, though their numbers are still not close to those of male faculty. Statistics from the Association to Advance Collegiate Schools of Business show that over the past 10 years, the percentage of female business school faculty rose from 23.6 percent in 2002 to 29 percent in 2011. But representation at higher faculty levels drops off considerably, and as women advance and obtain tenure, the gender gap widens. At schools of business, women make up:

- 40.6 percent of instructors
- 37.3 percent of assistant professors

- 29.1 percent of associate professors
- 17.9 percent of full professors

Women comprise 23 percent of U.S. college presidents, including the presidencies of four of the eight Ivy League universities. The number of female deans of business schools has steadily risen since the 1990s and now stands at nearly 17 percent of the 668 total.[19] This is an encouraging trend that I hope will continue.

Nonprofits

The proportion of female leaders is much higher in the U.S. nonprofit sector. This is understandable since nearly 75 percent of people employed by nonprofits are women. Several explanations for this have been offered. Some suggest that women have more compassion for societal issues than men. Others propose that many nonprofits are focused on traditionally female-related issues, such as education and healthcare. Or, it may simply be that women are less hesitant to accept the lower-paying jobs that nonprofits typically offer.

Many women do climb the career ladder all the way to the top at nonprofits. However, the larger the nonprofit, the less likely it is to have a female CEO. Women hold 57 percent of CEO positions at nonprofits with annual budgets of $1 million or less. But of those with budgets over $1 million, only 38 percent have female CEOs.[20] A 2009 Chronicle of Philanthropy survey finds that only 19 percent of CEOs at the 400 largest U.S. nonprofit groups were women.[21]

Politics

Global politics still lacks strong female representation. Of the world's 195 countries, there are only 10 female presidents and 8 female prime ministers, equaling 9.2 percent of heads of state. Roughly 19 percent of elected parliamentarians are women.[22] Seventeen percent of the U.S. Congress is female, with 76 women serving in the House and 17 in the Senate.

Business Owners

The number of new businesses in the United States started by women is increasing, but still not equal to those started by men. Women own 7.8 million nonfarm businesses in the United States, representing 28.7 percent of the total. Additionally, 4.6 million businesses are owned equally by men and women. Slightly over 30 percent of the women-owned businesses operate in the sectors of repair/maintenance/personal/laundry service and health care/social assistance.[23]

Of entrepreneurs seeking and obtaining angel funding, women are outnumbered by men. Women-owned businesses accounted for 21 percent of the entrepreneurs seeking angel capital in 2010, up from 13 percent in 2006. Women received funding at a lower yield rate, 13 percent, than the overall rate of 18.4 percent.[24]

Investors and Philanthropists

There is still a shortage of females in the business investor community who participate in funding startup companies as venture capitalists or angel investors. According to Ewing Marion Kauffman Foundation's 2006 report, of the estimated 225,000 active angels who invested $23.1 billion in 50,000 deals in 2005, no more than 8 percent were female.[25] This number rose slightly by 2010 to 13 percent of the total angel population.[26]

Women may choose to invest in start-ups because of the potential for an above-average rate of return on investment and to engage in the high-passion, high-energy world of entrepreneurship. As an angel investor, a woman is not simply sending a check, but can participate as a mentor and advisor to emerging companies. The impact of having more females invest in start-ups is in growing the number of women appointed to corporate boards of directors and support for the growth and development of women-owned businesses.

The venture capital industry is male-dominated, small, and geographically concentrated. Trish Costello, president of CVE Capital Corporation and founding CEO of the Center for Venture Education, says, "Most venture capitalists have a tight and trusted circle of business colleagues who act as gatekeepers for high potential deals, and women have rarely been networked into this small inner circle."[27]

Women are increasing their philanthropic participation in society. Philanthropy includes a wide range of activities related to volunteering and giving money. Women have traditionally been volunteers, and during the 1970s feminist movement, there were many organizations founded by women for the purpose of supporting female causes. Now, women are being recognized as independent philanthropic donors. They have taken a greater control of their personal finances and resources and are shaping the future of political, social, and economic arenas.

Because they live longer than men, women could oversee more than $41 trillion in the next 50 years. "Women in the country currently hold the majority of wealth," says Claire Costello, senior vice president and national foundation executive for Bank of America Merrill Lynch. "So it behooves everyone in the nonprofit sector to pay attention to the financial clout and moral imagination of women as they really determine where dollars go."[28]

Board Members

The purpose of a company's board of directors is to oversee and guide the activities of the company. This typically includes reviewing the annual budget, evaluating the CEO, and establishing company policies and objectives. The goal of these activities is to create economic gains and control the conduct of business in the interest of company shareholders.

Businesses diverse in race, gender, age, and life experiences have more resources to draw from. Board composition, likewise, benefits from diversity. A.G. Lafley, former chairman of Proctor and Gamble says, "A diverse organization will out-think, out-innovate, and out-perform an homogenous organization every time."[29]

Corporate boards lack diversity in several aspects, including age, gender, background, and tenure. When boards consist of a homogenous population, the individuals tend to fall into *groupthink*, a behavior supporting wrong ideas for the sake of agreeing with the group.[30] It is theorized that groupthink dominated in the lack of boardroom decision making at Enron.[31]

Groupthink may lead to:

- A sense of invincibility
- Belief in the inherent morality of goals
- Collective rationalization
- Stereotyping of out-groups
- Appearance of unanimity
- Self-censorship
- Pressures on dissenters
- Self-appointment as mind guards

"In many organizations, the group ends up being dumber than the individual members," says Keith Sawyer, professor of psychology and education at Washington University in St. Louis and author of the book *Group Genius*. Brainstorming isn't the solution to groupthink either. Creativity and innovation are the result of collaboration in diverse groups. Small sparks of ideas are collected, building one upon the other, leading to effective problem solving and appropriate decisions.[32]

However, adding a director for diversity's sake, without useful business or industry experience, won't result in any new benefits for the group. The arguments both for and against quotas are logical, and the practice is no longer just a hypothetical scenario. Norway passed a law in 2003 that required all publicly listed companies to reserve 40 percent of board seats for women by 2008. Spain, France, and The Netherlands have followed suit. The European Parliament passed a resolution in July 2011 calling for European Union–wide legislation stipulating that at least 40 percent of board seats be held by women by 2020.[33]

Despite evidence that shows solid economic benefit from diverse boards, quotas may be too drastic for achieving the desired outcome. Women that companies are compelled to put on boards are unlikely to be as effective as those they place there voluntarily. We shall soon see direct outcomes-based evidence of whether coercion benefits these European businesses.

New board members are recruited and nominated by existing board members. This may lead to endless cycles of men recruiting their male colleagues. But, even so, the slate of nominees goes before the shareholders for a vote. So, it is ultimately the responsibility of shareholders to evaluate the nominees objectively, based on their merits.

If there are no women on the ballot, then there may be an unwillingness, either acknowledged or subconscious, to invite a woman board member. How many votes are actually cast in board elections? Many proxy ballots are thrown away or assigned to fund managers. And how often are there more nominees on a ballot than positions available? In that common situation, the shareholder has no choice at all and an election is simply a rubber stamp.

There are 5,520 board members in the U.S. Fortune 500 companies. In 2011, women filled 16.1 percent of those board seats, up from 15.7 percent in 2010 and 15.2 percent in 2009. In both 2009 and 2010, more than 50 percent of companies had at least two women board directors, yet more than 10 percent had no women serving on their boards.[34]

In Europe, the percentage of female board members is lower. According to the annual Female FTSE Board report from Cranfield University School of Management, the proportion of women on the boards of FTSE-100 companies is only 12.5 percent, a marginal rise over the previous year. The Australian ASX200 has 8.3 percent female board members.[35]

There are many companies that have no women on their boards or in any high-level management position. As seen previously, the type of industry plays a part in the proportion of women in CEO positions. In particular, the U.S. oil and gas industries have very few women in leadership positions despite the fact that women are employed by these companies and have abundant industry knowledge and expertise.

Corporations with female CEOs have greater female representation on their boards.[36] In a Danish study, it was found that after a male CEO has his first daughter, the women in the company benefit from increased pay and benefits. The relationship was strongest if the first daughter born was also the first child.[37]

Women make 80 percent of consumer purchase decisions. That's a lot of financial power. This power could be wielded selectively to support the advancement of corporate women. *Impact purchasing* is the act of buying products from companies that behave according to your beliefs and ideals. *Impact investing* is the same principle related to investment choices.

In industries where women constitute the primary target consumer market, it would seem to be a no-brainer that the CEO should be a

Table 10.3 Percentage of Female Board Members in Top Companies with Primarily Female Consumers

Company (Fortune rank)	# Female	Total #	% Female
Procter & Gamble (26)	5	11	45.5%
Macy's (107)	4	10	40.0
TJX (119)*	3	9	33.3
Kraft (49)*	3	10	30.0
Johnson & Johnson (40)	3	12	25.0
Tyson Foods (93)	2	8	25.0
Kimberly–Clark (130)	3	12	25.0
Supervalu (61)	3	14	21.4
Kohl's (142)	2	10	20.0
Safeway (60)	1	10	10.0

*Kraft and TJX have female CEOs.

woman, and that women comprise at least 50 percent of the board of directors. This also applies to female-related healthcare and wellness product industries. However, this commonsense approach has not yet been realized in the top Fortune 500 companies (see Table 10.3). The average female representation among a sampling of ten companies having a predominant female market is 27.52 percent, and only two of them have women in the position of CEO.

Corporate boards of directors should have adequate female representation to oversee and guide company objectives. In the case of companies whose products are marketed *solely* to women, the need for female participation is paramount. As seen in Table 10.4, none of the selected companies have over 50 percent female board composition. The average female director representation among these ten companies is 29.22 percent, a slight increase over the companies shown in the previous Table 10.3. Both groups are above the average of 15.7 percent for all Fortune 500 boards.

The link between governance by the board of directors and the performance of a company is tenuous. At large firms, with many divisions, it's difficult to evaluate the effectiveness of the board. At Berkshire Hathaway, subsidiary companies are not required to have their own board of directors. Some of the 79 subsidiaries have boards, some have executive committees, and some have advisory boards.

Table 10.4   Percentage of Female Board Members in Selected
Cosmetics and Female Clothing Companies

Company	Female Board Members	Total Board Members	Percent Female
Revlon	3	11	27.3
Estée Lauder	7	15	46.7
L'Oréal USA	3	11	27.3
Avon*	5	10	50.0
Elizabeth Arden	1	7	14.3
Ann Inc. (Ann Taylor)*	4	9	44.4
Charming Shoppes, Inc. (Lane Bryant, Fashion Bug, Catherines)	2	10	20.0
J.Crew	1	5	20.0
Coldwater Creek	2	9	22.2
Limited Brands, Inc.	2	10	20.0

*Avon and Ann Inc. have female CEOs.

In the 2011 report "Bridging Board Gaps,"[38] Task Force Chair Charles Elson, cites four major points of improvement for the future of board governance:

1. Dissent is appropriate.
2. The default [for board structure] should be the split chair and CEO.
3. The board, when it feels it is necessary, should utilize third party advisors when appropriate.
4. There should be term limits in addition to director evaluations.

Elson, the Edgar S. Woolard, Jr., Chair in Corporate Governance and Director of the John L. Weinberg Center for Corporate Governance, University of Delaware, also says, "In my view, there are two critical governance factors which clearly show a relationship to performance:

1. Equity ownership of directors and
2. Independence of directors."[39]

Regarding equity, a director who has put their own money into a company is much more personally and emotionally invested in the company than a director who has been given stock through options.

Directors from outside a company bring value by having the freedom to think and act independently without risk of losing their job.

At worst, they may lose their board seat. At-large directors are able to view the company from an objective perspective, similar to the general public and consumer. Independent directors with some experience in the company industry are most precious.

Boards that are collections of CEOs and top executives from different industries provide strong leadership points of view, but often have too little industry-specific expertise and become far too supportive of management to adequately perform board duties, particularly in the area of risk assessment.

Being a board member requires a commitment of time. If stretched too thin, directors may be unable to effectively serve. Besides the typical quarterly board meeting, there are time-consuming board committees. The audit committee is the most time-intensive of any board committee. Retired individuals, in particular, may spend a significant number of hours participating on boards.

The Future

The statistics for female representation in various segments included in this book are in a constant state of flux. Business leadership in the United States will include more women in the future. This will result from two factors. The first is the intentional action to adopt a diverse management team. When attention is given to management and board composition by shareholders and consumers, companies are forced to respond. And in the case of some non–U.S. countries, governments are forcing a transition to gender balanced corporate governance.

The second cause for increased diversity is the passive natural evolution resulting from having a more gender-balanced education system and workforce than was in place 30 years ago. Women in middle management are gaining valuable knowledge and experience today that will make them attractive candidates for CEO and board positions in the future.

It is nearly impossible, and probably foolish, to attempt to predict who the future female leaders associated with Berkshire Hathaway might be. About half of newly appointed CEOs come from within a company and half from the outside. A review of the 79 subsidiary companies reveals no female in an obvious position to succeed a current male CEO, but there are several companies that appear to be likely to appoint a new CEO within a short period of time due to the current CEO's age. Whether that will be a female or male, is unknown and somewhat industry dependent. One thing is certain: The number of female CEOs, officers, and board members, both at Berkshire Hathaway and in corporate America in general, will increase in the future.

Notes

Introduction

1. Robert Hagstrom, *The Essential Buffett* (New York: John Wiley & Sons, 2001), 84.
2. Warren Buffett, *2006 Annual Report*, Berkshire Hathaway, Inc., February 28, 2007.
3. Warren Buffett, *Outstanding Investor Digest*, May 24, 1991.
4. Charles T. Munger, *Poor Charlie's Almanack* (Marceline, MO: Walsworth, 2005), 81.
5. "How Warren Buffett Manages His Managers," *CNNMoney*, CNN, October 12, 2009.
6. Warren Buffett, Letter to Shareholders, February 26, 2011.
7. Warren Buffett, Memo to Berkshire Hathaway Managers ("The All-Stars"), July 26, 2010.
8. Warren Buffett, 2007.
9. Eric Jackson, "Best in Class: America's Top Boards," Breakout Performance (blog), July 7, 2009, http://breakoutperformance.blogspot.com/2009/07/best-in-class-americas-top-boards.html.
10. Rachel Soares, Baye Cobb, Ellen Lebow, Allyson Regis, Hannah Winsten, and Veronica Wojnas, "2011 Catalyst Census: Fortune 500 Women Board

Directors," Catalyst December 2011. http://catalyst.org/file/533/2011_fortune _500_census_wbd.pdf. Accessed January 29, 2012.

11. Warren Buffett, Proxy Statement for Annual Meeting of Shareholders, Berkshire Hathaway, Inc., April 30, 2011.

12. Warren Buffett, 2011.

13. Warren Buffett, 2007.

14. Carol Loomis, interview with Warren Buffett, *Fortune* Most Powerful Women Summit, October 3, 2011.

15. Warren Buffett, Letter to Shareholders, Berkshire Hathaway, Inc., February 27, 2004.

Chapter 1   Rose Blumkin—Magic Carpet Ride

1. Carol Loomis, "The Inside Story of Warren Buffett," *Fortune*, April 11, 1988, 26.

2. Robert Batt, personal interview, August 2011.

3. Ibid.

4. Rose Blumkin and Dennis Mihelich, "Mrs. Rose Blumkin Interview," Douglas County Historical Society, August 30, 1983.

5. Joseph Schneersohn, "The Founding of Shchedrin." In *Tzemach Tzedek and the Haskala Movement* (Brooklyn, NY: Kehot Publication Society 1962), 10.

6. Robert Dorr, "Proud to Be a Jew," *Omaha World Herald*, April 1, 1979.

7. "Mrs. B's 100th Birthday," *Omaha World Herald*, December 9, 1993.

8. "Mrs. B Is 80," *Omaha World Herald*, January 24, 1974.

9. Robert Batt, 2011.

10. Alice Schroeder, "Rose," in *The Snowball: Warren Buffett and the Business of Life* (New York: Random House, 2008), 491.

11. "Shipping," *The Timberman*, Volume 15, (Miller Freeman Publications, Inc., August 1914), 45.

12. Robert McMorris, "Blumkin Business Phenomenon Began at Age 6," *Omaha World Herald*, July 9, 1967.

13. Rose Blumkin and Dennis Mihelich, 1983.

14. Ibid.

15. Ibid.

16. "The Life and Times of Rose Blumkin, An American Original," *Omaha World Herald*, December 12, 1993.

17. Rose Blumkin and Dennis Mihelich, 1983.

18. Robert McMorris, 1967.

19. David Perry, "Wanek Captures Three Industry Warriors in Bronze," *Furniture Today*, March 25, 2007.

20. Ibid.

21. Rose Blumkin and Dennis Mihelich, 1983.

22. Ibid.

23. Robert McMorris, 1967.

24. Rose Blumkin and Dennis Mihelich, 1983.

25. Jean Sullivan, "Rose Blumkin." Oral recording. Part of the American Jewish Committee's William E. Wiener Oral History Library. 1974.

26. "More about Mrs. B," *Omaha World Herald*, January 12, 1970.

27. Liz Reardon, "Lawsuit Says There's Only One Mrs. B," *Omaha World Herald*, January 14, 1984.

28. Jackie Kroeger, "Jury Awards Carpet Installers $10,000 in Suit against Mrs. B," *Omaha World Herald*, August 26, 1993.

29. Jean Sullivan, 1974

30. "The B? For Rose Blumkin It Ought to Stand for Busy," *Omaha World Herald*, July 14, 1989.

31. C. David Kotok, "At 90, Mrs. B Runs Store with Fervor," *Omaha World Herald*, December 12, 1983.

32. "Rose Blumkin," *Omaha World Herald*, January 4, 1979.

33. "Getting Personal—Mrs. Rose Blumkin," *Omaha World Herald*, June 1, 1977.

34. Sonja Schworer, "From Wheelchair, Mrs. B Plans Leasing Expansion," *Omaha Metro Update*, February 11, 1990, 23.

35. Robert Dorr, "Red Cross Gift Memorializes Mrs. B's Desire to Help People," *Omaha World Herald*, August 10, 1998.

36. Rose Blumkin and Dennis Mihelich, 1983.

37. Robert Dorr, "Farewell, Mrs. B," *Omaha World Herald*, August 11, 1998.

38. Robert Dorr, "Mrs. B Dismisses Idea of Retirement at Age 96," *Omaha World Herald*, July 7, 1990.

39. Robert Dorr, "Furniture Mart a Handshake Deal," *Omaha World Herald*, September 15, 1983.

40. "The Life and Times of Rose Blumkin, An American Original," 1983.

41. Warren Buffett, Letter to Shareholders, March 14, 1984.

42. Robert Dorr, "Sale of Blumkin Stock Will Avoid Friction," *Omaha World Herald*, September 16, 1983.

43. "My Hero Is," *Omaha World Herald*, November 30, 1986.

44. Robert Batt, 2011.

45. Warren Buffett, Letter to Shareholders, March 1, 1991.

46. C. David Kotok, 1983.

47. Robert Dorr, "Mrs. B: 'I Got Mad and Quit.'" *Omaha World Herald*, May 12, 1989.

48. Robert Dorr, "Son Says No One Wanted Mrs. B to Leave," *Omaha World Herald*, May 13, 1989.

49. Robert Dorr, "Mrs. B Would Strike a Deal to Regain Carpet Department," *Omaha World Herald*, May 16, 1989.

50. Steve Jordan, "Mrs. B: New Store 'To Let 'Em Have It.'" *Omaha World Herald*, September 15, 1989.

51. Robert Dorr, July 7, 1990.

52. Alice Schroeder, 2008, 495.

53. Ibid, 503.

54. Jim Rassmussen, "Healing Complete for Mrs. B," *Omaha World Herald*, April 23, 1993.

55. Rose Blumkin and Dennis Mihelich, 1983.

56. "The Life and Times of Rose Blumkin," December 12, 1993.

57. Robert McMorris, 1967.

58. Alice Schroeder, 2008, 504.

59. *Jewish Press*, "Rose Blumkin and Family Give One Million Dollars," January 23, 1981.

60. Rose Blumkin and Dennis Mihelich, 1983.

61. Dennis Burrow, "From Mrs. B to Mr. K: Do Not Underestimate Best Country in the World," *Omaha World Herald*, October 28, 1962.

62. Rose Blumkin and Dennis Mihelich, 1983.

63. "My Hero Is," *Omaha World Herald*, November 30, 1986.

64. Rose Blumkin and Dennis Mihelich, 1983.

65. Robert Dorr, "Nearly 104, Mrs. B Retires," *Omaha World Herald*, October 26, 1997.

Chapter 2   Susan Jacques—Puttin' On the Glitz

1. Elizabeth Taylor, *My Love Affair with Jewelry* (New York: Simon & Schuster, 2003).

2. Warren Buffett, "What You Should Know About the Jewelry Business," www.borsheims.com/borsheims/CustomerServices-Buffett.aspx, 2011.

3. Philip Durell, "Berkshire Hathaway Susan Jacques Interview/Chat," Motley Fool, May 13, 2005.

4. Ibid.

5. Gordon Munro, "Rhodesia History Summary," Our Rhodesian Heritage (blog), http://rhodesianheritage.blogspot.com/2010/02/rhodesia-history-summary.html, February 15, 2010.

6. Mary De Zutter, "Borsheim's Chief Credits Friedman as Retail Mentor," *Omaha World Herald*, June 26, 1994.

7. Philip Durell, 2005.

8. Gordon Munro, 2010.

9. "Zimbabwe Demographics Profile 2011," Index Mundi, www.indexmundi .com, accessed September 2011.

10. Mary De Zutter, June 26, 1994.

11. Ibid.

12. Susan Kuhlmann, "Borsheim's Jewelry Manager Finds This Country's Opportunity 'Phenomenal'," *Midlands Business Journal*, March 10–16, 1989, 3–4.

13. "About Susan Jacques," *USA Today*, May 10, 2000.

14. Donna Frischknecht, "Susan Jacques, Borsheims: Going Where Life Takes Her," *All Business*, May 19, 1997.

15. "Omaha's Crown Jewel," *The Reader, Keep Omaha Home*, 2007, 24–25.

16. Susan Kuhlmann, 1989.

17. Mary De Zutter, June 26, 1994.

18. Robert Dorr, "Sisters Hit Right Path in Omaha," *Omaha World Herald*, January 26, 1989.

19. Ibid.

20. Robert McMorris, "Borsheim Jewelry Business Sparkles in Downtown Store," *Omaha World Herald*, July 26, 1980.

21. Dana Parsons, "Big Board Gilds Golden Years," *Omaha World Herald*, January 21, 1976.

22. Robert Batt, personal interview, August 2011.

23. Dana Parsons, 1976.

24. Mary De Zutter, June 26, 1994.

25. *Omaha World Herald*, "Theft Victim Gets His Boy," August 8, 1967.

26. Al Frisbie, "Guard: Nobody Taking My Gun," *Omaha World Herald*, September 9, 1980.

27. Andrew Kilpatrick, "Borsheims: A Jewel," in *Of Permanent Value* (New York: McGraw Hill, 1998), 373.

28. Robert Hagstrom, *The Essential Buffett* (New York: John Wiley & Sons, 2001).

29. *Omaha World Herald*, "Ike Friedman's Life Glittering Success," September 13, 1991.

30. Warren Buffett, Letter to Shareholders, February 28, 1989.

31. Warren Buffett, Letter to Shareholders, March 2, 1990.

32. *Midlands Business Journal*, February 4, 1994.

33. Robert Dorr, "Buffett's Firm Buys 80 Percent of Borsheim's," *Omaha World Herald*, January 24, 1989.

34. Philip Durell, 2005.

35. Jim Rasmussen, "Borsheims Chief Ike Friedman Dies of Lung Cancer at Age 67," *Omaha World Herald*, September 12, 1991.

36. Robert Miles, "The Appointed One—Susan Jacques, Borsheims Fine Jewelry." In *The Warren Buffett CEO* (New York: John Wiley & Sons, 2002).

37. "About Susan Jacques," 2000.

38. Poppy Harlow, "The Woman behind Buffett's Bling," *CNN Money*, May 13, 2011.

39. Mary De Zutter, "Borsheims to Get New President, CEO," *Omaha World Herald*, January 6, 1994.

40. Warren Buffett, Letter to Shareholders, March 1, 1999.

41. Robert Miles, 2002.

42. Russ Banham, "The Warren Buffett School," Chief Executive.net, December 1, 2002, http://chiefexecutive.net/the-warren-buffett-school.

43. Philip Durell, 2005.

44. Ibid.

45. Anthony DeMarco, "Berkshire Hathaway Subsidiary to Buy Italian Jewelry Brand," *Forbes.com*, September 12, 2011, www.forbes.com/sites/anthonydemarco /2011/09/12/berkshire-hathaway-subsidiary-to-buy-italian-jewelry-brand.

46. "Berkshire Unit Richline to Buy Italian Jeweler," *Reuters*, September 10, 2011.

47. Philip Durell, 2005.

48. Robert Miles, 2002.

49. "Salesman Warren Buffett Gives Borsheims Best Weekend Ever," Borsheims Blog, May 4, 2011, www.borsheimsbrk.com/1903/salesman-warren-buffett -gives-borsheims-best-weekend-ever.

50. Michaela Saunders and Steve Jordon, "The Buffett Effect: Sales Records at Two Stores," *Omaha World Herald*, May 5, 2011.

51. "Omaha's Crown Jewel," 2007.

52. Ibid.

53. Mary De Zutter, June 26, 1994.

54. Ibid.

55. "Style Shot," *Omaha Magazine*, September/October 1999, 19.

56. Ibid.

57. Ibid.

58. Mary De Zutter, June 26, 1994.

59. "About Susan Jacques," 2000.

60. Robert Miles, 2002.

61. "About Susan Jacques," 2000.

62. Allison Edwards, "Borsheims Expands Sales Floor, Inventory," *Midlands Business Journal*, July 11–17, 1997, 1, 16.

63. Teresa Novellino, "Borsheims CEO Gives Career Advice at GIA Career Fair," *National Jeweler*, June 8, 2010.

64. Philip Durell, 2005.

65. Steve Jordon, "A Wish List for Hillary? Not at Borsheims," *Omaha World Herald*, December 27, 2000.

66. Maureen Dowd, "Liberties: Hillary's Stocking Stuffer," *The New York Times*, December 24, 2000.

67. Andrew Kilpatrick, 1998.

68. Steve Jordon, "Buffett Can Knock on Wood, Light 81 Candles," *Omaha World Herald*, August 28, 2011.

69. Philip Durell, 2005.

70. Richard D. Brown, "Borsheims Counters National Luxury Retailer Slump," *Midlands Business Journal*, November 27, 2009.

71. Michelle Leach, "Borsheims Adds to Product Mix, Reports Double-Digit Sales Gains," *Midlands Business Journal*, April 22, 2011.

72. Susan Kuhlmann, 1989.

73. Robert Miles, 2002.

74. Ibid.

75. "About Susan Jacques," 2000.

76. Ibid.

77. Michelle Leach, 2011.

78. Susan Kuhlmann, 1989.

79. Warren Buffett, "2009 Berkshire Hathaway Annual Report," February 26, 2010.

80. Christine Laue, "Borsheims' 13 Layoffs Are the First in Company History," *Omaha World Herald*, June 10, 2009.

81. Richard D. Brown, 2009.

82. Warren Buffett, 2010.

83. Warren Buffett, *Berkshire Hathaway Inc. 2010 Annual Report*, February 26, 2011.

84. "About Susan Jacques," 2000.

85. Russ Banham, 2002.

86. Teresa Novellino, 2010.

87. Robert Miles, 2002.

Chapter 3 Doris Christopher—Kitchen Counter Culture

1. Robert G. Hagstrom, *The Warren Buffett Way* (Hoboken, NJ: John Wiley & Sons, 2005).

2. Marc Hamburg, "Berkshire Hathaway to Acquire The Pampered Chef," press release, September 23, 2002.

3. Warren Buffett, Letter to Shareholders, February 21, 2003.

4. Doris Christopher, *Come to the Table* (New York: Warner Books, 1999).

5. Doris Christopher, *The Pampered Chef* (New York: Random House, 2005).

6. Lucinda Hahn, "Pampered Life," *Chicago Tribune*, January 18, 2005.

7. Jodi Heckel, "Pampered Chef Chief: Family Still Comes First," *The News-Gazette*, August 10, 2003.

8. S. A. Mawhorr, "Success Comes in the Shape of a Spatula," *Daily Herald*, July 24, 2000.

9. Lucinda Hahn, "Pampered Life," *Chicago Tribune*, January 18, 2005.

10. Robert A. Mamis, "Bootstrapping Lessons: Master of Bootstrapping Administration (MBA)," *Inc.*, August 1, 1995.

11. Michele Fitzpatrick, "Recipe for Success," *Chicago Tribune*, April 14, 1996.

12. S. A. Mawhorr, 2000.

13. Doris Christopher, 2005.

14. Ellyn Spragins, "Building a Company Warren Buffett Would Buy," *Fortune*, February 1, 2003.

15. Michele Fitzpatrick, 1996.

16. Doris Christopher, 2005.

17. Deborah Pankey, "Pampered Chef Founder Remembers 30 Years of Gadgets," *Daily Herald*, November 2, 2010.

18. Dimitra DeFotis, "Pampered Chef's Inventory Serves Up a Happy Kitchen," *Daily Herald*, March 20, 1996.

19. S. A. Mawhorr, 2000.

20. Doris Christopher, 1999.

21. Ellyn Spragins, 2003.

22. Robert A. Mamis, 1995.

23. Edison Nation, "The Pampered Chef—Doris Christopher," interview, August 16, 2011, www.youtube.com/watch?v=Uxpph-BYqAw.

24. Jane Edwards Creed, "Keeping the Dream Alive—How Great Leaders Do It," *Direct Selling News*, April 2009.

25. Doris Christopher, 2005.

26. Ibid.

27. S. A. Mawhorr, 2000.

28. Jay Christopher, *Come to the Basement* (Addison, IL: The Pampered Chef, 2001).

29. Ibid.

30. Ibid.

31. Jodi Heckel, 2003.

32. Dimitra DeFotis, 1996.

33. Michele Fitzpatrick, 1996.

34. Louis Johnston and Samuel H. Williamson, "What Was the U.S. GDP Then?" MeasuringWorth, 2011, www.measuringworth.org/usgdp.

35. Kathryn Grondin, "Pampered Chef Now Calls Addison Home," *Daily Herald*, October 19, 2002.

36. Doris Christopher, 2005.

37. "Company Spotlight: The Pampered Chef," *Direct Selling News*, September 2006.

38. DePaul University. Breakthroughs. *A Symposium of Business Owners*, Entrepreneurs & CEOs, Chicago, IL, October 28, 2010.

39. Rob Kaiser, "Pampered Chef Freed Founder from Schedule's Grind," *Chicago Tribune*, September 27, 2002.

40. Warren Buffett, "Forward." In Doris Christopher, *The Pampered Chef* (New York: Random House, 2005).

41. Warren Buffett, 2003.

42. Kathryn Grondin, 2002.

43. Larry Chonko and Raymond (Buddy) LaForge, "Academic Forum: Bringing Ethics to Light," *Direct Selling News* (July 2007).

44. Marc Hamburg, 2002.

45. Barbara Seale, "Direct Selling—A Changing Landscape," *Direct Selling News*, June 2009.

46. Michele Fitzpatrick, 1996.

47. Roger Lowenstein, "Nothing Charitable about Giving In," *The Washington Post*, July 20, 2003.

48. Alice Schroeder, "Oracle." In *The Snowball* (New York: Random House, 2008), 745.

49. Charles Storch, "Feeling the Heat, Warren Buffett Gives in on Giving," *Chicago Tribune*, July 25, 2005.

50. Warren Buffett, Letter to Shareholders, February 27, 2004.

51. Roger Lowenstein, 2003.

52. Laraine Spector, "Reflections on Leadership: Founder and Chairman of Pampered Chef Offers Her Insights," *Virtual Strategist*, Spring 2005.

53. S. A. Mawhorr, "The Pampered Chef in Addison Honored for Honesty, Integrity. *Daily Herald*, December 3, 1998.

54. Larry Chonko and Raymond (Buddy) LaForge, July 2007.

55. Doris Kelley Christopher, University of Illinois, http://brilliantfutures.illinois .edu/story.aspx?id=140.

56. Jay Christopher, 2001.

57. Doris Christopher, 2005.

58. Steven A. Camarota, "How Many Americans?" *The Washington Post*, September 2, 2008.

59. Larry Chonko and Raymond (Buddy) LaForge, "Academic Forum: Championship Customer Service," *Direct Selling News*, May 2007.

60. Robert A. Mamis, 1995.

61. Deborah Pankey, 2010.

62. *Wasserman v. Pampered Chef et. al. LC 063512*, Superior Court of Los Angeles County, Van Nuys, CA. (March 26, 2004).

63. Lucinda Hahn, "The Case of the TartMaster: Keeping Heat on Competition," *Chicago Tribune*, January 18, 2005.

64. Joanne Cleaver, "Pampered Chef Gets New Chief Exec," *Chicago Tribune*, January 21, 2003.

65. Michele Fitzpatrick, 1996.

66. Robert A. Mamis, 1995.

67. Doris Christopher, 1999.

68. Doris Christopher, 2005.

69. Jay Christopher, 2001.

70. Larry Chonko and Raymond (Buddy) LaForge, July 2007.

71. Edison Nation, 2011.

Chapter 4   Cathy Baron Tamraz—Distribution Evolution

1. Warren Buffett, Letter to Shareholders, February 26, 2011.

2. Janis Johnson, "Dollars and Sense," *Mills Quarterly*, Spring/Summer 2008, 10–12.

3. Ibid.

4. Ronald Chan, *Behind the Berkshire Hathaway Curtain* (Hoboken, NJ: John Wiley & Sons, 2010), 5.

5. Ibid.

6. Rachel Soares, Baye Cobb, Ellen Lebow, Allyson Regis, Hannah Winsten, and Veronica Wojnas, "2011 Catalyst Census: Fortune 500 Women Board Directors," Catalyst, December 2011, http://catalyst.org/file/533/2011 _fortune_500_census_wbd.pdf, accessed January 29, 2012.

7. Liz Claman, "Women at the Wheel: Business Wire CEO on Achieving Success, Working with Warren Buffett," Fox Business, May 10, 2011, http:// video.foxbusiness.com/v/4687290/business-wire-ceo-on-achieving-success- working-with-warren-buffett.

8. Greg Jarboe, "The 100th Anniversary of the Press Release," Searchengine watch.com, October 29, 2006, http://searchenginewatch.com/article/2067724 /The-100th-Birthday-of-the-Press-Release.

9. Cathy Baron Tamraz, "A Time-Honored Tradition for Transparency – The News Release," FinReg21.com, April 1, 2009, www.finreg21.com/blogs /a-time-honored-tradition-transparency-%E2%80%93-news-release.

10. "Final Rule. Interactive Data to Improve Financial Reporting." SEC. 17 CFR Parts 229, 230, 232, 239, 240, and 249 (2009).

11. Cathy Baron Tamraz, "Microsoft Needs to Get Its Head Out of the Cloud When It Comes to Disclosure," BusinessWired blog, November 3, 2010, http://blog.businesswire.com/2010/11/03/microsoft-needs-to-get-its-head -out-of-the-cloud-when-it-comes-to-disclosure.

12. Susan Pulliam and Karen Richardson, "Warren Buffett Unplugged," *Wall Street Journal*, November 12, 2005.

13. Warren Buffett, "Happy 50th Anniversary, Business Wire," Business Wire Video, July 12, 2011, www.youtube.com/watch?v=szkypJGiDcA.

14. Warren Buffett, *Berkshire Hathaway 2005 Annual Report*, February 28, 2006.

15. Dan Fost, "Buffett Seals the Deal," *San Francisco Chronicle*, January 18, 2006.

16. Greg Levine, "Buffett's Berkshire to Buy Business Wire," Forbes.com, January 17, 2006, www.forbes.com/2006/01/17/buffett-business-wire-cx _gl_0117autofacescan09.html.

17. Liz Claman, 2011.

18. Deb Subia, "April in Omaha: My Invitation to 2011 Berkshire Hathaway Annual Meeting," Business Wired (blog), May 6, 2011, http://blog.businesswire .com/2011/05/06/april-in-omaha-my-invitation-to-2011-berkshire-hathaway -annual-meeting.

19. Betsy Berkhemer and Renee Fraser, "Public Relations and Earned Media: CEO Interview with Cathy Baron Tamraz," *2 Minutes & More*, KFWB-AM, July 25, 2010.

20. Smart Business, "Cathy Baron Tamraz," January 1, 2007, www.sbnonline .com/2007/01/cathy-baron-tamraz-president-and-ceo-business-wire/?full=1.

21. Ibid.

22. Ibid.

23. Ibid.

24. Ronald Chan, 2010, 12.

Chapter 5   Marla Gottschalk—Consuming Passion

1. "Marla Gottschalk Named CEO of Pampered Chef," Business Wire, April 19, 2006, www.businesswire.com/news/home/20060419005767/en/Marla-Gotts chalk-Named-CEO-Pampered-Chef.

2. Ann Therese Palmer, "Numbers Added Up to Move into a Pampered Way of Life," *Chicago Tribune*, May 13, 2007.

3. Ronald W. Chan, "Looking Forward with Marla Gottschalk," in *Behind the Berkshire Hathaway Curtain* (Hoboken, NJ: John Wiley & Sons, 2010), 109.

4. Ibid, 110.

5. Ibid.

6. Ann Therese Palmer, 2007.

7. Ronald W. Chan, 2010, 111.

8. "The Pampered Chef, Ltd. Company Profile," Yahoo! Finance, http://biz .yahoo.com/ic/42/42750.html.

9. Warren Buffett, *2009 Berkshire Hathaway Annual Report*, February 26, 2010.

10. Jason Stipp, "Pampered Chef's Recipe for a Downturn," Morningstar, Inc. Video, www.youtube.com/watch?v=X2UVGIs-MXE, May 2, 2009.

11. Amy Bell, "In the Pink," *Direct Selling News*, October 2011.

12. Darren Dahl, "Taking the Direct Route to Sales Growth," *Inc.*, August 24, 2010.

13. L. Susan Williams and Michelle Bemiller, *Tupperware, Passion Parties, and Beyond* (Boulder, CO: Lynne Rienner, 2011).

14. "Company Spotlight: The Pampered Chef," *Direct Selling News*, September 2006.

15. Mark Moss, Shopping As an Entertainment Experience (Lanham: Lexington Books, 2007).

16. Thomas Hine, *I Want That! How We All Became Shoppers* (New York: Harper Collins, 2002).

17. Colin Campbell, *The Romantic Ethic and the Spirit of Modern Consumption* (Oxford: Basil Blackwell, 1987).

18. L. Susan Williams and Michelle Bermiller, 2011.

19. "Company Spotlight: The Pampered Chef," 2006.

20. Amy Bell, 2011.

21. Ibid.

22. Larry Chonko and Buddy LaForge, "Academic Forum: Bringing Ethics to Light," *Direct Selling News*, July 2007.

23. Dominique Xardel, *The Direct Selling Revolution* (Cambridge, MA: Blackwell, 1993), 157.

24. William Sluis, "It's My Party and I'll Sell if I Want To," *Chicago Tribune*, May 22, 2007.

25. The Pampered Chef, "Join Us! Get the More You're Looking For," Consultant Recruitment Brochure, 2011.

26. Tatiana Morales, "How Moms Are Making $$ At Home," *The Early Show*, CBS, February 11, 2008.

27. Leah Ingram, "Prevention at Work," *Delta Sky Magazine*, June 2011, 132–134.

28. Karyn Reagan, "The Pampered Chef," *Direct Selling News*, June 2008.

29. Karyn Reagan, "The Power of Pink," *Direct Selling News*, October 2011.

30. Karyn Reagan, 2008.

31. Ibid.

32. Karyn Reagan, 2011.

33. Karyn Reagan, 2008.

34. Ann Therese Palmer, 2007.

35. Ronald W. Chan, 2010, 119.

36. Ibid, 107.

Chapter 6   Beryl Raff—Precious Mettle

1. "Beryl Raff—Zale Corporation (ZLC)," *Wall Street Transcript*, April 10, 2000.

2. Thomas Bancroft, "Zale's Woes," *Forbes* 149, no. 13 (June 22, 1992): 46

3. Allen R. Myerson, Allen R. "Zale Names Chief after Long Stretch," *New York Times*, March 16, 1994.

4. "Jewelry Retailer Posts a 33 Percent Gain," *The Times-News*, February 17, 2000.

5. George William Shuster and Glen Beres, "Cornerstone Principles Will Guide Zale Growth, Says Raff," *Jewelers Circular Keystone*, January 2001.

6. Ibid.

7. "Beryl Raff—Zale Corporation (ZLC)," 2000.

8. George William Shuster and Glen Beres, 2001.

9. Ibid.

10. John Dicocco, interview with Alum Beryl Raff, CEO of Helzberg Diamonds, *Builders & Leaders*, Boston University School of Management, December 22, 2009.

11. Katie Hafner, "Canned Phrases for Making an Exit: Spend Time with the Family, Pursue Other Interests, the Dog Ate My ID," *New York Times*, December 23, 2006.

12. Maria Halkias, "Zale Posts Lower Earnings but Beats Reduced Estimates," *Dallas Morning News*, March 8, 2001.

13. Tara Murphy, "Zale Is a Diamond in the Rough," *Forbes*, November 27, 2001.

14. Katie Hafner, 2006.

15. Maria Halkias, "Leadership, Return to Diamond Basics Could Save Zale, Experts Say," *Dallas Morning News*, February 21, 2010.

16. Knight-Ridder News Service, "Former Zale Executive Takes Lead of J. C. Penney Fine Jewelry," *Times-News* (ID), May 10, 2001.

17. Glenn Law, "Ailing Whitehall Names Veteran Raff New CEO," *National Jeweler*, August 2005.

18. "Raff Is Whitehall CEO," *Professional Jeweler*, August 11, 2005.

19. Glenn Law, August 2005.

20. James P. Miller, "CEO Quits Before She Starts at Whitehall," *Chicago Tribune*, September 9, 2005.

21. Glenn Law, "Raff Resigns from Whitehall, Returns to Penney," *National Jeweler*, September 2005.

22. John Dicocco, 2009.

23. Barnett C. Helzberg Jr., *What I Learned Before I Sold to Warren Buffett* (Hoboken, NJ: John Wiley & Sons, 2003).

24. David Conrads, "Barnett Helzberg, Sr.," Missouri Valley Special Collections: Biography, 1999.

25. Barnett C. Helzberg, Jr., 2003.

26. Ibid.

27. Warren E. Buffett, Letter to Shareholders, March 1, 1996.

28. Andrew Kilpatrick, "Helzberg's Diamond Shops," in *Of Permanent Value* (New York: McGraw-Hill, 1998).

29. Jeffrey Comment, *Santa's Gift: True Stories of Courage, Humor, Hope, and Love* (New York: John Wiley & Sons, 2002).

30. "Beasley Will Lead Helzberg Diamonds," *Kansas City Business Journal*, November 2, 2004.

31. John Dicocco, 2009.

32. Maria Halkias, "Penney Jewelry Exec to Be Helzberg CEO," *Dallas Morning News*, April 7, 2009.

33. John Dicocco, 2009.

34. Cheryl Hall, "Jewelry Exec Treasures New Role," *Dallas Morning News*, May 6, 2009.

35. Maria Halkias, "Breaking Through: Retailers Pick More Women for Top Management Positions," *Dallas Morning News*, April 9, 2000.

36. Beryl Raff, "Rising to the Top: Managing It All," Women's Professional Lunch Series, Jewish Federation of Greater Dallas, October 11, 2006, Dallas, Texas.

37. Rob Bates, "Helzberg Diamonds Joining AGS," *Jewelers Circular Keystone*, July 28, 2010.

Chapter 7 Charlotte Guyman — Impact Creator

1. Warren Buffett, Letter to Shareholders, February 27, 2004.

2. Securities and Exchange Commission. 17 CFR PARTS 228, 229 and 249, [RELEASE NOS. 33–8177; 34–47235; File No. S7–40–02], January 24, 2003.

3. Ibid.

4. Forrest Krutter, Proxy Statement, Berkshire Hathaway, Inc., March 11, 2011.

5. Warren Buffett, Annual Shareholder's Meeting, Omaha, Nebraska, April 30, 2011.

6. Michael Cusumano, *Microsoft Secrets* (New York: The Free Press, 1995), 73.

7. Julie Bick, *All I Really Need to Know in Business I Learned at Microsoft* (New York: Simon & Schuster, 1997).

8. Paul Andrews, "Microsoft at Your Door," *The Seattle Times*, December 3, 1993.

9. Randall E. Stross, *The Microsoft Way* (New York: Addison-Wesley, 1996), 105–106.

10. Jim Erickson, "Microsoft Launches Drive for Expanded PC Market," *Seattle Post-Intelligencer*, 1994.

11. Paul Andrews, "Multimedia Battle Lines Are Drawn—Rollout of New Microsoft Software Line Challenges Controversial Patent Award," *The Seattle Times*, December 3, 1993.

12. Randall E. Stross, 1996.

13. Martin Campbell-Kelly, *From Airline Reservations to Sonic the Hedgehog.* (Cambridge, MA: The MIT Press, 2003), 261.

14. Jonathan Weber, "Two Small Software Firms Outwit Microsoft—Beating Bill at His Own Game," *The Seattle Times*, August 26, 1993.

15. Ted Lewis, "Emergent Behavior, Emergent Profits," *Computer*, July 1997.

16. Paul Andrews, "Microsoft Targets Consumers," *The Seattle Times*, August 26, 1993.

17. Julie Bick, 1997.

18. Greg Farrell, "Microsoft Sees On-Line Promise," *USA Today*, 1999.

19. Robert Slater, *Microsoft Rebooted* (New York: Penguin Group, 2004).

20. Microsoft. *Inside Out* (New York: Warner Books, 2000).

21. Ibid.

22. Cheryl Tsang, *Microsoft First Generation* (New York: John Wiley & Sons, 2000).

23. Microsoft, 2000.

24. Ibid.

25. Aaron Ricadela, "Deborah Willingham, Microsoft," *Women in Technology*, Informationweek.com, October 9, 2000.

26. Ibid.

27. Des Dearlove, "*Hire Very Smart People,*" in *Business the Bill Gates Way* (New York: AMACOM, American Management Association, 1999), 70.

28. Tina Kelley, "How to Keep the Best Workers Working at Their Best," *The New York Times*, October 26, 1997.

29. Kristi Helm, "Young Generation Redefines Culture of Microsoft Philanthropy," *The Seattle Times*, May 24, 2010.

30. Wendy Kaufman, "The Few, the Tech-Savvy Few: Option Millionaires," *All Things Considered*, National Public Radio, February 11, 2007.

31. Julie Bick, "The Microsoft Millionaires Come of Age," *The New York Times*, May 29, 2005.

32. Robert Slater, 2004.

33. Charlotte Guyman, "Visit to Save the Children Programs in Gaza and West Bank," Intersect, November 16, 2010, https://intersect.com/stories/1J8p2Nh6460R.

34. Patricia Sellers, "Melinda Gates Goes Public," *Fortune*, January 7, 2008.

Chapter 8 Susan Decker—Desire to Inspire

1. Miguel Helft, "Can She Turn Yahoo! Into, Well, Google?" *New York Times*, July 1, 2007.

2. Warren Buffett, Berkshire Hathaway Inc. 2006 Annual Report, February 28, 2007.

3. Alex Crippen, "Warren Buffett's Berkshire Blasts Benchmark S&P over Decade," CNBC, December 31, 2009.

4. Jamie McGee and Andrew Fry, "Buffett Takes $100,000 Berkshire Salary for 29th Straight Year," *Bloomberg Businessweek*, March 11, 2010.

5. Laura Saunders and Siobhan Hughes, "Buffett Builds His Tax-the-Rich Case," *Wall Street Journal*, October 13, 2011.

6. Julia Hanna, "The Fab Four," Harvard Business School, *Alumni Bulletin*, December 2009.

7. Deborah Blagg and Susan Young, "Five Honored for Missions Accomplished," *Harvard Alumni Bulletin*, September 2010.

8. Ben Elgin, "No Virtual Numbers for Yahoo!'s CFO," *Bloomberg Businessweek*, May 29, 2003.

9. Julia Homer, "Yahoo's Susan Decker," *CFO Magazine*, September 1, 2005.

10. Karen Angel, *Inside Yahoo!* (New York: John Wiley & Sons, 2002).

11. Ben Elgin, 2003.

12. Chris Kraeuter and Rachel Rosmarin, "Yahoo's Rising Star," *Forbes*, November 16, 2006.

13. Yahoo!, "Yahoo! Appoints New Chief Financial Officer," Yahoo! Media Relations, April 5, 2000.

14. John Battelle, *The Search* (New York: Penguin Group, 2005).

15. Julia Homer, 2005.

16. Chris Kraeuter and Rachel Rosmarin, 2006.

17. Julia Homer, 2005.

18. Chris Kraeuter and Rachel Rosmarin, 2006.

19. Stephen Taub, "Will CFO Decker Take the Reins at Yahoo?" *CFO Magazine*, December 6, 2006.

20. Elise Ackerman and Constance Loizos, "Popular Executive May Run Yahoo! One Day," *San Jose Mercury News*, January 1, 2007.

21. Ibid.

22. Miguel Helft, 2007.

23. Elise Ackerman and Constance Loizos, 2007.

24. Sarah Johnson, "Yahoo! Hands CEO Post to Yang, Not Decker," *CFO Magazine*, June 18, 2007.

25. Alix Stuart, "Secrets of Their Success," *CFO Magazine*, June 1, 2008.

26. Ben Elgin, 2003.

27. "Yahoo! President Susan Decker Takes Interest in Isarael," *Haaretz Israeli News*, May 20, 2008, www.youtube.com/watch?v=-E6eGSPtZ9Q.

28. Susan Decker, "Entrepreneurial Thought Leader Lecture," Stanford University, May 7, 2008.

29. Ibid.

30. Susan Decker, "Keynote Address," Advertising 2.0 Conference, New York, NY, June 4, 2008.

31. Susan Decker, "The Next Chapter," Yahoo! memo, January 13, 2009.

32. Eric Jackson, "Should CEOs Sit on Other Companies' Boards?" *Seeking Alpha*, April 23, 2009, http://seekingalpha.com/article/132716-should-ceos-sit-on-other-companies-boards.

33. Jessica Vascellaro, "Yahoo! Ex-President Returns to Harvard," *Wall Street Journal*, September 9, 2009.

34. Julia Hanna, 2009.

35. Laura Ratcliff, "Next Generation of Female Leaders Needs Strong Mentors," *The Glass Hammer*, May 25, 2011, www.theglasshammer.com/news/2011/05/25/next-generation-of-female-leaders-need-strong-mentors/.

36. Deborah Blagg and Susan Young, 2010.

37. Susan Decker, May 7, 2008.

38. Julia Hanna, 2009.

39. Jessica Vascellaro and Joann Lublin, "Departing Yahoo! President Has History of Missteps," *Wall Street Journal*, January 14, 2009.

40. Patricia Sellers, "Sue Decker Moves on from Yahoo!," *Fortune Postcards*, January 13, 2009.

41. Miguel Helft, 2007.

42. "Alumni Achievement Awards," Harvard Business School, 2010, www .alumni.hbs.edu/awards/2010/decker.html. Accessed January 31, 2012.

43. Julia Hanna, 2009.

Chapter 9   Katharine Graham—Capital Publisher

1. Jim Collins, "The 10 Greatest CEOs of All Time." *Fortune*, July 21, 2003.

2. Charlie Rose, "An Interview with Katharine Graham," *Charlie Rose, LLC*, February 5, 1997, www.charlierose.com/view/interview/5721. Accessed January 29, 2012.

3. "Philip Graham, 48, Publisher, a Suicide," *New York Times*, August 4, 1963.

4. Charlie Rose, 1997.

5. Madeleine Edmondson and Alden Duer Cohen, *The Women of Watergate* (New York: Simon and Schuster, 1975).

6. Alex S. Jones, "Katharine Graham at 70; One Woman, Two Lives, Many Memories," *New York Times*, July 1, 1987.

7. Peter Nulty, "National Business Hall of Fame," *Fortune*, April 5, 1993.

8. Katharine Graham, *Personal History* (New York: Alfred A. Knopf, 1997).

9. Alex S. Jones, 1987.

10. Bob Woodward, "Hands Off, Mind On," *Washington Post*, July 23, 2001.

11. Madeleine Edmondson and Alden Duer Cohen, 1975.

12. Agnes Meyer, "Women Aren't Men," *Atlantic Monthly*, August 1950.

13. Alex S. Jones, 1987.

14. Robin Gerber, *Katharine Graham* (New York: The Penguin Group, 2005).

15. Katharine Graham, 1997.

16. Warren Buffett, "Kay Graham's Management Career," Washpostco.com, 2001, www.washpostco.com/phoenix.zhtml?c=62487&p=irol-historykgraham. Accessed January 29, 2012.

17. Sally Jenkins, "Graham Blazed a Path, Sportswomen Saw the Light," *Washington Post*, July 19, 2001.

18. Carol Felsenthal, *Power, Privilege, and the Post* (New York: G.P. Putnam's Sons, 1993).

19. Patricia McCormack, "Most Powerful Woman in America," UPI—*Lowell Sun*, October 6, 1974.

20. Nora Ephron, "Paper Route," *New York Times*, February 9, 1997.

21. Cheryl Lanvin, "Celebrity World Q & A: Katharine Graham," *Wisconsin State Journal*, April 10, 1983.

22. Robert G. Kaiser, "The Storied Mrs. Graham," *Washington Post*, July 18, 2001.

23. Carol Felsenthal, 1993.

24. Robin Gerber, 2005.

25. Madeleine Edmondson and Alden Duer Cohen, 1975.

26. Alex S. Jones, 1987.

27. Robin Gerber, 2005.

28. Donald E. Graham, "Message from Don Graham," Washpostco.com, www.washpostco.com/phoenix.zhtml?c=62487&p=irol-ourcompanymessage. Accessed January 29, 2012.

29. Ira Berkow, "Washington Post Publisher Urged Watchdog to Bark," *Galesburg Register-Mail*, June 20, 1973.

30. Carl Bernstien, "Interview: Carl Bernstein," *Frontline News*, PBS, July 10, 2006.

31. Ira Berkow, 1973.

32. Ted Johnson, "For Presidents' Day: All the President's Men," *Variety*, February 21, 2011.

33. "Lower Profile, Press Advised," *Chronicle-Telegram*, September 12, 1974.

34. Madeleine Edmondson and Alden Duer Cohen, 1975.

35. Ira Berkow, 1973.

36. Robin Gerber, 2005.

37. Ibid.

38. J. Y. Smith and Noel Epstein, "Katharine Graham Dies at 84," *Washington Post,* July 18, 2001.

39. Ted Johnson, 2011.

40. Katharine Graham, *Katharine Graham's Washington* (New York: Alfred A. Knopf, 2002).

41. Charles Peters, *Tilting at Windmills* (Reading, MA: Addison-Wesley, 1988), 197.

42. Charlie Rose, 1997.

43. Charles T. Munger, *Poor Charlie's Almanack* (Virginia Beach, VA: The Donning Company, 2005), 197.

44. Charlie Rose, 1997.

45. Katharine Graham, 1997.

46. Charlie Rose, 1997.

47. Katharine Graham, 1997.

48. Donald E. Graham, The Washington Post Company Annual Report, February 23, 2011.

49. Ibid.

50. Katharine Graham, 1997.

51. Ibid.

52. Larry van Dyne, "The Bottom Line on Katharine Graham," *The Washingtonian*, December 1985, 204.

53. Ibid.

54. Katharine Graham, 2002.

55. Sruthi Ramakrishnan and A. Ananthalakshmi, "Dealtalk: Not for Sale? . . . *Washington Post*," *Reuters*, September 8, 2011.

56. Ibid.

57. Steven Mufson, "Warren Buffett to Step Down from Washington Post Co. Board," *Washington Post*, January 20, 2011.

58. Warren E. Buffett, Letter to Shareholders, February 28, 2007.

59. Warren Buffett, 2001.

60. Richard Perez-Pena, "Washington Post Names Publisher." *New York Times*, February 8, 2008.

61. Harry Jaffe, "Katharine the Second." *The Washingtonian*, August 1, 2008.

62. Richard Perez-Pena, 2008.

63. Harry Jaffe, 2008.

64. David S. Broder, "Farewell Katharine Graham," *The Times-News*, July 19, 2001.

65. Charlie Rose, 1997.

Chapter 10   Women at the Top and at the Table

1. Peter Cappelli and Monika Hamori, "The New Road to the Top," *Harvard Business Review*, January 2005.

2. Georges Desvaux, Sandrine Devillard-Hoellinger, and Pascal Baumgarten, *Women Matter: Gender Diversity, A Corporate Performance Driver*, McKinsey & Company, 2007.

3. Katherine Phillips, Katie A. Liljenquist, and Margaret Neale, "Better Decisions through Diversity," *Kellogg Focus on Research*, Kellogg School of Management, October 2010.

4. Taylor H. Cox and Stacy Blake, "Managing Cultural Diversity: Implications for Organizational Competitiveness," *Academy Management Executive* 5, no. 3 (August 1991): 45–56.

5. Sylvia Ann Hewlett, "Executive Women and the Myth of Having It All," *Harvard Business Review* 80 (April 2002): 66–73.

6. Kerry Hannon, "Boomer Women Flunk Mentoring," Forbes.com, October 25, 2011, www.forbes.com/sites/kerryhannon/2011/10/25/boomer-women -flunk-mentoring-new-linkedin-survey.

7. "Women MBAs," Catalyst, Inc., August 9, 2011, www.catalyst.org/publi cation/250/women-mbas.

8. Sylvia Ann Hewlett, Carolyn Buck Luce, and Peggy Schiller, "The Hidden Brain Drain: Off Ramps and On Ramps in Women's Career," *Harvard Business Review* 83 (March 2005): 31–57.

9. George Desvaux, et. al. 2007.

10. Australian Government EOWA, "Gender Workplace Statistics at a Glance," Annual Report. 2009, www.eowa.gov.au/Information_Centres/Resource _Centre/EOWA_Publications/Gender_stats_at_a_glance.pdf.

11. Adrian Wooldridge, "The Daughter Also Rises," *The Economist,* Schumpeter, August 27, 2001, 58.

12. Hu Yuanyuan, "China Ranks High in Women CEOs," *China Daily*, August 3, 2011.

13. Ricardo Hausmann, Laura D. Tyson, Yasmina Bekhouche, and Saadia Zahidi, "The Global Gender Gap Index 2011," Global Gender Gap Report, World Economic Forum, 2011.

14. Rachel Soares, Jan Combopiano, Allyson Regis, Yelena Shur, and Rosita Wong, "2010 Catalyst Census: Fortune 500 Women Executive Officers and Top Earners" and "2010 Catalyst Census: Fortune 500 Women Board Directors," Catalyst, Inc., December 2010.

15. "Women in Business Education," The Graduate Management Admission Council, 2011, http://gmac.mediaroom.com/index.php?s=55.

16. Susan M. Adams, Atul Gupta, Dominique M. Haughton, and John D. Leeth, "Gender Differences in CEO Compensation: Evidence from the USA," *Women in Management Review* 22, no. 3 (2007): 208–224.

17. U.S. Department of Education, "Degrees in Business Conferred," *Digest of Education Statistics*, July 2010.

18. "Women in Business Education," The Graduate Management Admissions Council, 2011.

19. Association to Advance Collegiate Schools of Business (AACSB), 2008.

20. Guidestar "Nonprofit Compensation Report," 2010, http://www2.guidestar .org/rxg/products/nonprofit-compensation-solutions/guidestar-nonprofit-com pensation-report.aspx.

21. Shifra Bronznick and Didi Goldenhar, "Flexibility and More Mentors Will Expand the Number of Female Nonprofit CEOs," *The Chronicle of Philanthropy*, November 12, 2009.

22. Global Fund for Women, "Status of Women Fact Sheet," 2011, www.global fundforwomen.org/impact/media-center/fact-sheets/status-of-women-fact -sheet.

23. U.S. Census Bureau, 2007 Economic Census. Survey of Business Owners— Women Owned Firms, www.census.gov/econ/sbo/get07sof.html?12.

24. Jeffrey Sohl, "The Angel Investor Market in 2010: A Market on the Rebound," Center for Venture Research, April 12, 2011.

25. Ewing Marion Kauffman Foundation, "Women and Angel Investing: An Untapped Pool of Equity for Entrepreneurs," April 2006, www.kauffman .org/uploadedFiles/women_and_angel_investing_100906.pdf.

26. Jeffrey Sohl, 2011.

27. Candida Brush, Nancy Carter, Elizabeth Gatewood, Patricia Greene, and Myra Hart, "Gatekeepers of Venture Growth," Diana Project Report, Kauffman Foundation, 2004, www.kauffman.org/research-and-policy/gate keepers-of-venture-growth.aspx.

28. Kathleen Kingsbury, "Controlling Trillions, Women Drive Charitable Giving," Reuters, December 12, 2011.

29. Bud Simpson, "Doing Business with Alaska Native Corporation," *Business Law Today*, July–August, 2007, 41.

30. Sylvia Hewlett, "What the U.S. Can Learn from Europe about Gender Equality in the Workplace," *Harvard Business Review*, May 2010.

31. Marleen A. O'Connor, "The Enron Board: The Perils of Goupthink," *University of Cincinnati Law Review* 71 (2003): 1233–1257.

32. Keith Sawyer, *Group Genius* (New York: Perseus, 2007).

33. "The Wrong Way to Promote Women," *The Economist*, July 23, 2011, 11–12.

34. Rachel Soares, Baye Cobb, Ellen Lebow, Allyson Regis, Hannah Winsten, and Veronica Wojnas, "2011 Catalyst Census: Fortune 500 Women Board Directors," Catalyst, December 2011, http://catalyst.org/file/533/2011 _fortune_500_census_wbd.pdf. Accessed January 29, 2012.

35. "Gender Workplace Statistics at a Glance," 2009.

36. Douglas Branson, *The Last Male Bastion* (New York: Routledge, 2010).

37. Michael S. Dahl, Cristian L. Dezso, and David Gaddis Ross, "Like Daughter, Like Father: How Women's Wages Change When CEOs Have Daughters," March 1, 2011, Social Science Research Network: http://ssrn.com/ abstract=1774434.

38. Charles Elson, Glenn Hubbard, and Frank Zarb, "Bridging Board Gaps," Report of the Study Group on Corporate Boards, Columbia Business School, 2011.

39. Eric Jackson, "Three of America's Best Boards," *Seeking Alpha*, July 7, 2009, http://seekingalpha.com/article/147414-three-of-america-s-best-boards.

About the Author

Karen Linder was born in Omaha, Nebraska, and raised in nearby Lincoln. She earned a bachelor's degree in Biology from Nebraska Wesleyan University and trained in Cytotechnology at the Des Moines School of Cytotechnology. She worked as a cytotechnologist for 29 years in three pathology laboratories, including the company she founded, Heartland Pathology, Inc. She is a former faculty member of the University of Nebraska Medical Center (UNMC) and founder of the UNMC School of Cytotechnology.

Karen is a past President of the American Society for Cytotechnology (ASCT), and twice past President of the Iowa Society of Cytology. She received the Marion and Nelson Holmquist Cytotechnologist Achievement Award from the ASCT and the Cytotechnologist Award for Outstanding Achievement from the American Society of Cytopathology.

Karen's interests include art, science, literature, and entrepreneurship. She is a member of the Nebraska Angels, a group of investors that provides funding to start-up companies, and a member of Women Investing in Nebraska, a philanthropic group that provides funds to Nebraska nonprofit organizations.

Karen is Founder and President of Linspiration, Inc. a Nebraska-based company that supports creativity and entrepreneurship. She serves on the boards of directors of the Museum of Nebraska Art, The KANEKO, and SkyVu Entertainment.

As Karen A. Allen, she has written numerous scientific journal articles and edited two textbooks: *A Guide to Cytopreparation* (1995) and *Risk Management for the Cytology Laboratory* (2002). She founded the Allen Writing Award, presented annually by the ASCT. She previously self-published the children's book *Jack the Curly Black Dog: Goes to the Beach* (2010). *The Women of Berkshire Hathaway* is her first business/biography book.

Karen and her husband, Jim Linder, live in Omaha, Nebraska, and Montecito, California. They have six adult children. You can follow Karen on Twitter at @karenlinder and learn more about this book at www.womenofberkshire.com.

Index